S2l   WP
C 22
S23 .

S15

D1464835

Exploring Psycho-Social Studies Series
Published and distributed by Karnac Books

Other titles in the Series

Object Relations and Social Relations: The Implications of the
Relational Turn in Psychoanalysis
  Edited by Simon Clarke, Herbert Hahn, and Paul Hoggett
Researching Beneath the Surface
  Edited by Simon Clarke and Paul Hoggett

Orders

Tel: +44 (0)20 7431 1075; Fax: +44 (0)20 7435 9076

E-mail: shop@karnacbooks.com

www.karnac books.com

SOCIAL SYMPTOMS OF IDENTITY NEEDS

Why We Have Failed to Solve Our Social Problems, and What to Do About It

Mark Bracher

KARNAC

First published in 2009 by
Karnac Books Ltd
118 Finchley Road, London NW3 5HT

British Library Cataloguing in Publication Data

A C.I.P. for this book is available from the British Library

ISBN 978 1 85575 654 0

Edited, designed and produced by The Studio Publishing Services Ltd
www.publishingservicesuk.co.uk
e-mail: studio@publishingservicesuk.co.uk

Printed in Great Britain

www.karnacbooks.com

CONTENTS

ACKNOWLEDGEMENTS

I want to thank Simon Clarke and Paul Hoggett, directors of Karnac's Explorations in Psycho-Social Studies Series, for their support of this book and their valuable editorial advice. Thanks also to Jeff Berman and Bob Samuels for their ongoing support of the work that finds its expression here, and to my friend and department chair, Ron Corthell, for maintaining conditions in which intellectual work could be done. Most of all, I wish to thank my long-time friend and collaborator Marshall Alcorn for his intellectual and political camaraderie and moral support over the years. It was Marshall who persuaded me many years ago that psychoanalysis deserved a hearing, who co-authored with me my first psychoanalytic article, and who has made major personal and professional sacrifices over the past fifteen years to establish, protect, and nurture the Association for the Psychoanalysis of Culture and Society (APCS). *Social Symptoms of Identity Needs* is dedicated to Marshall and to APCS, an organization devoted to solving social problems, whose annual conferences and journal provided impetus and opportunities for me to develop the understanding of social problems and their solutions presented in this book.

Permissions

Quotations from *Violence* by James Gilligan, © 1996 by James Gilligan, are used by permission of Grossett & Dunlap, Inc., a division of Penguin Group (USA) Inc., Brockman, Inc., and James Gilligan.

Thanks also to The Ohio State University Press for permission to reprint portions of my "Editor's Column: Social Symptoms". *JPCS: Journal for the Psychoanalysis of Culture & Society*, 5(1) (Spring 2000): 1–27, © The Ohio State University 2000.

ABOUT THE AUTHOR

Mark Bracher is Professor of English and Director of the Center for Literature and Psychoanalysis at Kent State University. His previous books include *Radical Pedagogy: Identity, Generativity, and Social Transformation* (2006), *The Writing Cure: Psychoanalysis, Composition, and the Aims of Education* (1999), *Lacan, Discourse, and Social Change: A Psychoanalytic Cultural Criticism* (1993), and *Being Form'd: Thinking Through Blake's* Milton (1985).

*Dedicated to
Marshall Alcorn,
The Association for the Psychoanalysis of Culture and Society,
and the work of social transformation.*

PREFACE

I have written *Social Symptoms of Identity Needs* because of my growing frustration and conviction that we not doing nearly as much as we could and should be doing to solve our most serious social problems. The project originated during my tenure as editor of the interdisciplinary journal *JPCS: Journal for the Psychoanalysis of Culture & Society* (now *Psychoanalysis, Culture, and Society*). My editorial role engaged me in reading and writing about a wide range of social and cultural issues in relation to multiple psychological factors and schools. Through this work, I began to realize that the most important causes of our most troubling social problems are going unrecognized and unaddressed.

Social Symptoms of Identity Needs aims to remedy this deficiency, and I believe its findings have profound and wide-ranging implications for a broad range of cultural practices and social policies. Based on research from multiple disciplines, the book explains how our major social problems, including crime, violence, terrorism, war, poverty, substance abuse, and prejudice, are primarily the result of efforts on the part of their perpetrators to maintain a secure identity, or sense of self. It demonstrates, further, how our ineffective and counterproductive responses to these problems—including

the War on Drugs, the War on Crime, and the War on Terrorism—
are themselves the result of the fact that we do not really want to
solve them, because they serve as means for us, the general public,
to maintain our own identities. The book locates the root causes of
these social problems and counterproductive responses in certain
trauma-generating phenomena of culture and society, which render
people's identities vulnerable and prone to defend and maintain
themselves by any means necessary. It concludes by explaining
social and cultural interventions that can prevent the social problems by preventing, repairing, or compensating for the identity
problems that give rise to them. *Social Symptoms of Identity Needs*
distinguishes itself from other analyses of social problems in a number of important ways. First, while the majority of inquiries into the
causes of and solutions to social problems focus on single problems
and their supposedly specific causes and/or solutions, the present
investigation finds that our major social problems ultimately arise
from the same root causes and, thus, can all be addressed through
the same basic social and cultural interventions. More specifically,
Social Symptoms of Identity Needs uncovers a previously unrecognized common fundamental cause for all of these problems: identity needs. In contrast to most treatments of the psychological
causes of antisocial behaviours, which invoke varying and often
disjunctive motives and theories of motivation, *Social Symptoms of
Identity Needs* draws on psychoanalytic, psychological, neurological, and sociological research on identity and the self to develop a
comprehensive model of identity that explains how our most serious social problems are all motivated by the need to protect and
enhance a vulnerable identity, or sense of self.

The next question is: what causes vulnerable and antisocial
identities? Although genetic endowment is obviously a factor in all
psychological dispositions, research in multiple disciplines clearly
demonstrates that the key factors in the construction of character
and personality are to be found in the material, social, and cultural
environments. The literature of sociology is replete with such explanations. However, most of these accounts fail to specify the nature
of the causal (psychological) links between environment and
behaviour. The present analysis, in contrast, reveals identity needs
and vulnerabilities as the key causal links between environment
and behaviour, explaining how various social and cultural factors

damage (traumatize) identity and thus render it unable to maintain itself by more benign means. For example, while standard explanations of crime focus on environmental causes such as poverty, inequality, unstable neighbourhoods, and family problems, my analysis, drawing on ethnographic and clinical studies of criminals, explains that these environmental conditions do not, in and of themselves, lead directly to crime. Rather, they lead to crime if and only if they produce identities for which, and conditions in which, crime is the best (or only) feasible option for maintaining one's sense of self. This step provides a crucial link missing from most environmentalist explanations of social behaviour, and it demonstrates that effective solutions to social problems must address the social and cultural environments *in ways that affect the identities* of the individuals engaging in the socially problematic behaviours.

Social Symptoms of Identity Needs takes one additional step in its analysis of social problems: it inquires into the causes of those collective behaviours—including public policies, social and cultural institutions and practices, and material and economic practices and structures—that are responsible for the social and cultural conditions that both form and mobilize the immediate perpetrators of social problems. Most significantly, it asks why we pursue "solutions" to our major social problems that are clearly not only ineffective but also counterproductive. Other discussions of this question (which are exceedingly uncommon) locate the cause in the special (material and power) interests of the dominant class. *Social Symptoms of Identity Needs*, in contrast, shows how counterproductive responses such as the War on Crime, the War on Drugs, and the War on Terrorism are motivated at bottom by the identity needs of both the policy-makers and the general public. This same motivation is shown to underlie the social, economic, political, and cultural practices, institutions, and structures that maintain poverty, inequality, exploitation, and insecurity. These practices and conditions create various types of subalterns—denigrated Others— that help maintain the identities of dominant groups by functioning as suitable objects for the identity-maintaining mechanisms of downward social comparison, displacement (scapegoating), and externalization (escaping one's own negative qualities by locating them in the inferior Other). In short, *Social Symptoms of Identity Needs* reveals that the main reason for our failure to solve our social problems is because the overwhelming majority of individuals in our society rely on these problems, in one way or another, to maintain their own (surprisingly traumatized and hence vulnerable) identities.

Finally, the understanding that *Social Symptoms of Identity Needs* provides of the motivational primacy of identity maintenance, of the social and cultural conditions that are optimal for identity development and maintenance, and of the multiple levels of causality in which identity and its formative and maintenance conditions are involved, enables the formulation of more effective strategies for preventing these social problems. While other social and cultural remedies for social problems are based on mere correlations (either observed or only anticipated) between interventions and results, *Social Symptoms of Identity Needs* explains the causal paths by which social problems are produced (i.e., by harming or impeding identity) and by which successful interventions work (i.e., by supporting and developing identity), and this understanding enables much more effective formulation and implementation of interventions for reducing or eliminating our major social problems.

PART I

IDENTITY AND THE CAUSES
OF SOCIAL PROBLEMS

The causes of social problems

"The true criterion of reform is ... whether it goes to the roots and attempts to change causes—or whether it remains on the surface and attempts to deal only with symptoms"

(Fromm, 1955, p. 273)

Social symptoms

"Psychical symptoms", as defined by Freud, are "acts detrimental, or at least useless, to the subject's life as a whole, often complained of by him as unwelcome and bringing unpleasure and suffering to him" (Freud, 1916–1917, p. 358), but which are, none the less, "found to be *useful in asserting the position of the self* and becom[e] more and more closely merged with the ego and more and more indispensable to it" (Freud, 1926d, p. 99, my italics). Social symptoms, similarly, are collective actions that are detrimental to a society's life as a whole, often complained of by people as unwelcome and bringing unpleasure and suffering to them, but which are, none the less, indispensable to them in maintaining their identity, or "asserting the position of the self". There are three basic types of social symptom:

1. Harmful behaviours, including crime, delinquency, violence, war, terrorism, and addictions.
2. Ineffective or counterproductive efforts to prevent or reduce these behaviours, such as the War on Crime, the War on Drugs, and the War on Terrorism.
3. Production of (or acquiescence in) material, political, social, and cultural conditions that are both unjust and traumatogenic, the elimination of which would significantly reduce the first two types of symptom. Such conditions include hunger, poverty, homelessness, unemployment, and lack of adequate health care, child care, and education.

These social problems continue to exist mainly because we have failed to take the necessary steps to solve them, despite having the knowledge, the resources, and the avowed desire to do so. The very fact that we have the knowledge, the resources, and the express desire to reduce problems like crime, violence, substance abuse, terrorism, war, and poverty and yet have not done so suggests that some part of us does not want to solve these problems.

A central argument of this book is that people avoid knowledge of how to solve social problems because solving these problems is threatening to them. Indeed, many people are threatened by the mere understanding of these problems, or, more precisely, by a comprehensive understanding of their causes. Such an understanding is easy enough to come by, for researchers have compiled substantial bodies of evidence for the causes of all of our major social problems. While the causes are often multiple and various, the matrix of variables in each case is usually no greater than that involved in numerous cognitive tasks that most people are quite capable of performing, as they often do, for example, in troubleshooting a malfunctioning tool, appliance, or motor vehicle, perfecting a recipe, starting a small business, or analysing the performances of their investment portfolio or favourite sports team. Yet, when it comes to social problems, many people fail to recognize the full array of causes, both proximal and distal, that combine to produce the social problem at issue. Instead, they attribute social problems to the supposedly flawed characters of certain segments of the population (Schorr, 1988, p. xxvii). Thus, crime is seen as caused by immoral and violent people, the drug problem by self-indulgent people, poverty by lazy people, and so on. Simply put, people like to assume that social problems are caused by harmful behaviours and that these harmful behaviours are themselves caused by flawed character, period:

Flawed character → Harmful behaviours → Social problems

As William Ryan pointed out several decades ago, most public policy concerning social problems in the USA is based on this (usually tacit) view that their ultimate cause lies in the individual character of their immediate perpetrators or bearers, and efforts to solve social problems therefore consist of various interventions to eliminate, incapacitate, or reform these individuals (Ryan, 1971, pp. 3–29).

This cognitive symptom—the truncated view of the causes of social problems—protects people's sense of self, or identity, by enabling them to avoid recognizing their own role in producing the social problems, a recognition that would undermine their self-image as innocent, socially productive, generous people. Sociologist Michael Lewis argued several decades ago that our ineffective and counterproductive social policies are not failures at all, but resounding successes, accomplishing exactly what the majority of Americans want and need: the production of various types of "inferior" people in relation to which the rest of us can feel successful (Lewis, 1993, pp. 51–79). Closer examination in later chapters of some of these "failed" policies will explain how these "failures"—either to take any action or to take effective action, as the case may be—are motivated by our need to maintain our identities, or sense of self, and how solving these problems would thus constitute a significant threat to many "normal, law-abiding" members of society by depriving them of powerful scapegoats and foils for establishing and maintaining their own identities.

Our pursuit of ignorance and failure

This refusal to recognize the root causes of social problems supports two basic strategies by which we avoid solving them. The first is to make little or no effort to solve them. This response is often rationalized by asserting that certain problems, such as poverty, crime, and delinquency, cannot be solved, and berating and ridiculing efforts to do so. It is nowadays often claimed that programmes such as those of Franklin D. Roosevelt's New Deal and Lyndon Johnson's Great Society were fundamentally misguided, ineffective, and even counterproductive, and that we need to abandon such efforts and instead provide "tax relief" and "get big Government off people's backs". Such claims turn a blind eye to irrefutable evidence that government efforts to promote justice and equality, reduce poverty, provide health care, and rehabilitate drug addicts and violent criminals not only can work but actually have worked quite remarkably in many instances to lift people out of poverty, improve their health, and provide them with other opportunities to flourish (Currie & Skolnick, 1997, pp. 9–11; Schorr, 1988, pp. xxiv–xxvi, 1998, pp. xxv–xxvi). Ignoring such evidence allows people to believe that nothing can be done to relieve certain types of human suffering and injustice, and this belief enables them to perpetuate social problems with a clear conscience.

The second strategy we use to avoid solving our social problems is to take some action apparently aimed at solving them, but to ignore available knowledge of how to do so and to pursue instead policies that are ineffective and even counterproductive. Lisbeth Schorr notes, for example, that "the nation's rich body of knowledge about improving the life prospects of disadvantaged children remains largely unutilized" (Schorr, 1998, p. 19). The same is true of knowledge about how to rehabilitate criminals and drug addicts, help people get out of poverty, and prevent teen pregnancy (Currie & Skolnick, 1997, p. 10; Schorr, 1998, pp. 169, 194, 234ff.), and also to prevent war and terrorism.

The War on Drugs is a prominent instance of such a symptomatic, counterproductive response, based on the failure of the American public and policy-makers to identify and address the key causes of the problem. Policy-makers and the general public have correctly recognized two proximal causes that are individually necessary and jointly sufficient to produce the drug problem: a demand for drugs and a supply of them. And they have correctly concluded that eliminating either the supply of drugs or the demand for them will eliminate the drug problem. Problems arise, however, with the next logical step: how to eliminate the supply and/or the demand. Rather than enquiring into the causes of the behaviours of production and consumption (that is, the psychological needs and environmental circumstances that give rise to these behaviours), policy-makers and the general public simply assume that the causes are character flaws in the users, producers, and distributors of the substances. More precisely, they assume that greed and pleasure are the prime motivators of both the production and the consumption of drugs. From this it follows that both the supply of and the demand for drugs could be eliminated by decreasing the pleasure they produce, a conclusion that supports the idea that the problem can be solved by prohibition, which reduces the net pleasure gained by drug production and consumption by inflicting severe unpleasure for such behaviours. Hence the three primary interventions of the USA's drug policy, which are three forms of pleasure reduction: (1) incarceration for possession of illegal drugs, which dramatically alters the net pleasure resulting from their production and use; (2) moral condemnation (including the "just say no" slogan), which aims both to produce the displeasure of social censure and to inculcate an internal source of displeasure in the form of a superego opposition to drug production and use; and (3) education concerning the physiological, psychological, and social harm that can result from drug use, which aims to produce an awareness of future suffering that production and consumption may effect.

Unfortunately, these programmes, like Prohibition in the 1920s, have proved largely ineffective. The major reason is because the fundamental assumption about human motivation on which they are all based—the assumption that people produce and consume illegal drugs because of an excessive desire for pleasure inadequately controlled by ego and superego constraints—is invalid. As we will see when we examine the research on addiction and substance abuse, drug use is caused not primarily by the desire for pleasure but rather by the need to maintain a sense of self, or identity, in the face of threatening internal or external circumstances.

The other front in the USA's drug war, the supply side, suffers from a similar failure to understand the deep motivation of drug production and trafficking. Here, too, it is assumed that the pleasure principle—in this case, in the form of greed—is the fundamental motivation of the manufacturers and distributors. From this assumption, it follows that the way to eliminate or reduce drug manufacture and trafficking is to reduce the yield of pleasure such behaviours produce, by arresting the producers and traffickers and finding and destroying their supplies and production facilities. Here, too, however, the primary motivation is not pleasure, but the need for an identity, for a sense of self as a force that matters in the world, which drug trafficking can provide much more readily and powerfully than any of the other (often severely limited) options available to those who engage in these illegal activities. This point will become clear when we investigate the motivations of criminal activity in general.

The failure to recognize the motivations of drug users and producers is a major reason we have not formulated a more successful drug policy in the USA. To prevent a persistent behaviour it is always helpful and often necessary to alter its motivations. Concerning the drug problem, we need to recognize what motivates people to produce and consume drugs in spite of the significant risk of dire consequences for such behaviours. But this level of causation–motivation is rarely if ever given careful consideration by policy-makers or the public at large.

Why is this the case? Why, moreover, do policy-makers, along with most of the general public, continue to support a drug policy that has not only failed to solve the problem of drug abuse but has actually created new problems, such as the development of organized and violent crime around drug production and distribution, the criminalization and incarceration of large segments of the population (particularly young black men), and the expenditure of considerable public resources for enforcement of the laws prohibiting drug manufacture, distribution, and possession? What are the causes of this socially harmful behaviour of policy-makers and ordinary citizens: that is, their/our insistence on sticking with an ineffective and counterproductive policy and their/our failure to recognize and understand the psychological needs that cause substance abuse, as well as the environmental causes of these psychological needs?

Ironically, the failure to recognize the most fundamental motivation driving drug production and consumption and the resulting continued pursuit of our failed drug policy are themselves caused by the same fundamental psychological need that motivates drug production and consumption: the need to maintain one's identity, or sense of self. The War on Drugs supports the identities of "normal" people, first, by freeing them of all responsibility for the drug problem, helping them to believe that their own behaviours— their voting choices, consumption habits, business practices, cultural activities, and so on—play no role in producing the behaviours of substance abusers, and second, by providing them with the image of a depraved Other in comparison with whom they can feel morally pure and (in many cases) blissfully unaware of their own addictions to, and abuses of, various substances, such as alcohol, tobacco, food, entertainment, commodities, money, and so on.

This same deep motivation—the need to maintain one's identity—is responsible for the fact that policy-makers and the public rarely inquire into the (material, social, and cultural) environmental causes of drug production and consumption, both current environmental circumstances that serve to trigger, and past environmental factors that have created, the psychological needs (including "character flaws") driving individuals to produce or consume drugs. As later chapters will substantiate, the reason the more effective, environmental interventions are not emphasized by policy-makers and the general public is not because the knowledge of environmental causes is not available to them; rather, it is because locating the causes of substance abuse primarily or even solely in the producers and consumers of illegal drugs answers a fundamental psychological need of "good, normal, law-abiding citizens": the need to maintain a strong identity, or sense of self.

This same dynamic is motivating the War on Terrorism. The necessity of discovering and addressing the root causes of terrorism, and the refusal of the Bush administration to do so, have been noted by many social scientists and other observers (e.g., Mack, 2002; Perlman, 2002; Rubenstein, 2003). Rather than inquiring into the motives, and the causes of the motives, of the terrorists' actions, George W. Bush rushed to declare the perpetrators evil and their actions incomprehensible, thus reducing the attacks to a single, inscrutable cause: evil, irrational individuals. Subsequently, on the relatively rare occasions that Bush and the public in general have acknowledged that the terrorists' motives had causes, the causes have usually been reduced to the single factor of fanatical, fundamentalist Islamic religious teaching. Ignored are past and present events of Western military intervention, economic and political hegemony, and cultural imperialism and the psychological impact of these actions on many Muslims.

Such failure to acknowledge the full array of causes that are responsible for a social problem is perhaps the most fundamental and damaging of social symptoms, for, without taking into account the full battery of causes responsible for a social problem, it is very difficult to formulate effective policies to combat it. Dissolving this symptom can thus make an important contribution toward the solution of social problems. But how can one combat the unconscious defences against recognizing these causes?

There are three levels of intervention. The first is to make explicit, continuously and forcefully, in the face of denials and diversions, all the significant causes that contribute to social problems. The second is to expose the defences against acknowledging these causes and explain what is motivating these defences—that is, explain how they are working to maintain the identities of those who use the defences. And the third and most fundamental level of intervention is to help people develop identities that relieve them of the need to resort to such defences in order to maintain their identities. I will discuss the second and third levels of intervention in later chapters. Here, I focus on the first, not only because it is the simplest and easiest to enact, but also because having a grasp of the entire network of a social problem's causes is a prerequisite for detecting when specific social views or policies are functioning defensively as a means of avoiding one or more causes and their concomitant interventions.

The web of causality producing social problems

What, then, are the key causes, both proximal and distal, that produce social problems? The most immediate and obvious, as we have already discussed, are the behaviours that constitute these problems and that are the focus of our responses to substance abuse and most other social problems as well. Most policies aimed at ameliorating social problems take into account only these most proximal causes: the behaviours constituting or producing the social problem and the presumed immorality or character flaws of

those who engage in these behaviours. But such attribution of problematic behaviours to character faults and/or moral deficiencies
provides little or no explanation of the causes of the behaviours; in
a tautological move, it simply assumes that bad actions are caused
by bad people. How do we know that people who commit bad
actions are bad? Because they commit bad actions. No insight is
offered about either the internal causes (motivations) or the external causes (situations and circumstances) of such behaviours.

Psychological causes

To prevent or alter the behaviours responsible for social problems,
we need to do more than simply attribute these behaviours to a
presumed moral deficiency or flawed character of those who
engage in them. We need to understand the psychological forces
that motivate their harmful behaviours and/or prevent them from
engaging in alternative, more benign behaviours. This means
understanding the deepest motivations. Most policies aimed at
solving social problems fail to recognize and engage these motivations. Instead, they attempt to change the problematic behaviours
through some form of force, overlooking more productive and less
coercive alternatives such as (a) altering the perpetrators' psychological needs (motivations) so that they express themselves through
more benign behaviours in the prevailing circumstances, or (b)
changing the perpetrators' circumstances so that they can satisfy
their psychological needs through more benign behaviours made
possible by the altered circumstances.

Current environmental circumstances

This alternative addresses the other proximal cause of socially
harmful behaviours—that is, the specific circumstances (physical,
material, interpersonal, social, political, cultural) with which they
are confronted. A small percentage of preventive measures attempt
to address this additional cause by altering situations to make it less
likely that individuals will engage in socially problematic behaviours. Such alterations include the provision of incentives and
opportunities for individuals to pursue alternative, benign behaviours—such as opportunities for youth to engage in sports (e.g.,

midnight basketball) or artistic activities (e.g., music, dance)—and the removal of incentives and opportunities to engage in the harmful activities (through, for example, reducing poverty and oppression, installing locks and security systems, imposing curfews, and disbanding gangs). But while there does exist in some quarters a tacit acknowledgement of the causal role played by circumstance in the production of social problems, this recognition does not inform public policy in the rigorous and systematic manner it should. The crucial importance of circumstances in triggering harmful behaviours is largely ignored by politicians and the general public. This is most unfortunate, because, to the extent that we can understand how certain circumstances tend to elicit socially problematic behaviours in vulnerable identities, we can reduce the social problem by altering the circumstances.

Taking the perpetrator's psychological needs and environmental circumstances into account yields the following view of the causes of social problems:

$$\text{Psychological needs} \times \text{environmental circumstances} \rightarrow$$
$$\text{harmful behaviour} \rightarrow \text{social problem}$$

When we understand these two proximal causes of the problematic behaviours constituting social problems, we can take steps to prevent the behaviours by eliminating one or both of the causes—specifically, the motivation and/or the environmental triggers and constraints.

Formative environmental causes

More enlightened social policy (unfortunately, quite rare) recognizes yet another level of causality, often referred to as "root causes": the factors of an individual's formative environment that cause the development of the particular psychological needs (including "character flaws") that predispose certain individuals to engage in socially harmful behaviours. This perspective recognizes that while an individual's psychological needs (whether or not involving a "flawed character") are a necessary cause of the social problems, these needs do not arise *ex nihilo*, but are, rather, produced by an interaction of the individual's genetic endowment with his or her formative environment. This "root cause" perspective operates with the following understanding of the causes of social problems, in which genetic factors interact with formative environmental factors to produce an individual's psychological needs, which then interact with the individual's current environmental circumstances to produce harmful behaviours that constitute social problems (see Figure 1).

This more comprehensive understanding of the causes of behaviour enables interventions far upstream of a social problem, most notably interventions in the formative environments of individuals, to prevent them from developing the psychological vulnerabilities and needs ("character flaws") that predispose them to engage in the sorts of behaviours that constitute social problems. Examples of the rare but highly effective programmes addressing the formative environmental factors include early childhood intervention programmes in Murfreesboro, Tennessee, in Ypsilanti, Michigan, and in Harlem, each of which produced significant reductions in dropouts, crime, substance abuse, and teen pregnancy by providing various forms of psychological support for children during their formative years (Schorr, 1988, pp. 193–197, 272).

Despite the proven effectiveness of such environmental interventions, most public attention and public policies are focused on preventing or containing individuals' socially harmful behaviour, primarily through forcefully intervening in their psychological needs and/or current environmental circumstances. In recent

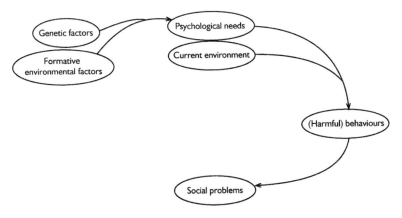

Figure 1.   Environmental and psychological causes of social problems.

decades, social policy in the USA has actually decreased, rather than increased, programmes for changing the formative and situational environments. Conservatives have been quite successful in rationalizing their resistance to root-cause thinking and discrediting such an approach to social problems. They have done so by insisting that such an approach is ineffective and oppressive. Sometimes branding such efforts as "social engineering", they attempt to associate them with the ruthless totalitarian tactics of Nazi Germany and Stalinist Russia. At the very least, they claim that the persistence of problems like poverty and crime in the aftermath of New Deal and Great Society social programmes proves that root-cause approaches to such problems are ineffective or even counterproductive.

But just because some root-cause approaches to social problems have not completely solved the problem does not mean they have been counterproductive or even ineffective. On the contrary, many of these programmes have produced significant human benefits (Schorr, 1988, 1998). And even if the programmes had been utter failures, that fact would not prove in the least that root-cause interventions could not succeed. Abandoning root-cause thinking concerning social problems makes no more sense than abandoning root-cause thinking when it comes to trying to prevent disease. Abandoning root-cause thinking concerning social problems now would be like medicine abandoning the search for the causes of disease in the nineteenth century and continuing to treat patients by bleeding them, or opposing inoculation on the grounds that it victimized the innocent. If such a conclusion had been drawn from similar initial failures in other fields, we would be lacking most vaccines, antibiotics, and surgical procedures, our preferred modes of transportation and telecommunication, most of psychotherapy, and countless other benefits besides. To give up in the face of failures or limited successes with root-cause social interventions thus demonstrates not realistic thinking, but wishful thinking: a thinking governed by the wish not to eliminate, reduce, or even understand the true causes of our social problems, but, rather, to perpetuate them.

There are a number of reasons root-cause thinking is resisted. One is the perceived economic cost of addressing root causes: the rich and powerful perceive such interventions (incorrectly, in most cases) as costing more money than they save and thus resulting in a net financial loss for themselves. But the most powerful resistance

to root-cause thinking comes from the fact that it implicates everyone in social problems and therefore threatens their (our) identities.
For a rigorous pursuit of the root causes of social problems cannot
stop after locating the causes of harmful behaviours in the perpetrators' formative and triggering environments. Rather, it must
enquire into the causes of both of these causes—that is, the causes
of these environments. And when it does so, it encounters the fact
that, while both the harmful formative and the triggering environmental conditions are due in part to chance, contingency, or
"fortune", which includes factors over which no one has any
control, they are also caused to a large degree by the behaviours of
other individuals, especially policy-making behaviours, including
voting for certain political candidates rather than others. That is, the
social and political behaviours of "normal people", "law-abiding
citizens", cause the material, social, political, and cultural realities
that constitute a large part of both the formative environments and
the triggering environments of the immediate perpetrators of social
problems. Addressing the root causes of social problems thus
means taking into account not only the psychologically formative
and the triggering environments of the immediate perpetrators, but
also the behaviours of "normal" people that produce these environments. Adding these behaviours to the picture produces a more
complete model of the causes of social problems (Figure 2).

Finally, a complete understanding of the causes of social problems must also take into account the causes of the "environment-
constituting" behaviours of "normal", "law-abiding" people, which
means understanding, first, the psychological needs and personal
circumstances that converge to produce these behaviours, and
second, the formative environmental factors that combine with
their genetic endowment to produce their psychological needs.
What we have, then, are the following layers of causes.

1. Social problems are caused most immediately by certain harm-
    ful behaviours of certain individuals.

2. These harmful behaviours are caused by the individuals'
    particular psychological needs interacting with their current
    environmental circumstances.

3. These psychological needs are caused by individuals' particu-
    lar genetic endowments interacting with their particular
    formative environments.

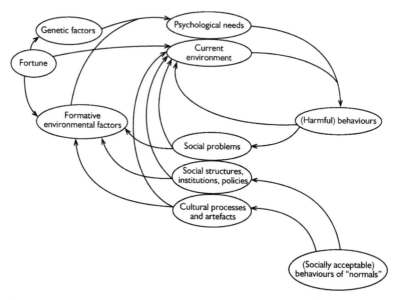

Figure 2. Root causes of environmental and psychological causes of social problems.

4. Both the formative environments and the current environmental circumstances are caused jointly by "fortune" and by environment-constituting behaviours, primarily the behaviours of "normal, law-abiding" individuals.

5. The environment-constituting behaviours of "normal, law-abiding" individuals are caused by their particular psychological needs interacting with their environmental circumstances.

6. "Normal" individuals' psychological needs are caused by their particular genetic endowments interacting with their particular formative environments.

7. "Normal" individuals' formative environments and current environmental circumstances are caused jointly by "fortune" and by environment-constituting behaviours, primarily the behaviours of these same "normal, law-abiding" individuals.

As Figure 3 indicates, these various causes constitute a system of potentially self-perpetuating circular causation—represented by the continuous circulation of each factor through the figure eight of the diagram—with a given cause contributing to a chain of effects

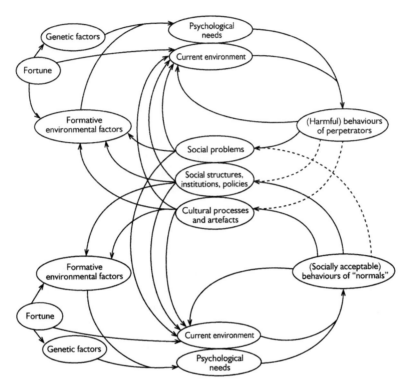

Figure 3.   Vicious circle of causes of social problems.

that eventuates in (re)producing this same cause. Thus, for example, criminal behaviour (as we will see in more detail in Chapter Two) produces social conditions that elicit "crime-fighting" behaviour from many voters, policy makers, law enforcement officials, members of the legal system, corrections officers, and so on in the form of harsher punishment, and this harsher punishment (part of the "social condition") contributes to formative environments and current environmental circumstances of perpetrators that produce greater psychological predispositions in them toward criminal behaviour, thus constituting a vicious circle.

But, while such a vicious circle does operate in many social problems, it is not inevitable. The system of causes producing social problems is not closed, and thus social problems are not necessarily self-perpetuating. In fact, the good news to be derived from this comprehensive understanding of the causes of social problems is

that each of the multiple causes constitutes a possible point of intervention. For example, changes in the environmental circumstances
of individuals can prevent socially harmful behaviours, as can alteration of the psychological needs that are motivating the harmful
behaviour.

Social solutions through identity interventions: a new strategy for social change

Reducing the harmful behaviours that constitute social problems
thus requires, first, recognizing the vicious, spiralling circle that
exists between such behaviours and the production of environments that variously produce and trigger the psychological vulnerabilities motivating these behaviours, and second, intervening to
prevent or reduce these psychological vulnerabilities and thus eliminating the need to engage in these harmful behaviours. The aim of
this book is to promote this process by explaining:

1. identity's motivational role in social problems—that is, how
   identity needs cause (motivate) the behaviours that constitute,
   both directly and indirectly—social problems;
2. the nature of identity—that is, the components and dynamics
   involved in its development and maintenance;
3. the social and cultural forces that produce the identity deficiencies that lead to behaviours that constitute social problems;
4. interventions to support and/or develop identity in ways that
   will help prevent these behaviours that constitute the social
   problems.

Social symptoms draws on research in multiple disciplines to
show that our major social problems, including crime, violence,
terrorism, war, substance abuse, and prejudice, are largely the result
of efforts on the part of their perpetrators to maintain a secure identity, or sense of self. The investigation reveals, further, that our
society's ineffective and counterproductive responses to these problems—including the War on Drugs, the War on Crime, and the War
on Terrorism—are themselves the result of the fact that we do not
really want to solve them, because they serve as means for the rest

of us, the general public, to maintain our own identities. And, at a third level, underlying both the first-order social problems and the failure of adequate responses to them, the analysis finds certain trauma-generating social conditions and cultural forces which render identity vulnerable and prone to defend and maintain itself by any means necessary. The analysis further reveals that these social and cultural forces, like the first and second levels of social problems, are themselves social symptoms, maintained for the identity support they provide, primarily to the more privileged classes.

Having explained the identity dynamics underlying these three levels of social problems, the book concludes by identifying social and cultural interventions that can help solve or mitigate these social symptoms by preventing or repairing the identity problems that give rise to them. The understanding that *Social Symptoms* provides of the motivational primacy of identity maintenance, of the social and cultural conditions that are optimal for identity development and maintenance, and of the multiple levels of causality in which identity and its formative and maintenance conditions are involved, enables the formulation of more effective strategies for preventing these social problems. While other social and cultural remedies for social problems are based on mere correlations (either observed or only anticipated) between interventions and results, the present study explains the causal paths by which social problems are produced (i.e., by harming or impeding identity) and by which successful interventions work (i.e., by supporting and developing identity), and this understanding establishes a foundation for the formulation and implementation of more effective interventions for reducing or eliminating our major social problems.

In order to solve our social problems, we thus need first to understand the identity needs—of both the immediate perpetrators and the general public—that are responsible for the various behaviours that produce these problems. Chapter One presents a comprehensive model of identity that allows us to see how harmful behaviours, the environmental factors giving rise to them, and the failed efforts to prevent them all function unconsciously to maintain the identities of the people involved.

Part II exposes the specific identity needs motivating the perpetrators of some of our most significant social problems and explains how the behaviours that constitute these problems are ways of maintaining the identities of their perpetrators. Chapter Two explains the identity vulnerabilities and deficiencies of various types of delinquents and criminals, and demonstrates how their respective antisocial behaviours serve in one way or another to maintain their identities. Chapter Three provides a similar analysis of terrorists and warriors.

Part III explains how our failure to solve our most pressing social problems is the result of efforts to maintain our identities through establishing and maintaining subalterns, including drug addicts, criminals, enemy nations, terrorists, poor people, and others. Chapter Four shows how the War on Drugs, the War on Crime, and the War on Terrorism, as well as prejudice and group hatred, function to defend the (perhaps surprisingly) vulnerable and deficient identities of "normal, law-abiding citizens" by serving as targets on which these more privileged individuals can simultaneously externalize and enact their own unacknowledged and rejected elements of self, particularly their aggression. Chapter Five exposes the traumatogenic conditions of contemporary American society and culture that are largely responsible for the respective identity vulnerabilities of both subaltern and privileged individuals and that therefore need to be reduced in order to reduce the identity needs that produce social symptoms. Each type of trauma—physical, institutional, structural, and cultural—is seen to be the result of an effort to protect or repair an identity that has itself been injured by one or more of these same types of trauma. Thus, we find at the core of our most pressing social problems an unending chain of trauma, whereby those who are traumatized inflict trauma, directly or indirectly, on others (and ultimately also on themselves), who repeat the infliction on victims of their own, *ad infinitum*. Solving these social problems thus requires breaking the chain of trauma by reducing the need for traumatized identities to maintain themselves through activities—physical, institutional, structural, or cultural violence—that are themselves traumatogenic. And this requires providing alternative, more benign ways for traumatized identities to repair and maintain themselves.

Part IV develops these strategies. Chapter Six sketches out several ways of shifting individuals' investments away from malignant, violence-entailing contents (such as the traditional masculine qualities of toughness, independence, and dominance) and towards more benign, prosocial contents (such as gentleness, fairness, and caring). Chapter Seven presents a strategy for deactivating the collective identity defences that contribute significantly to various social symptoms. In addition to decommissioning cognitive distortions that are harmful *per se*, such an undermining of defences also enables the integration into identity of rejected impulses, ideas, wishes, and fantasies, the exclusion of which renders identity vulnerable in a number of ways. Chapter Eight articulates several cultural interventions that can promote integration of these excluded elements of self and thus make identities stronger and less in need of socially harmful ways of maintaining themselves.

Social Symptoms' analyses of identity and its relation to social problems lead to the conclusion that our society must engage in a systematic effort to protect, support, and promote the identities of all its members, as well as those of other nations, for four basic reasons.

1. Providing identity support and development is the best, and ultimately the only, way to solve our most serious social problems.
2. Social justice requires optimal identity support and development opportunities for everyone.
3. If we want to be moral and to have others behave morally, we must protect them and ourselves from identity damage and insecurity and promote identity development, because consistently moral behaviour is possible only on the foundation of a secure and adequately developed identity.
4. Our own individual, personal fulfilment requires helping others achieve optimal identity security and development.

CHAPTER ONE

The nature of identity and its role in social problems

"The need to feel a sense of identity stems from the very condition of human existence, and it is the source of the most intense strivings. Since I cannot remain sane without the sense of "I," I am driven to do almost anything to acquire this sense. . . . [The need for identity] is sometimes even stronger than the need for physical survival"

(Fromm, 1955, p. 63)

"Maintenance of identity in [humans] has priority over any other principle determining human behaviour. . . . The identity principle . . . is absolutely compelling"

(Lichtenstein, 1977, pp. 59, 116)

"People will sacrifice anything to prevent the death and disintegration of their individual or group identity"

(Gilligan, 1996, p. 97)

As we saw in the Introduction, effectively addressing social problems requires understanding the causes of human behaviour: first, the causes of those behaviours that constitute social problems, and second, the causes of those behaviours that cause the causes of these primary behaviours. And since all human behaviour is the result of a person's motives interacting with his or her circumstances, understanding human motivation is a prerequisite for understanding and effectively intervening in social problems. This chapter sketches out a more adequate and comprehensive account of human motivation than is present in most social theories, all of which are based on a more or less explicit and comprehensive theory of human motivation (Carveth, 1984, p. 44; Turner, 1987, pp. 15ff.). The central principle of this theory is that all human behaviour is ultimately motivated by the need to maintain one's identity, which I define as the sense of oneself as a force that matters in the world. Our behaviour is the result of our continuous effort to maintain or enhance this identity, or sense of self.

In its most basic form, identity is simply the sense that one *is* (Lichtenstein, 1977, p. 8; Rangell, 1994, p. 27). Erik Erikson, who brought the concept to prominence in both academic and public discourse, provides a more extended definition of identity as "a sense of psychosocial well-being" (Erikson, 1968, p. 19), which involves "a subjective sense of an invigorating sameness and continuity" (*ibid.*, p. 50) and "a feeling of being at home in one's body, a sense of 'knowing where one is going', and an inner assuredness of anticipated recognition from those who count" (*ibid.*, p. 165). Identity as one's sense of oneself, which Erikson sometimes refers to as ego-identity, is to be distinguished from both social identity and personal identity, each of which, however, contributes to ego-identity, or one's sense of oneself. Most discussions of "identity", in both public discourse and academic discourse, concern social identity, which refers to an individual's various memberships in social groups and categories, such as those of race, ethnicity, religion, class, gender, sexuality, occupation, political affiliation, age, and so on. While social identity is of great importance to most individuals, it is not itself the prime mover of individual and social action that it is sometimes taken to be (Gaertner, Sedikides, Vevea, & Iuzzini, 2002). Rather, it is important only in so far as it either contributes to, or undermines, an individual's ego-identity, or sense of self. The same is true of personal identity, which denotes those qualities that distinguish an individual from other individuals: our differences from others matter to us only to the extent that they bear in one way or another on our sense of self.

Maintaining this most fundamental (ego) identity, or sense of self, is our most basic need and the ultimate motivation behind all our actions, both individual and collective. Heinz Lichtenstein, the other major psychoanalytic theorist of identity after Erikson, concludes that "maintenance of identity in [humans] has priority over any other principle determining human behaviour" (Lichtenstein, 1977, p. 59), including the pleasure principle, the repetition compulsion, and the instinctual drives of libido and aggression, all of which, according to Lichtenstein, are particular manifestations of a more fundamental principle: identity. Lichtenstein views instincts as "guarantors of biological identity", and sees "nonprocreative sexuality" as a means of acquiring "a primary identity" (ibid.) by achieving "an ecstatic climax of the sense of being" (ibid., p. 41). He argues that Freud's "repetition compulsion is a manifestation of the necessity for maintenance of the 'theme of identity'" and that "the maintenance of the identity theme does indeed appear to have priority over any other principle, including the pleasure principle" (ibid., p. 103). Indeed, "identity establishment and maintenance must be considered basic biological principles" (ibid., p. 114). Establishing and maintaining an identity, or sense of self, is more important than anything else, including biological survival. Even homeostasis is subordinate to "the necessity of maintenance of identity" (ibid., p. 115).

Other psychoanalysts, while not as systematic as Lichtenstein in their exposition of the identity principle, also note its motivational primacy. Erich Fromm observes that

> the need to feel a sense of identity stems from the very condition of human existence, and it is the source of the most intense strivings. Since I cannot remain sane without the sense of 'I', I am driven to do almost anything to acquire this sense. . . . [The need for identity] is sometimes even stronger than the need for physical survival. [Fromm, 1955, p. 63]

(See also Lichtenberg & Schonbar, 1992, p. 11; Pine, 1990, pp. 81–96; Rangell, 1994, p. 36.)

Even the work of Jacques Lacan, which focuses on conflicts and discontinuities of the self, recognizes the fundamental motivation to maintain a sense of self in (1) the endless quest for a sense of bodily unity, coherence, and integrity; (2) the unflagging devotion to certain systems of knowledge and belief; (3) the ongoing attempt to embody certain ideals; (4) the repeated enactment of certain fundamental fantasies; and (5) the repeated and automatic gratification of certain unconscious drives (Lacan, 1966).

That the need to maintain one's identity or sense of self is the ultimate motive driving human behaviour has been noted by other researchers as well. Kristen Renwick Monroe, who began her career as a rational action theorist, was led by her research on rescuers of Jews during the Holocaust to recognize "the tremendous power of identity to constrain critical political and moral choice" (Monroe, 2004, p. 77) and has concluded that the nature of one's identity was "the critical factor for both perpetrators and for the rescuers" (ibid., p. 81). Psychiatrist James Gilligan concluded, after working many years with violent criminals, that "people will sacrifice anything to prevent the death and disintegration of their individual or group identity" (Gilligan, 1996, p. 97). John Burton reached a similar conclusion based on his research into basic human needs: "Individuals in society have always employed whatever means are currently available to them to attain recognition and identity" (Burton, 1997, p. 10). Kenneth Hoover, a political scientist and identity theorist, echoes this view. "Identity is not optional", he declares. "People will act on their promptings toward identity in whatever theatre is available" (Hoover, 2004a, p. 5). "People will seek an identity whether by fair means or foul, constructive or destructive" (Hoover, 2004b, pp. 107–108).

These claims for the motivational primacy of identity maintenance made by clinicians and other qualitative researchers are supported by numerous quantitative studies demonstrating the operation of processes such as self-affirmation, self-enhancement, self-verification, self-assessment, self-improvement, and the pursuit of self-esteem (on these motives, and the difference between identity and self esteem, see Appendix II). Self-affirmation theory, developed by Claude Steele, posits that whenever the self feels threatened, a global self-affirmation system directs cognition and behaviour in ways that protect and restore one's sense of self. In several experiments, Steele and his colleagues found that, when identity is threatened, people use whatever means are available to re-establish its integrity. In one study, subjects were told that the people in their community (and hence, by implication, they themselves) were either (1) bad drivers, (2) unco-operative with community projects, or (3) co-operative with community projects. They were then asked, two days later, if they would provide a list of everything in their kitchens in order to assist in the development of a food co-op in their community. Those individuals whose identities had earlier been threatened—by being told either that they were bad drivers or that they were unco-operative—agreed to this request at a rate twice as high as that of individuals whose identities had not been threatened. From this and other similar experiments, Steele concludes that when our identity is threatened, we will use any means available to re-establish its integrity. Sometimes, this involves addressing the threat, but when such a response is not feasible or cost-effective, we will instead affirm aspects of identity that were unaffected by the threat, such as when individuals whose identity as good drivers was threatened responded by demonstrating not their driving skills but, rather, their co-operative natures (Steele, 1999, pp. 374–375).

Identity contents

What, then, is the nature of this identity that is the prime mover of human behaviour? The most important elements of identity are its contents, which are more diverse and complex than has been recognized by either most researchers or laypersons. The dominant notion concerning identity contents is that they consist of one's social roles (e.g., father, mother, teacher, psychologist), demographic categories (e.g., race, gender, age, socio-economic class), group memberships (e.g., national, regional, community, political, religious), and/or ideals and values (e.g., kindness, courage, intelligence). While such identity-bearing categories—which can be reduced to linguistic signifiers—are essential to our sense of self, they are not by themselves sufficient to sustain it. In the linguistic register alone, our sense of self is also heavily dependent on certain systems of belief or knowledge that we have invested in, and on certain identity-bearing scripts or narratives that we have adopted. Moreover, these three forms of linguistically based identity contents are themselves based on, and incapable of functioning without, two non-linguistic forms of identity content: images and affective–physiological states. As the neurologist Antonio Damasio explains, the foundation of our sense of self derives from a continual, pulse-like neurological mapping of our biological condition, including our skin, our skeletal muscles, and our viscera. This physiological mapping is then re-represented in imagistic form, in connection with images of the internal and external objects, and this continuous imagistic representation constitutes our core sense of self, including our sense of sameness and continuity despite the changes that we undergo across our lifespan and sometimes even moment to moment: since our body's fundamental structure and its basic systems and organs persist through our life, neurological mappings and imagistic representations of our self also remain more or less the same (Damasio, 2000, pp. 22–23, 125–153). Our most comprehensive identity, or fullest sense of self, derives from the neurological mappings and imagistic representations of our body together with the linguistic representations given to some of them as well as to selected patterns and abstractions of our self (see Damasio, 2000, p. 173).

As Damasio's account indicates, our sense of self requires an integration and sustained activation of three different registers of experience and memory: the affective–physiological, the perceptual–imagistic, and the conceptual–linguistic. The affective-physiological register sustains identity through the body's adequate physiological functioning, including the processing of sensory information, and through the periodic repetition of what Daniel Stern (1985) has called "vitality affects", such as excitement, joy, quiescence, and anger. Imagistic register identity is a function of an individual's body image, felt sense of bodily unity, agency, and efficacy, and visual–spatial orientation in the external world. And identity in the conceptual–linguistic register is composed of ideals, values, social roles, demographic categories, and group memberships, which are themselves based on certain identity-bearing signifiers, such as "man", "woman", "civilized", and "intelligent", as well as on systems of signifiers, such as specific bodies of knowledge, belief systems, scripts, and narratives.

Affective–physiological identity contents

Thus while the linguistically based identity contents focused on by most identity theorists and the general public may be the most familiar, they are not the most primal or fundamental contents. That position belongs to certain affective–physiological states that become established early on as optimal for us. Such states develop out of, and remain tied to, our experiences of our basic metabolic functions. They are

the many "forms of feeling" inextricably involved with all the vital processes of life, such as breathing, getting hungry, falling asleep and emerging out of sleep, or feeling the coming and going of emotions and thoughts. [Stern, 1985, p. 54]

These processes, which operate as long as we are alive, manifest themselves in the form of "activation contours" involving different types, degrees, and trajectories of affective–physiological arousal. These optimal affective–physiological states can differ significantly from one individual to another, and from one group to another. Some people experience their most intense sense of self when they are in the hypervigilant state brought on by pressure or danger, while for others the most secure sense of self is based on a state of calmness or relaxation such as that produced by immersion in a supportive, stable, highly predictable environment. But whatever particular vitality affect(s) lie at the core of one's identity, every individual is constantly operating in such a way as to reproduce those affects and their activation contours. This is because the reproduction of the affective–physiological states that are most familiar and reassuring to us is one of the most powerful ways we all have of supporting our identity.

The importance of maintaining optimal affective–physiological states is evident from the continual monitoring and numerous adjustments and techniques that we direct toward these states, activities that include but also far exceed what is necessary for our mere biological well-being. In Western cultures, there are at least five basic techniques for maintaining optimal, identity-bearing affective–physiological states, and post-industrial societies provide multiple venues and resources for engaging in each of them. These techniques include:

1. ingesting physiology-altering substances (alcohol, recreational drugs, caffeine, nicotine, sugar, chocolate);

2. stimulating the body to produce endorphins or adrenaline (sex, exercise, risk taking);
3. cultivating mood-altering sensory and perceptual experiences (music, sight-seeing, aromatherapy, massage, bathing, showering);
4. engaging in affect-regulating social activities (parties, sports, games, meetings);
5. engaging in affect-regulating cultural activities (attending concerts, religious events, sports spectatorship).

Most people employ one or more of these techniques multiple times, and/or for an extended period of time, on any given day. Not all individuals have the access or ability to employ only socially benign techniques, and, as a result, some attempts to maintain one's identity-bearing affective–physiological state cause harm to oneself or to others. Violence and criminality are prime examples. As we will see in the next chapter, some criminal activities (in addition to the consumption of illegal substances) are engaged in for the rush they provide, and some warriors and terrorists, as we will see in Chapter Three, become addicted to their violent activity because of the rush it brings. But the fact that, as Stern notes, any given affective–physiological state can be produced by a number of different types of experience—for example, a rush can be produced by experiences as various as danger, joy, intense sensual stimulation, the consumption of chemical stimulants, or an intellectual or artistic breakthrough (Stern, 1985, pp. 55–58)—means that socially destructive behaviours that are engaged in (partly or totally) for the purposes of maintaining a certain identity-bearing affective–physiological state might be reduced by providing opportunities to engage in socially benign behaviours that produce much the same affective–physiological state. This fact has important ramifications for social problems and social policy.

Imagistic identity contents

Identity in the imagistic register is the sense of oneself as "a single, coherent, bounded physical entity" (Stern, 1985, p. 82). Imagistic identity is a function, most notably, of our bodily form and efficacy in relation to our physical surroundings. We are constantly seeking to support our imagistic identity by maintaining our sense of bodily integrity and efficacy and by enhancing our physical form, as well as by altering our body's physical environment to render it more supportive of these maintenance efforts. A number of psychological researchers and clinicians have come to view "the body self and body image as basic foundations for a psychological sense of self" (Krueger, 1989, p. xi), such that "an individual's healthy mature sense of self contains, at its core, a cohesive, distinct, and accurate body self" (*ibid.*, p. x). As Krueger states,

> The body and its evolving mental representation are the foundation of a sense of self. . . . In order to experience a stable sense of self, one must first have experienced the integrity of one's own body space and boundaries. [*ibid.*, p. 38]

The necessity of a stable body image for a secure sense of self has been demonstrated by, among other things, the fact that when individuals are deprived of their body image through sensory deprivation (by, for example, being suspended motionless in water in a dark, absolutely quiet room), their "sense of self [is] radically dissipated" (Fisher, 1974, p. 22).

Three key components of the bodily sense of self have been identified. Most fundamental is the sense of a body boundary, which separates inside from outside and determines our sense of where we end and other people and the world at large begin. This boundary is the basis for the sense of bodily integrity and coherence that we gradually develop throughout childhood and adolescence and into adulthood. The body boundary is also a factor in the second component of our bodily sense of self, our visual image of our appearance and the degree to which it approximates or falls short of the appearance ideals we develop (largely on the basis of being socialized into our culture's ideals). The third component of our bodily sense of self is our sense of bodily agency and efficacy, the experience of our body as an origin or centre of initiative that can make things happen in the world. Each of these three basic factors of our bodily sense of self has a number of subsidiary elements through which it can be seen to motivate a multiplicity of behaviours aiming at maintaining and/or enhancing our bodily identity.

The most obvious concerns for our body image involve our appearance. Most Americans continually monitor and intervene in the shape, size, colour, and texture of multiple body parts, including numerous facial features, arms, chest, abdomen, thighs, buttocks, and multiple types of bodily hair, all for the purpose of conforming to a particular cultural ideal appearance and thus eliciting positive feedback from others. We often go to great pains—sometimes literally—and expend considerable money, time, and effort to acquire such feedback concerning our bodies, either through numerous types of display, or through actual physical alteration. As Seymour Fisher observes, "It is difficult to think of any human enterprise to which greater quantities of effort, money, and ingenuity are devoted than that involved in converting one's body into an acceptable and understandable companion" (Fisher, 1974, p. xii). When camouflage cannot produce the results we desire, we often turn to various techniques for altering the body itself (*ibid.*, p. 80). One of the most common techniques is dieting. Most adults in the USA have dieted at one time or another, and many have done so multiple times. Multi-billion-dollar industries have grown up around these efforts (and have, of course, played a major role in promoting the efforts), including diet foods, diet books, diet programmes, and diet consultants.

Another prominent technique for altering the body's appearance is exercising, which has also increased dramatically in the last three decades in our society. Here, too, the fact that multiple multi-billion-dollar industries are involved indicates the importance of this activity to us. And when neither diet nor exercise can produce the optimal body appearance, individuals increasingly resort to the most radical form of alteration: surgery. Once involving only a few procedures (nose jobs, breast implants) indulged in primarily by movie stars and the super-rich, cosmetic surgery has grown to involve dozens of procedures and is undergone by many ordinary, middle-class individuals as well. In addition to breast implants and nose jobs, procedures now include altering the size or shape of virtually every part of the face (lips, chin, cheekbones, jawbone, eyelids, eyebrows, brow, hairline, ears), liposuction of most parts of the torso and thighs, implants for the buttock, pectoral, and calf muscles, penile implants, hair transplants, and more.

Deficiencies in one's body image or sense of self produce significant human costs through the resources they take away from other, more beneficial activities. And, in addition to such passive harm or acts of omission, our body-image vulnerability also motivates harmful acts of commission, in the form of prejudice and discrimination directed towards individuals whose bodily appearance and/or ideals deviate from our own. Instances include racism, sexism, homophobia, and discrimination towards individuals who are obese or who have physical handicaps (Fisher, 1974, p. 73).

While our devotion to our bodily appearance may be more evident, maintaining a sense of our bodily integrity is even more important, and perhaps also more destructive. Our sense of bodily integrity begins with the sense that our body has a distinct and stable boundary, separating us from the world, inside from outside. The importance of a sense of bodily boundary is demonstrated by the fact that, as Fisher notes, "people expend enormous energy in setting up defensive boundaries" (ibid., p. 22), and "[e]ach person battles day and night to maintain his borders" (ibid., p. 40). Research, Fisher reports, indicates "that the greater a person's uncertainty about the protection provided by his own body border the more he will seek compensatory ways of reaffirming that border" (ibid., p. 22). Many of these efforts involve fairly benign manipulations of the skin, which is the key organ defining the body's border. Such manipulations include stimulating the skin to enhance our sensation of it (and hence our bodily boundary), emphasizing it visually to increase our own as well as others' perceptions of it (and hence of our boundary), and adopting various types of auxiliary skin (Fisher, 1974, pp. 23, 27, 70, 91, 103; Krueger, 1989, p. 10). We also adopt various types of auxiliary skin to emphasize our bodily boundary, including clothing, skeletal musculature, and fat (Krueger, 1989, pp. 10, 27), as well as buildings and motor vehicles (Fisher, 1974, p. 23).

While these forms of bodily boundary enhancement seem to be more or less harmless, this is not always the case. For one thing, the establishment and maintenance of some auxiliary boundaries can lead to violence, on either a small or a large scale, such as when gang members fight any non-members who may venture on to what they have declared to be their turf, or when nations fight wars to expand their boundaries or to prevent feared intrusion from another nation. Moreover, as Fisher points out,

> a person who doubts the strength and integrity of his body may express this feeling by being chronically afraid that intruders will break into his house (or perhaps even that the borders of his country will be invaded). [*ibid.*, p. xiii]

In addition to our appearance and boundary security, our bodily sense of self is also derived from our sense of bodily agency, efficacy, power, control, competence, and mastery (see Krueger, 1989, pp. 18–21), which is also the foundation of the more general senses of agency, efficacy, and competence that are important aspects of our identity as a whole. The motivational force of this identity need can be seen not only in the dogged determination of infants and children to master their bodies in crawling, standing, walking, running, jumping, and climbing, but also in the time, expense, and effort that many adults devote to improving their backhand or their putting stroke. It can also be seen in our acquisition and use of all sorts of prosthetic devices and surrogate bodies—tools, machines, appliances, motor vehicles, and so on—as well as in our spectatorship of sports and arts performances in which we achieve vicarious gratification from the bodily mastery and efficacy of accomplished athletes and artists.

Once again, since these enactments and displays of bodily agency and efficacy are so common and appear to cause little harm, they are rarely criticized. But the pursuit of bodily agency and efficacy can play a significant role in violence of all types. Interpersonal physical violence—which, as we shall see, is usually motivated by men's efforts to protect a vulnerable sense of their own manhood—constitutes a readily available and incontrovertible means of demonstrating (to oneself as well as to others) one's bodily agency, efficacy, power, control, and mastery. Participation in group violence is also motivated by a need to demonstrate one's bodily power.

Given the harm that results from various prominent strategies for defending and enhancing our bodily, imagistic sense of self, it is clear that one way of reducing the social problems to which these efforts contribute—including inadequate health care and education for millions of people, as well as prejudice and discrimination, interpersonal violence, and war—would be to provide alternative, more benign means of identity support to substitute for these harmful means.

Linguistic identity contents

There are three basic types of linguistic or conceptual identity contents: identity-defining words or signifiers, identity-bearing systems of knowledge or belief, and narratives, stories, or scripts that articulate our sense of self through time or in action. Identity-defining words include, as noted earlier, the names of our various demographic groups, organizations, social roles, and character traits, as well as those ideals, virtues, and values that we have identified with and attempt to embody (e.g., kind, courageous, strong, intelligent, etc.). The identity-bearing function of these signifiers can be inferred from the effort we put forth to (a) protect and enhance their status, (b) enact or embody them, and (c) be recognized as being them, as well from as our feelings of depression, anxiety, or anger when we are unsuccessful in one or more of these aims. Thus, when someone makes a disparaging remark about one of our identity categories or character traits, as in a racial or ethnic slur, we often feel threatened or anxious and may bristle or even attack this person. The same is true when someone fails to confirm our embodiment of one of our identity-bearing signifiers, either through express denial (e.g., "you're not very intelligent") or through omission (as when a politician fails to praise or even mention our group in his or her speech). And, when we fail to embody or enact one of our identity-bearing signifiers, we feel distraught, ashamed, anxious, or depressed. Conversely, when the status of such signifiers is enhanced, or we successfully embody or receive recognition for being one of these signifiers, we feel invigorated and swell with pride and self-confidence.

As we will see in greater detail in later chapters, these identity-bearing signifiers can motivate behaviours that are quite harmful. Some identity-bearing signifiers (e.g., outlaw, rebel) can lead fairly directly to social problems, while others (e.g., altruist, philanthropist, peacemaker) can lead to social benefits. Attempts to maintain or enhance the status of one's identity-bearing demographic categories often result in competition with other groups, which in turn can result in conflict and even violence. Studies in what is known as "minimal group theory" have shown that dividing a relatively homogeneous and friendly group of individuals into two arbitrary categories (such as lovers of Klee and lovers of Kandinski) activates a strategy of identity enhancement in which members of each group begin to perceive members of the other group in increasingly negative terms and take pains to establish the superiority of their own group, whether through the unequal distribution of resources or through acts of aggression against the other group. The same dynamic can be seen in inter-city sports rivalries, inter-ethnic tensions, and international conflicts.

The importance of systems of belief and knowledge for maintaining our sense of self manifests itself in a similar manner: here, too, we go to great efforts and extremes to maintain (a) the general social status of these systems, (b) our embodiment or inhabitation of these systems, and (c) our recognition as embodying or inhabiting these systems. As Cohen, Aronson, and Steele explain:

> [B]eliefs can constitute valued sources of identity. They may thus be given up only with great reluctance, and they may be embraced even when they conflict with the demands of fact, logic, or material self-interest. . . . Capital punishment proponents, for example, might cling to a belief in the death penalty's deterrent efficacy in large part because it reinforces their identity as political conservatives. . . . Evidence that challenges the validity of such cherished beliefs presents a self-threat insofar as giving up that belief would entail losing a source of esteem or identity. To neutralize that threat, people are apt to evaluate evidence defensively. [Cohen, Aronson, & Steele, 2000, p. 1151]

Studies in what is called system justification theory have found that many people who are harmed by the social system in which they live will, none the less, attempt to justify that system (Jost & Banaji, 1994). The reason they do so is because, in all likelihood, their sense of self is dependent in crucial ways on this system. Thus, in the USA, many of the individuals who suffer most from the predatory practices of capitalism are ardent supporters of "free enterprise", "individualism", "self-reliance", and "independence", and adamant opponents of welfare, a single-payer healthcare system, more progressive taxation, and more government regulation of business and management practices, which they perceive as "socialism" and thus as inherently bad. That systems of belief constitute an important component of one's sense of self is also indicated by empirical studies demonstrating that when people's sense of self is threatened by reminders of their mortality, they will not only embrace and defend their beliefs with greater fervour in an effort to maintain their threatened identity, they will also discriminate against those with a different belief system by evaluating them more harshly and behaving with greater hostility towards them (Pyszczynski, Greenberg, & Solomon, 1999, pp. 836–837).

Protecting one's identity-bearing beliefs, then, can easily lead to conflict. Prominent among the social problems resulting from attempts to maintain and enhance one's identity-bearing systems of belief are the various kinds of conflict, from interpersonal tensions, skirmishes, and physical fights to religious and ideological wars, that have been engaged in for the primary purpose of enhancing the stature of a particular belief system. Examples include the vilification, persecution, and even execution of individuals who dared to present scientific knowledge or an ethical system that contradicted a society's dominant religious beliefs. Socrates, Jesus, Galileo, Copernicus, Darwin, Marx, and Freud are notable historical instances. But the same thing is going on today, not only in parts of the world controlled by Islamic fundamentalists, but in the American government, which was, during the administration of George W. Bush, populated by right-wing Christian fundamentalists who ignored, marginalized, or dismissed scientific knowledge and systems of practice that contradicted their religious beliefs, particularly those concerning the origin of the human species, the beginning of individual life, and the nature and causes of homosexuality.

In addition to identity-bearing signifiers and systems of belief, our sense of self also depends heavily on certain narratives, stories, or scripts. Identity-bearing narratives, stories, or scripts function to operationalize our identity-bearing signifiers, such as "the good mother" or "the good husband" (Atwood, 1996, p. xvi) that is, to translate them into behaviours enacting them. As Joan Atwood observes,

> Scripts provide us with a general idea of how we are supposed to behave and what is supposed to happen. . . . Scripts are the "blueprints for behaviour", that specify the whos, whats, whens, and whys of behaviour. [Atwood, 1996, pp. xvi, 13]

Freud observed the power of such scripts in what he called transference, the tendency of individuals to perceive or manipulate people and situations in order to repeat early, formative relationships and interactions with significant others (primarily their parents). Since Freud, other psychoanalysts have recognized that this urge to repeat key scenarios extends beyond transference with the psychoanalyst into all areas of life. Marshall Edelson (1992), for example, argues that much human behaviour is directed by an unconscious fantasy or "master story", which, he says, is like "a movie stored and playing in the mind" (p. 107) and which "determines [our] responses to and interactions with external reality" (ibid., p. 108). Since they constitute an important element of our sense of self, we seek to enact and receive recognition for our identity-bearing scripts or narratives whenever possible. Thus, the types of situations, events, and other people we choose to engage with, as well as which aspects of these engagements we attend to, which we ignore, and how we construe them, are all motivated by our need to enact our identity-bearing narratives (Trzebinski, 1995, pp. 73–76). As Atwood observes,

> Human beings expect their lives to follow certain scripts, and they make efforts to follow these scripts. Human beings try to make their experiences congruent with these scripts, sometimes even reinterpreting their reality so as to make it fit them better. [Atwood, 1996, p. xvi]

Harm occurs when we try to force reality, and especially other people, to conform to our identity-bearing scripts. Freud noted how individuals in transference tried to manipulate other individuals—particularly the analyst—into playing a role in their personal transference script or unconscious fantasy. Even greater harm can result when some people try to manipulate other people into validating or playing roles in certain collective or cultural scripts. Great harm has been produced by the most extensive identity-bearing cultural scripts, those of religion, which, in narrating the origin and destiny of the cosmos, the human species, and/or a particular racial or ethnic group of people, constitute a major source of the sense of self of people who have embraced them. Consequences include the tenacious resistance of many fundamentalist Christians to the theory of evolution, which is seen to contradict the biblical myth of the origin of the human species, as well as to other scientific evidence, such as that concerning the origin of the universe, which also contradicts the biblical myth. Jewish and Islamic myths have been similarly destructive, as is witnessed by, among many other things, the conflict over who is the rightful possessor of Jerusalem. Stories of the origins or history of one's national or ethnic group, or of one's extended or immediate family, as well as fictional or fantastic stories, can also constitute a significant dimension of one's identity, defining the trajectory of a good (or sometimes a bad) life and demonstrating the character qualities needed to follow that trajectory. Thus, many Americans who grow up on rags-to-riches stories—"real" and fictional—aspire to become rich and/or famous by working hard in business, entertainment, or sports, just as the "real" or fictional characters did in the stories they have consumed. The harm done to individuals who futilely try to enact such myths, as well as to others whose lives intersect with theirs, is considerable, though generally overlooked.

Some identity-bearing cultural scripts do harm by dictating various forms of violence and injustice. One well known historical example, vestiges of which persist, is the racist scripts prescribing a host of behaviours of deference and subservience for black people in relation to white people. Another instance is scripts concerning gender and sexuality. One researcher, noting that "cultural-level scripts have been shown to guide real-life sexual behaviour and to perpetuate gender inequality", concludes that "sexual scripts in popular media may have profound real-life effects" (Carpenter, 1998, p. 158). Other researchers have found that cultural "scripts for the ways in which males and females are to behave" play "a causal role" in keeping women in abusive relationships (Vandello & Cohen, 2003, p. 1008). And another team of researchers has identified men's masculinity scripts as contributing to various social problems, including violence against women, gays, and competitors, as well as alcoholism, risk-taking behaviours such as reckless driving, and general indifference towards others (Mahalik, Englar-Carlson, & Good, 2003, pp. 124–126).

Identity maintaining strategies

In order to maintain a sense of self, one must continually enact or receive recognition for one or more of these identity contents in each register. There are several basic strategies for maintaining and enhancing one's identity, including:

1. engaging in behaviours that more fully enact one's identity contents;
2. engaging in behaviours that elicit greater recognition of one's identity contents;
3. transforming the environment to make it offer more opportunities for enactment and/or recognition;
4. transferring to a new environment that offers more opportunities for enactment and/or recognition;
5. adopting new identity contents for which recognition and/or enactment opportunities are more readily available;
6. engaging in biased information processing regarding one's identity in order to exaggerate the degree of enactment or recognition achieved.

Every act we engage in embodies one or more of these identity-maintaining strategies.

Identity-enacting behaviours

The most direct way of maintaining one's identity or sense of self is to engage in behaviours that are themselves enactments of one's identity contents. Thus, people for whom the qualities of intelligence, kindness, or courage are important elements of identity can maintain or enhance their identities by engaging in acts of intelligence, kindness, or courage. When we detect a deficiency in one of our identity-bearing qualities, we respond by engaging in behaviour that enacts the quality (Burke, 1991, p. 839; Wicklund & Gollwitzer, 1981, pp. 89–114). Thus, if our sense of self includes being intelligent and we do something that we or other people perceive as stupid, our internal monitor will signal a shortcoming in the area of intelligence and we will seek to engage in behaviour that either enacts intelligence or compensates for this shortcoming by enacting another identity content. Some contents, such as kindness and generosity, entail behaviours that are mostly helpful rather than harmful, while other contents, such as dominance and toughness, entail harmful behaviours that produce social problems. This process plays a significant role in much violent behaviour, since violence is a readily available means for men to enact qualities defining their masculinity, such as aggression, toughness, and dominance, whenever they feel deficient in any way.

But enacting identity contents is also implicated in social problems in other ways that are generally not recognized by policy makers and the general public. For one, the enactment of other types of contents besides ideals and values can also play a significant role in producing socially harmful behaviours—contents such as body images and intense affects. For example, vitality affects centred on the activation contour of the rush may incline people more to activities like drug abuse and violent behaviour than do vitality affects of quiescence or mutual attunement. Similarly, body-imagistic identity contents such as massive size and muscularity, like linguistic-conceptual identity components such as "masculine", incline one more towards competition, aggression, and violence than do body images of grace and agility.

Identity contents also contribute to social symptoms indirectly: when it is difficult for people to enact a particular content, it renders their identity vulnerable. Certain master signifiers, beliefs, scripts, body images, and affective–physiological states are more difficult to enact than others, either because individuals lack the capacity to enact them or because individuals' social positions and/or cultures fail to provide them with the opportunities or resources necessary for enactment. For example, enacting a traditional definition of masculinity is more difficult for men who are small and frail than for men who are big and strong, and enacting thoughtfulness or intelligence is more difficult for individuals who are deprived of education, information, and the leisure to think than for those who have ready access to these resources.

In addition, identity contents that many people see as positive—for example, contents such as "successful" and "courageous"—are often coded (by a particular individual, group, or society) in ways that require or enable their enactment through behaviours that are quite harmful and destructive. Thus, in the USA, the ideal of "success" has motivated many exploitive and ruthless business practices, and the ideal of courage has sent many males into all sorts of violent confrontations, ranging from playground fights to warfare. Such harmful enactments of neutral or even largely benign contents occur when individuals lack either the ability or the opportunity to enact them through benign behaviours.

Recognition-seeking behaviours

Despite the existence of direct feedback from the enactment of identity contents, recognition from others is also crucial for maintaining one's identity, and much behaviour is motivated by the need to elicit recognition. Recognition by others is necessary for an identity to be established in the first place (Lichtenstein, 1977, pp. 11, 13, 78) and also for identity, once it is established, to sustain itself (Erikson, 1968, p. 105). The indispensability and motivational force of the need for recognition have been recognized by philosophers for centuries. Adam Smith called recognition "the most ardent desire of human nature" (quoted in Todorov, 2001, p. 15). Building on Smith's observations about recognition, Tzvetan Todorov states that "the need for recognition is the fundamental human fact" (p. 16) and observes that its absence is "the worst evil that could befall us" and that "there is no price we are not prepared to pay to obtain it" (p. 15). No matter how much recognition one has received, one always needs new experiences of it, Todorov argues:

> The recognition of our existence . . . is the soul's oxygen. The fact that I breathe today does not dispense with the need for air tomorrow, and past recognitions will not be sufficient for me in the present. . . . We can be indifferent to the opinion others have of us, but we cannot remain insensitive to a lack of recognition of our very existence. [*ibid.*, pp. 57, 82]

Recognition-seeking behaviour is fundamental and ubiquitous, and psychologists have devoted an entire sub-field, under the name of self-presentation, to its study (Leary, 1996). Numerous strategies and tactics have been documented by which people attempt to obtain recognition, leading to the conclusion that "self-presentational motives underlie and pervade nearly every corner of interpersonal life" (*ibid.*, p. xiii). Certain behaviours designed to elicit recognition constitute social problems, including teen pregnancy, shoplifting, robbery, and various gang activities, such as tagging, vandalism, intimidation, and violence, as Lichtenstein notes (Lichtenstein, 1977, pp. 314, 312). The same can be said for terrorism and war.

In addition to contributing to social problems, the need for recognition also motivates the quest for social justice. Eliciting recognition is an obvious function of certain political behaviours, such as marches, protests, demonstrations, and sit-ins. The same is true of identity politics, as the philosopher Charles Taylor observes. Noting that "our identity requires recognition by others" (1991, p. 45), Taylor goes on to point out that the absence of equal recognition can, in the view of many, "be a form of oppression" (*ibid.*, p. 49) and "inflict damage on those who are denied it" (*ibid.*, p. 50), thus prompting political demands to provide the lacking recognition for identity.

But identity politics and public protests are not the only political activities that seek recognition as a means of maintaining identity. Frankfurt School Director Axel Honneth argues that all major social and political struggles and movements have as their fundamental aim the elicitation of greater recognition for certain groups of people who perceive themselves, or are perceived by others, as receiving inadequate recognition from the social order. In *The Struggle for Recognition: The Moral Grammar of Social Conflicts*, Honneth (1995) notes that, in the prevailing view,

> the motives for rebellion, protest, and resistance have generally been transformed into categories of "interest", and these interests are supposed to emerge from the objective inequalities in the distribution of material opportunities without ever being linked, in any way, to the everyday web of moral feelings. [*ibid.*, p. 161]

Contrary to this assumption, Honneth contends, drawing on historical and psychological research, "that motives for social resistance and rebellion are formed in the context of moral experiences stemming from the violation of deeply rooted expectations regarding recognition" (*ibid.*, p. 163). Indeed, the experience of social injustice as such, Honneth argues, is basically the experience of inadequate recognition from society. "What subjects expect of society," Honneth says, "is above all recognition of their identity claims" (Fraser & Honneth, 2003, pp. 131–132).

The French philosopher Emmanuel Renault goes even further, arguing that not only political struggles and movements, but all politics as such, are quests for recognition. Renault maintains that all instances of harm deriving from the social order, ranging from lack of money or status to fear of losing one's job, are experienced as a denial of recognition (Renault, 2004b, p. 54) and that politics is in its essence a demand for recognition (*ibid.*, p. 96). "It is the need for recognition of personal identity," he contends, "that explains resistance, revolt, and their political expression" (*ibid.*, p. 97). All instances of political protest and struggle and social action are thus recognition-eliciting behaviours in support of identity maintenance.

Environment-altering behaviours

In addition to eliciting recognition, political protests and movements also usually aim to alter political, social, or cultural structures, institutions, or practices in ways that reduce identity threats and increase opportunities for identity enactment and recognition for certain groups of people. We can thus expand the Frankfurt School view by defining politics as an attempt to alter the physical, social, or cultural environment in one of three basic ways:

1. increasing opportunities for recognition;
2. increasing opportunities for enacting identity contents;
3. removing perceived threats to identity.

In the USA, the Civil Rights, Women's Liberation, and Gay Rights movements have all sought to remove certain socially and legally sanctioned forms of disregard or denial of recognition—such as the absence of certain rights (to vote, own property, marry, etc.) and the presence of negative cultural images—as well as to institute equal opportunities for members of these identity groups to enact and be recognized for their identity contents by working, owning property, marrying, raising children, and so on.

Socially harmful behaviours, too, are sometimes motivated by the aim to change one's environment to make it more supportive of one's identity. Interpersonal violence is often an effort to halt or eliminate people or activities that one experiences as harmful or threatening. Perpetrators often perceive their violent behaviours to be acts of self-defence or justified vengeance. The same is true of much collective violence. Islamic terrorists attack the USA because they perceive its foreign policy, military presence, and/or cultural imperialism as forces destructive of Islamic identity, and ethnic and religious groups war with each other because they see the other group as a military, political, economic, cultural, and/or psychological threat to some aspect of their own identity. And increasingly, conservative Christian groups in the USA are attempting to restrict personal freedoms by making certain of their core identity contents (e.g., beliefs that abortion and homosexuality are wrong) into law, thus providing institutional recognition for key identity-bearing beliefs.

Transferring to a new environment

In addition to transforming our environment, we also enhance our identity by switching environments when we experience our current environment as threatening or unsupportive of our identity (Baumeister & Vohs, 2001, p. 206; Crocker & Park, 2003, pp. 297–299, 302). Such switching can be partial or domain-specific, or it can be total and comprehensive. Howard Kaplan has found that individuals whose identities are not adequately recognized by the dominant social order are more likely to participate in both social movements and socially deviant behaviours, such as various forms of delinquency. Both social movements and deviant social groups offer an alternative environment in which one's identity finds greater support in the form of social recognition, new opportunities for identity enactment, and greater experience of self-efficacy (Kaplan & Liu, 2000, pp. 218–221). Kaplan finds that the social movement or deviant behaviour an individual engages in may or may not be related to the specific aspects of the individual's identity that are threatened by the dominant social order; all that is necessary is that the new order provide alternative, more effective means of identity-maintenance overall (*ibid.*, pp. 218–219).

Adopting new identity contents

The absence of sufficient opportunities for enactment or recognition of one's current identity contents can lead one to adopt alternative contents for which such opportunities are greater. Thus, lack of social support for benign contents will often result in the adoption of malignant contents—or what Erikson referred to as a negative identity—that are easier to enact than the benign contents. Prominent examples include underprivileged youth who turn to delinquency "where conditions of economic, ethnic, and religious marginality provide poor bases for any kind of positive identity" (Erikson, 1968, p. 88). In such cases, antisocial behaviours such as crime and violence elicit attention and fearful recognition not only from peers and community members but also from authorities, and this latter recognition can be decisive in an individual's adoption of a negative identity, as Erikson explains: "If such 'negative identities' are accepted as a youth's 'natural' and final identity by teachers, judges, and psychiatrists, he not infrequently invests his pride as well as his need for total orientation in becoming exactly what the careless community expects him to become" (Erikson, 1968, p. 88).

This dynamic can also work in the opposite direction. A culture, or certain of its institutions, can promote the replacement of malignant identity contents with more benign ones by decreasing recognition and enactment opportunities for the former and increasing such opportunities for the latter.

Identity-maintaining defences

In addition to behaviours designed to maintain, in various ways, our sense of self, we also try to maintain our identity through certain cognitive operations, the psychological defence mechanisms which downplay or distort identity threats and exaggerate identity enactments and recognition. These defences are employed not only by individuals but also by groups in order to protect certain shared identity contents from shared threats. Both the individual and the collective forms of defences play a major role in producing and maintaining most of our social problems.

Avoidant defences

One of the most fundamental and pervasive forms of defence is avoidance of identity-threatening perceptions, thoughts, feelings, or impulses. Avoidant cognition includes *repression*, which prevents awareness of aspects of oneself that threaten or contradict one's sense of self. An example can be found in the general lack of awareness among American citizens of the feelings of greed, fear, and aggression that underwrite much of the USA's foreign and domestic policy. *Denial*, which rejects awareness of identity-threatening elements of external reality, is rampant in American politics, particularly regarding failed policies, a fact amply documented in Bob Woodward's account of the Iraq War debacle, *State of Denial* (Woodward, 2006). *Reaction formation*, which avoids an identity-contrary feeling or impulse by inducing its opposite, is operating when groups under siege "keep a stiff upper lip", or "put on a happy face", as well as when individuals and groups transform their *Schadenfreude* at an adversary's ill fortune into sympathy or grief. *Displacement*, which avoids an identity-threatening target of one's feeling or impulse by switching to an alternative, less threatening target, can be seen in the blame for economic woes that many Americans direct towards illegal immigrants rather than towards the real culprit, the American plutocracy and its policies. *Undoing* attempts to avoid negative conclusions about oneself by reversing the identity-threatening negative effects or implications of one's behaviour—for example, a nation's providing food and medical care for victims of its military or economic aggression allows its citizens—to maintain their collective identity as kind and generous despite blatant evidence to the contrary.

Minimizing defences

Minimizing defences function not to block or avoid disturbing information concerning identity, but, rather, to reduce the degree of threat to insignificant or at least manageable proportions. *Intellectualization* minimizes the identity-threatening impact of an action or event by blocking awareness of its more concrete and indefeasible aspects or implications. Public discourse on war is often extremely intellectualized, omitting all reference to the exploding bodies, bowel- and bladder-emptying terror, and shrieks of agony that constitute the concrete reality of war. A closely related defence is the use of *euphemisms* to name realities that contradict important aspects of one's sense of self. Thus, categorizing a screaming child whose legs have been blown off by a mortar round as a "casualty" or "collateral damage" helps maintain a nation's collective sense of self as "a peaceful, freedom-loving people" in the face of horrible contradictory evidence. *Rationalization* reduces the discrepancy between reality, one's behaviour, or contrary elements of oneself, on the one hand, and identity contents on the other. Examples include blaming others, or external conditions, for one's failures. *Sublimation* minimizes the intensity and destructive consequences—and hence the threat to identity—of identity-dystonic impulses by directing these impulses towards objects that are more socially acceptable and that also, in many cases, elicit a more moderated expression of the impulses, as, for example, when one engages in violence on the athletic field rather than on the street, or shoots other people with paint balls rather than bullets.

Externalizing defences

Externalizing defences protect identity from threatening elements of self by attributing these elements to someone else, which then allows one to focus on this other as a way of convincing oneself that it is the other, and not oneself, who possesses this negative attribute. In *externalization*, one finds another individual or group that actually does possess certain identity-contrary elements of one's self, and one focuses on this other as a way of escaping awareness of these same elements in one's self. When such an other is lacking, one may resort to *projection*, which attributes a negative quality of one's own to an other who does not actually possess this quality. Some circumstances of this sort will also allow *projective identification*, in which one manipulates the other in such a way as to bring the other to actually embody one's own rejected, despised element. Externalizing defences, which are prominent in most intergroup conflicts, including terrorism and war, enable beliefs such as George W. Bush's that "we" are a peaceful, freedom-loving people and "they" are evil and hate freedom.

Dissociative defences

A fourth basic type of defence, dissociation, protects identity by preventing or breaking identity-undermining links between perceptions, ideas, feelings, and attitudes. *Compartmentalization* involves the sequestration of mutually conflicting identity-bearing perceptions, thoughts, feelings, or behaviours into separate domains of one's life, such as when an individual is calm, controlled, and rational at work and lively, spontaneous, and impulsive at home, or kind and loving to family members and pets at home, but a cold and ruthless executioner at work in the concentration camp. *Isolation of affect* allows one to think about a disturbing reality and to experience the emotional disturbance, but not at the same time. Thus, one may, in one moment, think about problems in one's life without feeling distraught, and in another moment feel anxious, angry, or depressed without knowing why. A related defence, *affectualization*, involves flooding the mind with affect as a way to avoid making cognitive connections that would lead to identity-threatening realizations. Political rallies and demonstrations almost always activate this defence to some degree. *Dyselaboration* (Horowitz, Milbrath, Reidboc, & Stinson, 1993) involves distortion of information in ways that prevent the formation of a complete, comprehensive, coherent picture of an event or behaviour in relation to all its causes and consequences, because such a picture would implicate one in an identity-threatening manner. Political propaganda is rife with this defence.

Defences against reality or elements of the self that conflict with identity contents can thus contribute significantly to, and in some cases directly produce, serious social problems. It follows that one important way to help reduce social problems is to reduce identity defences. While dissolving defences is usually associated with individual psychoanalytic treatment, there is no reason that certain defences—particularly those that are collectively shared and that are enabled by social and cultural institutions and practices—could not be eliminated or significantly reduced through various social and cultural interventions, as we will see in Chapter Seven.

Identity inclusiveness and integration

Inclusiveness of individual contents

Defences, as well as harmful behaviours, are increased when identity contents exclude or oppose significant elements of the self. For example, when the identity content "man" is construed as excluding gentleness, tenderness, dependency needs, or feelings of vulnerability, the result is an identity that is (a) more constricted, (b) more vulnerable, and (c) more defensive. Such identities are more constricted in that they can be maintained only by a very limited number of behaviours. A traditional "man" can maintain his identity by being tough and aggressive, but not by being tender and gentle. Because of this limitation, a constricted identity is also more vulnerable: when a traditional "man" experiences feelings of gentleness or tenderness, not only does he receive no fulfilment, he actually feels threatened. And when people feel threatened, they often become defensive and respond with aggression and even violence against the perceived threat. Thus, when a traditional "man" experiences gentle or tender feelings for another man, he may exhibit homophobia, externalizing his own feelings of tenderness on to the other man and then behaving aggressively, and sometimes even violently, towards the other man.

Inclusiveness of the totality of contents

In addition to the nature of one's identity contents, the number of contents and their relations to each other are also important determinants of identity security and, hence, of behaviour, including defensiveness. Identity is very much like an investment portfolio, in that diversification is the best way to maintain security over the long run. If one invests one's entire sense of self in a particular signifier (e.g., athlete), bodily factor (e.g., muscularity or strenuous physical activity), and/or affective state (e.g., excitement or anger), one's chances of maintaining a secure identity, or sense of self, are considerably less than if one's sense of self is distributed across multiple and diverse identity contents in each of the three registers. If circumstances—such as injury, ageing, or lack of athletic ability or opportunity—prevent one from enacting and being recognized for these identity contents, one will be left without an identity leg to stand on and may experience depression or anxiety and turn to quick fixes, such as drugs, gambling, or even crime to try to maintain a sense of self. One can see such results not only at the end of some athletic careers, but also at the end of the careers of other individuals whose sense of self has been primarily a function of their work.

The benefit of identity diversification has been verified empirically by Patricia Linville, who argues that such diversification—or self-complexity, as she terms it—serves as "a buffer against stressful life events" (Linville, 1985, p. 115) and reduces depression. She, therefore, advises interventions to increase such diversification. Much the same point is made in Heinz Kohut's psychoanalytic self psychology, which emphasizes that a secure sense of self requires multiple and diverse selfobjects, which can be defined as any human or non-human entities or processes that enable the enactment or recognition of an identity content (see Gilbert, 1994).

The degree of emotional fulfilment or depletion one feels is a function of the sum of identity support flowing in from all one's identity contents. Thus, when enactment or recognition of a given identity content is prevented, a person with a large number of diverse identity contents will sustain less severe identity depletion than an individual with a small number of diverse contents. As research in self-affirmation theory demonstrates, when we suffer a blow to one of our identity contents, we usually have recourse to one of four means of maintaining our sense of self (Steele, 1999):

1. we will reaffirm this content, if there is an opportunity to do so. If such an opportunity is lacking,
2. we will enact another benign, prosocial content. If neither of these opportunities is available,
3. we will enact a negative (antisocial) content, or
4. we will resort to denigration of, or even aggression toward, other individuals or groups.

Providing opportunities for individuals to develop and enact diversified (benign) identity contents can thus make a significant contribution to solving social problems, in so far as it enhances their identity security and thus reduces their need to embrace malignant identity contents and resort to harmful behaviours in order to maintain their sense of self.

Conflicts among identity contents

While having a multiplicity and diversity of identity contents renders identity more inclusive and hence more secure, it also introduces a new type of identity threat: an internal threat, in the form of conflict between different identity contents. Such conflict can take several different forms. The simplest and perhaps most inevitable form is conflict over time (Burke, 1991, p. 842): at any given moment, some identity contents will be cultivated, enacted, or recognized and others will not be. For example, many adults experience time conflicts between their familial and professional identity contents: time spent working often reduces the amount of time one can spend with one's family, and vice versa. Similar time conflicts can exist between different family roles (e.g., spouse, parent, sibling, child), or between familial or professional identity contents, on the one hand, and identity contents such as political activist, volunteer, musician, or amateur athlete, on the other.

In addition to conflicts over time, some identity contents are inherently mutually contradictory. A man who is a clergyman, for example, might experience a contradiction between the toughness and aggression traditionally associated with masculinity and the kindness and gentleness that are important elements of being a clergyman (Burke, 1991, p. 842). Sometimes, such contradictory elements inhabit the same register, such as the linguistic categories of "man" vs. "pastor", or affective states of a rush versus calmness, but in other cases they may reside in two different registers, such as the linguistic content of "pastor" vs. an imagistic content of a tough, powerful, impenetrable body or an affective–physiological content of anger. The most familiar sort of inter-register conflicts are those between id impulses and superego restraints, or the pleasures of the flesh and one's conscience. Religion and morality often set up oppositions between these two registers, in particular, by labelling certain impulses (e.g., "sin") with signifiers antithetical to the most prized identity-bearing signifiers (e.g., "saint").

A third form of conflict between identity contents involves the entailment of two mutually incompatible behaviours. Here, the individual may experience a conflict not between the contents themselves, but, rather, between the respective behavioural demands of the two contents. For example, the linguistic content of a long-distance runner and the complementary imagistic content of a lean, well-conditioned body will conflict with the affective–physiological states produced by smoking, heavy drinking, or substance abuse—not because of inherent contradictions between contents but because engaging in the latter behaviours will prevent one from engaging in the behaviours necessary to enact the former contents. Such conflicts can take a temporal form, in which a present wish or impulse entails behaviours which, if engaged in, will prevent the enactment of certain identity contents in the future, as is demonstrated by the fable of the grasshopper and the ant, in which present gratification and future gratification (and survival) entail mutually incompatible present behaviours (eating and relaxing *vs.* working and storing food for the winter).

In addition to conflicts among identity contents, there are also conflicts between identity contents and elements of the self that have not been incorporated into one's identity. An example is the conflict many people in our society have between unconscious murderous wishes or impulses (Strean & Freeman, 1991) and identity contents such as civilized, kind, and gentle. This type of conflict is often a central cause of both social problems and the failure to solve them. There are two basic ways of responding to such conflicts. The first, and most damaging, is with defence, which protects both elements (though not to an equal degree) by constricting identity in ways that keep the opposing elements from coming into direct confrontation with each other. The second type of response, which is usually more personally and socially productive than the first, is expansion of identity so as to better accommodate both the conflicting elements. Expansion of the boundaries of identity—that is, of what is included in one's sense of self—can either involve the modification of old identity contents so that they are no longer antithetical to certain heretofore excluded elements of self, or it can take the form of incorporation of new contents into identity. An example of the first way would be the redefinition of masculinity to include gentleness, sensitivity, and kindness, which reduces the conflicts many men experience between such traits, feelings, and impulses, on the one hand, and their maintenance of "masculinity" on the other. Examples of adopting a new identity content that incorporates previously excluded and conflictual elements of self occur when a man embraces the new identity of "father" as including tenderness and gentleness, or when a man acknowledges that, in addition to his masculine identity, he also has a "feminine" side. Such expansions of masculine identity have been shown to reduce violent behaviour in men who have been convicted of violent crimes (see Gilligan, 2001).

A similar expansion took place in the second half of the twentieth century with regard to female identity, when many women rejected "lady" as an identity-bearing signifier because it excluded important elements of their self, such as strength, assertiveness, and sexual desire and enjoyment. Before the second wave of feminism, many women experienced significant conflicts between their sexual desire, ambition, and aggression, on the one hand, and, on the other hand, their identity as a "lady", which entailed demureness and selflessness. Some women consciously struggled with this conflict, while others repressed their "unladylike" qualities at an early age and suffered psychological symptoms such as depression and anxiety, or physical symptoms such as lethargy or various somatoform disorders. A way out of this impasse was created when certain women rejected "lady" as an identity-bearing signifier and instead embraced "woman", which included their previously excluded qualities and was generally less prescriptive and proscriptive of behaviour, thus allowing greater autonomy and flexibility in general.

While these expansions of gender identities have produced social benefits, additional expansions of the identities of "normal, law-abiding" individuals to include their laziness, selfishness, greed, lustfulness, and even murderous wishes and impulses are probably necessary if we are to solve our greatest social problems. If the great "Moral Majority" of Americans recognized and owned these negative qualities in themselves, they would not need to externalize and attack them in such others as the poor, the homeless, the unemployed, the addicted, gangstas, criminals, and terrorists. Ironically, the official identity proclaimed by most of the "Moral Majority"—"Christian"—includes, in its doctrine of original sin, the recognition that these negative qualities are a part of everyone and not just the special possession of members of certain demonized groups. Most "normal, law-abiding" Americans, however, no matter how "Christian" they might be, are largely ignorant of just how similar they are in the depth of their selves or souls to those they consider to be the dregs of humanity: terrorists, murderers, child molesters, rapists, addicts, derelicts, and so on. "There but for the grace of God go I" is a recognition that every believer should have whenever he or she encounters a member of one of these demonized, denigrated, or marginalized groups. Today, however, this dictum is little known and rarely practised, even among the most fervently religious Americans.

If we ask why this is the case—why so many Americans have forgotten this basic tenet of their religion at the very time when they have embraced other tenets of Christianity all the more fervently—we must conclude that a significant part of the reason is their lack of a sufficiently complex identity, an identity that could maintain its moral virtues while also incorporating recognition and ownership of these other unpalatable and even repugnant qualities that are present in everyone. In order to be able to contain and own, rather than externalize and attack, the psychological qualities most responsible for social harm, individuals must have a prosocial identity that is not only strong enough but also complex enough to incorporate these negative qualities without allowing them to determine behaviour.

Complexity and comprehensiveness of self schemas

What is needed is more complex self schemas. A self schema is "an organized compendium of meanings that a person attributes to his or her self . . . a pattern of nonconscious associations between various units of belief about self-attributes" (Horowitz, 1998, pp. 87–88). Stated in terms of the identity model we are developing here, a self schema is a constellation of multiple identity contents from all three registers, including identity-bearing values, ideals, knowledge, beliefs, narratives, scripts, body images, and affects. Most people have multiple self schemas, organized hierarchically, and an individual's identity security depends to a considerable extent on how well differentiated and integrated these schemas and their respective identity contents are (ibid., pp. 89–90). A well integrated hierarchy of self schemas reduces intrapsychic conflict—and thereby personal suffering and socially harmful behaviours—by providing a time, a place, and a mode for all elements of the self. The importance of temporal integration is articulated in the famous passage from Ecclesiastes (incorporated into a popular song by The Byrds in the 1960s) stating that there is a time for everything. An identity that incorporates past and future as well as the immediate present is more stable and secure than a sense of self that is limited to the immediate present. Such temporal diversification is even more crucial than the diversification of identity contents discussed above, for, in its absence, an individual is hostage to the contingencies of the immediate present. An identity lacking temporal extension and integration will be subject to the impulse or emotion of the present. If the situation is aversive, the individual or group may be consumed with anxiety, depression, or rage and engage in desperate and destructive actions, such as suicide or homicide, unaware that "tomorrow is another day", or that help may be "just around the corner", two popular sayings that encourage and enable temporal extension of one's sense of self beyond the present moment. And, if the situation and mood are agreeable, the individual or group is in danger of dancing blithely into the future, like the grasshopper into winter or a lamb to the slaughter. Thus, the collective American identity, composed largely of contents involving invulnerability and dominance, was more severely traumatized—and reacted much more destructively—to the attacks of 9/11 than might have been the case if it had incorporated, rather than repressed, its own vulnerability and culpability for the suffering of others—not to mention its own hatred and murderous wishes regarding the Other.

The importance of an inclusive and temporally extended identity for overcoming social problems is evident from the fact that many addicts and criminals have what are sometimes referred to as impulsive personality structures, in which harmful behaviours such as violence, substance abuse, gambling, and drunk driving are engaged in without foresight or forethought, as a direct and instantaneous expression of the individual's momentary state of mind. Various treatment programmes for such individuals, including twelve-step programmes for alcohol and substance abuse and also anger management training, help the individuals to develop greater temporal extension of their identity, so that their sense of self at any given time is a function not just of their immediate circumstances and the affects and wishes they provoke but also of their past (both proximal and distal) senses of self and the various different future senses of self that they are able to anticipate (and either wish for or dread) as the respective consequences of several different behavioural responses that they might make to the immediately present circumstances.

In addition to being necessary for survival, the temporal extension of identity also enables the mutual accommodation of contrary emotions and attitudes, which is essential for modulating emotions, attitudes, and behaviour and is, thus, also crucial for personal and social well-being. For example, persons operating with a self-schema that has integrated love and hate, or empathy and anger, will be able to tolerate and respond more productively to situations of interpersonal and intergroup conflict—including international conflict—than will people for whom the experiences of such mental states are mutually exclusive. As Horowitz observes, individuals with "supraordinate [self] schemas that integrate many associations . . . can anticipate going through a mood cycle . . . [and can thus] tolerate periods of ambivalence between self and other without impulsive estrangement" (Horowitz, 1998, p. 148).

This greater identity complexity, moreover, enables one to recognize a similar complexity in others. An individual with a well-integrated hierarchy of self-schemas

> has an expectation of state variation in the other person and can tolerate shifts in warmth and coldness, closeness and distance, empathy and misunderstanding. Insults do not lead to enduring revenge fantasies . . . Love may ebb and flow, but it seldom turns into hate. Well-modulated restraints, renunciations, sublimations, and rational choices occur. [*ibid.*]

More complex self schemas of this sort can involve not only temporal extension and alteration but also conceptual co-ordination and prioritization. In some cases, a supraordinate self schema can be constructed around a supraordinate concept that unites conflicting identity-bearing concepts. Men, for example, can construct a more complex self schema around concepts such as androgyny, or yin and yang, which incorporate opposing elements of self and subordinate them both (in varying degrees) to a larger unity.

In addition to temporal and conceptual co-ordination of conflicting elements of self, more complex identities also make use of subordination and prioritization. Thus, for example, the recovering alcoholic owns, as part of his identity, both the craving for alcohol and the striving for sobriety, but subordinates the former to the latter, such that when the two intentions conflict, only the striving for sobriety is allowed to be directly enacted as behaviour. More generally, anyone who has mature, positive relations with other people will feel both affection and aggression (love and hate) toward any given individual at various times, but will subordinate the aggression to the affection. Thus, one may criticize a friend or loved one, or express anger towards him or her, but always within a context, evident to both parties, of an overriding and ongoing love or affection. Thus positive, prosocial identity contents coexist in identity with negative, antisocial elements: i.e., the individual has owned, accepted as part of himself, these negative, antisocial feelings, impulses, and qualities, but the negative, antisocial contents are monitored or chaperoned by stronger positive, prosocial contents, which contain and moderate their influence on behaviour. The same principle operates in relations between nations and other groups.

In the absence of complex self schemas, individuals and groups can protect their prosocial identity contents from harmful and antisocial contents only through recourse to the various defences discussed earlier. People lacking an identity sufficiently complex to enable such integration of opposing feelings or attitudes and the resulting experience of ambivalence towards others (e.g., feeling threatened by, and hence angry at, another's actions but still secure enough to feel a relationship or kinship with the other as a human being) will be likely to behave in extreme, unproductive, and harmful ways, declaring the other to be "evil" and attacking the other with little thought for the long-term consequences of such actions. Such people will also find it much more difficult to acknowledge the ambivalence and complexity of others (Westen & Heim, 2003, p. 658), resulting in declarations such as George W. Bush's "If you're not with us, you're against us!"

Inclusiveness of identity structures

Robert Kegan, drawing on the developmental theories of Piaget, Erikson, Loevinger, and others, has constructed a model of psychological development composed of five increasingly extensive and complex forms of self, or identity structures. Each stage of Kegan's model involves the development of a more comprehensive identity that extends its boundaries both temporally and interpersonally in such a way that resolves contradictions or impasses inherent in the previous form of identity (Kegan, 1982, 1994).

In the first stage, which is most prominent during infancy, one's sense of self resides only in impulses and perceptions, which change from one moment to the next. Past and future states are excluded from one's sense of self, so there is no continuity between one impulsive state and the next and no connection between one's (impulsive) actions and their consequences. There is also no integration of different impulses and perceptions in the present, and only the most rudimentary apprehension of otherness.

While most individuals develop a more extensive and organized self schema, some individuals—primarily those characterized as borderline, sometimes referred to as having an impulsive character structure—operate much of the time with a highly impulsive sense of self. As noted above, such individuals can be quite volatile and even violent. Impulsive identities can easily become violent because (a) in so far as such individuals *are* their impulses, any thwarting of these impulses is experienced as a destruction of their sense of self, or identity; (b) there is no internal factor that can regulate the intensity and expression of their aggression; and (c) their lack of attunement to others results in their antagonizing other people by enacting their own impulses in oblivion of others' needs and wishes. The violent behaviour produced by such an identity tends to be volatile rather than calm, and reactive rather than premeditated. Toddlers and other people operating with this structure lash out indiscriminately, and sometimes violently, whenever their currently operating identity content is threatened.

In the second stage, the imperial, identity is located not in discrete impulses and perceptual states but in enduring dispositions, needs, interests, intentions, and wishes. However, although one's momentary impulses are connected with—and thus regulated by—past and future self states, one's various ongoing dispositions or wishes remain largely dissociated from each other. Although the imperial structure takes account of other people, the other's subjectivity is not included in one's sense of self. Other people are apprehended not as other people, but merely as obstacles or instruments related to one's own identity needs. Such identity thus produces manipulative, utilitarian relations with others. Kegan has found a significant correlation between the imperial structure of identity and sociopathic forms of violence, which are characterized by their apparent non-impulsive, calculating cold-bloodedness. He notes that the various characteristics of sociopaths—their lying, selfishness, manipulativeness, callousness, charm, naiveté, and unreliability—are also characteristic of ten-year-olds, most of whom have an imperial identity structure (Kegan, 1986). Since people with this structure *are* their ongoing needs, projects, and roles, any interference with their projects or roles is experienced as a threat to their identity and is thus met with aggression. Much political manoeuvring—including *Realpolitik*—operates out of this identity structure. Examples include the Bush administration's unilateralism and exceptionalism in foreign policy and its monarchical conception of the executive branch of government.

The third stage, the interpersonal, mends these disjunctions, making identity itself a function of its interpersonal relationships, and self-consciousness of one's own roles and subjectivity in relation to those of other people becomes central to one's sense of self. This form of identity centres on strong, one-to-one relationships of mutuality and reciprocity, and manifests itself, for example, in the "all you need is love" mentality. Interpersonal identity is limited, however, by its inability to adjudicate among, and co-ordinate, conflicting roles and relationships. Moreover, while it embraces some people as integral components of itself, it relates to people beyond this inner circle with much the same indifference as the imperial identity does, and it has no concern for, or even significant awareness of, the group as a whole. This identity structure can be seen in George W. Bush's fierce loyalty to personal friends (Attorney General Alberto Gonzales, White House Counsel Harriet Myers, FEMA Director Michael Brown, etc.) in utter disregard of the harm caused by their incompetence and malfeasance. The interpersonal structure leaves people vulnerable to authoritarianism and to committing violence in the service of a particular authority in relation to which their sense of self is constituted. Anything that threatens an interpersonal identity's authority figure or relation to that authority is met with aggression. Moreover, aggression fomented by the authority is often eagerly embraced by his interpersonally structured subjects. Hence, the violence perpetrated by gangs, cults, militia groups, and entire nations in thrall to charismatic leaders such as Charles Manson, Jim Jones, Hitler, Mussolini, and countless lesser known figures throughout the ages.

The limitations of the interpersonal structure are overcome in the institutional, or systemic, form of identity. Here, rather than being a multiplicity of more or less independent roles and relationships, identity takes the form of a system or institution that integrates these different roles and relationships into a more or less coherent unity. Identity is now able to involve not only self-consciousness, but also self-regulation and self-formation, which are guided by the ideological system at the core of identity. This systemic form of identity, though, is unable to reconcile the opposing claims of different systems, and it can thus be instrumental in perpetrating some of the same forms of violence as the interpersonal. Individuals operating with an institutional identity structure, however, commit violence not primarily out of interpersonal loyalty to a charismatic leader, but out of loyalty to the particular group or system with which they have identified. Thus, the Holocaust was perpetrated not only by individuals personally devoted to Hitler, but also by dispassionate bureaucrats committed to the Third Reich. And similarly today, much of the greatest violence is perpetrated not by bloodthirsty individuals or members of gangs or terrorist cells, but, rather, by "innocent" citizens whose devotion to maintaining the current social system overrides their awareness of the tremendous suffering and injustice produced by this system and sometimes occurring right under their noses (e.g., in the form of children and elderly people without adequate care) as well as around the world (e.g., in the form of economic systems and policies that result in 1.1 *billion* people living in extreme poverty and 20,000 of these people dying *every day* from this condition (Sachs, 2005)). Thus, while group loyalties, including ethnocentrism and nationalism, can foster valuable prosocial behaviours, even the most generous instances of this identity structure—as expressed, for example, in John F. Kennedy's famous exhortation, "Ask not what your country can do for you, ask what you can do for your country"—leave one indifferent to most of the suffering in the world.

In the final, fifth form of identity, the interindividual or trans-systemic structure, this problem is overcome by identity's assuming a position supraordinate to all institutions and systems. Kegan does not have much to say about this form of identity, because it is actualized by only a small number of people, and by most of them only occasionally and in certain domains of life. We can, however, provide an account of this form of identity by drawing on Erik Erikson's notion of an identity that is "self-aware, all-human" (Erikson, 1974, p. 44), "species-wide" (Erikson, 1964, p. 242), and "world-wide" (Erikson, 1968, p. 42), as well as our own experience and observation of this structure in action. For, although most of us do not operate with this sense of self continuously, or perhaps even frequently, most of us appear to have at least begun to develop such a structure and to occasionally enact it, such as when we transcend partisan conflicts and understand the perspective of the other side, feel their suffering, mourn their losses, or desire their well-being. The interindividual form of identity involves, in the words of the Upanishads, seeing "all beings in [one's] own self and [one's] own self in all beings" (quoted in Erikson, 1964, p. 221). It is also at the heart of the African notion of *ubuntu*, "I am because you are." In the interindividual form of identity, my sense of self includes not only my impulses, my ongoing desires and projects, my interpersonal relationships, and the institutions and systems I identify with, but also every other human being, past, present, and future, and perhaps non-human beings as well. Maintaining such an identity coincides with "what in Hinduism is called the maintenance of the world" (Erikson, 1974, p. 124). For such an identity, taking care of oneself means taking care of everyone else, and vice versa. This caring for others, which Erikson calls generativity, involves "the responsibility of each individual for the potentialities of all generations and of all generations for each individual" (Erikson, 1964, p. 157). When I have an interindividual identity, every other human being is an essential component of my sense of self, such that when anyone else suffers, I suffer, and when anyone else experiences joy or contentment, so do I, through that person. Parents enact this identity structure whenever they care more for their children's well-being than for their own; at such times their children's well-being is the most important element of their own well-being. And many people experience and enact this expanded identity with regard to complete strangers as well, such as when they feel sympathy for suffering people they have never met, or try to help a stranger in need, sometimes risking their own lives to do so, as in the case of many Holocaust rescuers (Monroe, 1996, 2004). For most people, this interindividual self emerges only sporadically, in certain domains and with regard to certain types of people, but the existence of such moments in most people is evidence that it is not a mere fantasy, and that if we put our minds to it, we should be able to understand how to promote its more frequent and extended activation. For only this interindividual form of identity is sufficiently comprehensive and integrated to avoid being implicated in one way or another in significant social problems, including violence.

* * *

In the exposition to this point, we have seen various ways in which identity issues lead to socially harmful behaviours. The most obvious way is through the enactment of malignant identity contents that entail such behaviours. Examples include masculine identity contents in all three registers that contribute to various forms of violence: identity-bearing master signifiers such as man, dominant, and tough; beliefs of male superiority; narratives of competition, triumph, and dominance; ideal body images of great size, strength, and toughness; and affective–physiological states such as anger, rage, and adrenaline-infused excitement. In addition, some socially harmful behaviours (e.g., many types of aggression and violence) are motivated by the need for recognition. We have also seen how defending against perceived external threats to one's identity can lead to behaviours that do harm to others and to oneself, and how internal threats resulting from inadequate integration of conflicting elements of the self can motivate the activation of cognitive distortions of self, others, and the social world that enable socially harmful behaviours, such as prejudice and discrimination. And, finally, we have seen how identity structures that are inadequately inclusive of both other people and elements of oneself can allow and even promote serious social harm, including various forms of violence.

Each of these identity factors—malignant identity contents, the need for recognition, harmful defences, and inadequate identity inclusiveness and structure—is a causal factor in many social problems, including the second-order "meta-problem" of failure to deal effectively with first-order social problems. This fact will be demonstrated in Part Two with regard to a number of our worst social problems, including multiple forms of violence. Part Three will make the same point about poverty and inequality, explaining how the subalterns produced by such conditions function as important means by which "normal", "successful", "law-abiding" individuals maintain their identities. However, such conditions also, it will be shown, constitute traumatogenic forces that undermine the identities of virtually all members of society, including the identities of "good" individuals, thus leading them to perpetuate poverty, inequality, and the other social problems resulting from them as a way to maintain their own damaged or vulnerable identities. Part Four will outline a strategy for solving these social problems by addressing the identity problems at their root.

PART II

SOCIAL PROBLEMS AS
SYMPTOMS OF IDENTITY NEEDS

CHAPTER TWO

Delinquency, crime, and violence

"[T]he exercise of violence [is] ... a symptom ... which, if properly read, could expose the central motives and concerns of violent men"

(Toch, 1969, p. vi)

"[P]roblems of violence can be traced to the pursuit of human needs of recognition and identity"

(Burton, 1997, p. 31)

I dentity maintenance would seem to be a minor or even totally non-existent cause of many social problems, such as teen pregnancy, shoplifting, substance abuse, vandalism, and violent crimes including robbery, assault, rape, and murder. Teenage pregnancy is often thought to be the result of ignorance and carelessness regarding sex; shoplifting and robbery are assumed to be motivated by the desire for material possessions; substance abuse is regarded as mere pleasure-seeking self-indulgence; and vandalism and other violent crimes are attributed to the expression of aggressive and violent character. Ethnographic research into the perpetrators of these problems, however, has revealed a very different reality: it demonstrates that these commonly attributed motives are themselves covers for or expressions of the need to maintain, defend, or enhance a deeply vulnerable, needy, or deficient identity.

Teenage pregnancy

A common misconception regarding teenage pregnancy is that it is not motivated at all but is rather the product of accident and the ignorance of teenage girls concerning sex and contraception. As Leon Dash, a *Washington Post* reporter who wrote a book on the subject, puts it, "I thought they got pregnant because of ignorance of birth control or because they were manipulated by boys". What he discovered, however, "was that they wanted the babies" (quoted in Mirow, 1989, 1-C). The most fundamental reason most teenage mothers want a baby is because they see it as the best—and often only—means available to them for establishing a more secure and substantial identity. As Judith Musick discovered in her research,

> Identity issues explain why so many girls, even those with considerable promise, become mothers while still in their teens. . . . Although identity formation is a continuous process throughout the life cycle, it has its crisis during the adolescent years. Shaped by what went before and shaping what comes after, identity is the primary motivational force of adolescence. Because of this, it is the primary motivational force of adolescent childbearing. . . . The desire for motherhood grows out of and is intimately connected to the adolescent's sense of herself and where she fits into the world. [Musick, 1993, pp. 64, 68]

The intense need to establish a secure identity in adolescence is universal (*ibid.*, p. 63), but adolescent girls who have babies have been found to differ in several crucial ways from most other girls: in the area of internal resources, their identity strength, contents, and maintenance strategies are often greatly impoverished, and in the area of external identity support, their resources and opportunities for establishing secure, substantial identities are severely limited. Concerning their internal resources, because of mothers (often themselves quite young and overwhelmed with mother-hood) who were angry, depressed, or otherwise unresponsive, and because of sexual abuse, many teenage mothers lack a strong sense of self and self-worth, with the result that they are extremely needy, desperate for closeness and connection (*ibid.*, pp. 100–101). This desperation predisposes them to seek identity and identity support primarily from interpersonal relationships. In addition, many teenage mothers have never experienced a loving and trusting rela-tionship with a man: many have never known a father (*ibid.*, p. 81), and many have been sexually abused by fathers, stepfathers, uncles, or mothers' boyfriends (*ibid.*, pp. 86ff.). Such experiences create identity-bearing scripts of passivity and victimization in which sexuality is paramount (*ibid.*, pp. 92ff.), which then cause these girls to give greater emphasis to sexual activity and repro-duction in their relationships with men (*ibid.*, 1993, pp. 97, 104). The abuse, moreover, enhances the girls' need for closeness and connec-tion, while simultaneously defining such qualities in terms of sex (*ibid.*, p. 99). "Young females arriving at early adolescence with unmet dependency and affiliative needs," Musick notes, "are at considerable risk for exploitation and early initiation of sexual activity. How can these girls resist men's sexual advances if there is the implicit (or explicit) promise of love, closeness, or being cared for?" (*ibid.*, p. 102).

In addition to such internal impediments to the establishment of a secure identity, teenage mothers are also confronted with bleak objective possibilities for enacting, and receiving recognition for, substantial identity contents. Many can see no way other than motherhood to enact a substantial identity and be recognized as somebody. Despite the lack of all other opportunities, motherhood can always be counted on to provide an identity and its attendant recognition. Not surprisingly, Dash found that motherhood was especially appealing to girls who were doing poorly in school: "While the better students strove for a diploma," he reports, "the poorer students achieved their form of recognition with a baby" (Dash, 1989, p. 10). Musick concludes:

> At the developmental crossroads of adolescence, when everything in her life seems up in the air, in an environment that offers no chance to explore other options, no other models or avenues out,

motherhood promises a path to personhood, a path to her own place in the world. Having a baby means the adolescent no longer need wonder who she is: she knows—she is a mother. [Musick, 1993, p. 70]

For some girls, in short, motherhood is "the only identity imaginable" (ibid., p. 140).

Having a baby provides identity support in a number of powerful ways. In the linguistic register it transforms the adolescent "girl" into a "woman". Dash observes that having a baby "is one way of announcing: I am a woman" (Dash, 1989, p. 9). Having a baby also transforms a "woman" into a "mother". Both transformations offer an increase in recognition by the generalized other: in the patriarchal social order, a "woman" is more somebody than a "girl" is, and a "mother" is more somebody than a "woman" is. Having a baby is thus a quick way to embody two signifiers bringing with them considerably more recognition than the previous identity-bearing signifier "girl". "I like it when people notice I'm having a baby," one pregnant teenager confided. "It gives me a good feeling inside and makes me feel important" (quoted in Musick, 1993, p. 109). Another teenage mother wrote to her daughter, "You make me feel special and needed. With out you my life was boring and almost meaningless" (ibid., p. 10).

The identity components involving body images are also significant in teenage pregnancy. The novel sensations and changing form of her body during pregnancy, together with the change in others' responses to her appearance, can promote a resubjectification of her body for her—a heightened sense of herself as a unified, centred, productive physical agent. In addition, the changes in a woman's physical appearance during pregnancy, along with the new wardrobe that inevitably accompanies pregnancy, imagistically enact the new, more substantial identity and also elicit new embodied responses from other people. Visibly pregnant women often receive more attention than they did before, even from strangers, and the attention is of a different kind: whereas before, the woman's body may have been viewed, by both men and women, as an object of (primarily) male desire, during pregnancy a woman's body is seen much more as an active, productive agent rather than just a passive object. As an act of creation—of another body, another person—pregnancy is in many ways the ultimate instance of bodily agency. This enhancement of agency is extended to the life-sustaining care the girl gives her baby after it is born, through nursing, holding, bathing, comforting, and protecting it. And, in this relationship, the baby further enhances the girl's imagistic identity by functioning as a kind of prosthetic and surrogate body for her, an extension or an avatar of herself in the world.

Motherhood also provides powerful identity-bearing affective-physiological states, in the form of profound emotional experiences. One aim of many teenage mothers, Musick reports, is to find the emotional sustenance that they desperately yearned for but failed to receive from their own mothers (Musick, 1993, p. 111). One adolescent mother stated: "My mother used to treat me like shit, that's why I had a baby. So I can show the best possible love always towards my baby than anyone has ever given me" (quoted in Musick, 1993, p. 15). Another confided, "When I was about 11 or 12 I was very lonely so then I went to having sex and then I got pregnant and that was my way of curing my loneliness [by] having kids" (ibid., p. 111).

A baby may thus represent virtually the only means available for some poor teenage girls to experience a substantial sense of self, and, as such, it constitutes the primary motivation for having a baby. It follows that if efforts to reduce teenage pregnancy are to be effective, they must provide alternative means of identity establishment and maintenance (Musick, 1993, pp. 30, 66).

Addictions

Identity vulnerability as cause of addiction

That social problems arise from efforts to maintain one's identity can also be seen quite clearly in the case of addictions, which involve an attachment to substances and/or activities that clearly provide a significant boost to one's sense of self. This, rather than a purely physiological need for a substance, is the reason addictions are often so hard to overcome, both individually and socially. That addiction to alcohol and other drugs is motivated by the need to support a vulnerable identity is clear from studies of addicts.

According to Jerome Levin, "Addicts lack a firm sense of identity
... [and] identity disturbances are ubiquitous among substance
abusers" (Levin, 1999, pp. 113, 118). Often the identity disturbance
manifests itself as low self-esteem: "There are no serious substance
abusers who do not have abysmally low self-esteem" (Levin, 1999,
pp. 61, 83–84). The powerful feelings of shame that substance
abusers typically experience, and which they turn to drugs in order
to escape (ibid., p. 116), also point to identity vulnerability, since
shame is the feeling that the self is worthless. Other manifestations
of identity deficiency include the feeling of inner emptiness and
lack of a sense of control common among addicts (ibid., pp. 113, 46),
both of which express a lack of identity, the sense of oneself as a
force that matters in the world.

The fundamental role of identity vulnerability in addiction can
also be inferred from the deficiencies of identity support in the past
and present environments of many addicts, and from the fact that
the beginning of substance abuse often occurs during the identity
disruptions brought on by adolescence, family crises, or experiences of disappointment, abandonment, humiliation, or betrayal by
friends, lovers, schoolmates, and co-workers (Wurmser, 1995,
p. 114). That abusers abuse substances primarily as a means of
maintaining identity in identity-threatening circumstances can also
be inferred from the fact that many American soldiers in the
Vietnam war turned to heroin as a way to maintain their identities
under the most extreme of threats, and that when they returned
home and these threats no longer obtained, over 90 per cent gave
up the drug (Zinberg, 1997, pp. 151, 160).

In addition to external threats, various identity deficiencies can
also produce identity vulnerability. Studies of addicts have revealed
a number of specific identity deficiencies that lead to addiction. One
is lack of adequate integration among elements or registers of the
self. "The basic defect, the basic dilemma in the life of the drug-
dependent individual, such as the alcoholic," Krystal maintains,
"... is that he is unable to claim, own up to and exercise various
parts of himself" (Krystal, 1994, p. 302). Levin agrees. "Substance
abusers are highly psychophobic," he says. "They externalize and
act out in every possible way to avoid contact with their inner
worlds" (Levin, 1999, p. 94). A major manifestation of the deficient
integration found in many addicts is their inability to give adequate

verbal or imagistic representation to the major affective-physiolog-ical elements of the self. One of the more severe forms of this fail-ure is alexithymia, a condition in which individuals are unable to name, or even consciously have, specific feelings; instead of feeling anxiety or depression, for example, they experience various bodily sensations (Krystal, 1997, pp. 109–110). Many addicts are also unable even to give imagistic expression, in the form of fantasies, to their mental states (*ibid.*, p. 110). Being out of touch with their feel-ings deprives these individuals of the most fundamental evidence of their ongoing being, the core of their sense of self (Levin, 1999, p. 138). It also produces a somatic tension that many individuals find unbearable: "Feelings that cannot be verbalized are over-whelming, and one of the most common ways of dealing with the inability to withstand the tension of unverbalized affect is to drink or drug it away" (*ibid.*, p. 56). Khantzian suggests, in the same vein, "that the painful, repetitious aspects of drug use and dependence represent attempts to work out painful affect states for which there are no words, memories, or other symbolic representation" (Levin, 1999, p. 228).

Underlying lack of integration are inadequate identity struc-tures, which prevent the inclusion and integration of (and hence access to and control of) multiple and variegated identity contents, including affective states. Such structural deficiencies manifest themselves in a number of ways, including intrapsychic conflicts, deficiencies in the ability to care for oneself, interpersonal prob-lems, excessive need for external recognition, and externalizing, impulsive, and antisocial behaviours (*ibid.*). The impulsive and anti-social behaviours, in particular, indicate that addicts frequently embody Kegan's impulsive and imperial identity structures, res-pectively. In so far as one's sense of self includes only one's imme-diately present state, as in the impulsive structure, then one *is* nothing more than one's immediate, present impulses, and one thus experiences delay of gratification as tantamount to annihilation. Moreover, in so far as one's sense of self excludes other people and their needs, as both the impulsive and the imperial structures do, then one will lack both the motive and the capacity to behave in a benevolent or considerate manner. One will also have, as many addicts do, an excessive need for external recognition, since the others who provide recognition have not been internalized and integrated into one's sense of self (Khantzian, 1999, p. 92; Levin, 1999, p. 107).

One particularly acute manifestation of lack of adequate structure and integration is the presence of powerful affects such as anxiety, depression, rage, shame, and loneliness (Khantzian, 1999, pp. 88–89). Such powerful, out of control affective states are both manifestations of, and threats to, an insecure identity. In such cases, many individuals turn to drugs as a means of preventing or reducing these threatening affects (*ibid.*, p. 187). "An addict's main motivation for drug dependence," Khantzian argues, "is to use the effects of drugs to relieve or change feelings that are experienced as painful or unbearable" (*ibid.*, p. 226). Khantzian reports that opiates, such as heroin, are usually sought as a means of avoiding identity-threatening affective states such as aggression and rage (*ibid.*, 1999, p. 193).

Enacting identity contents through drug use

In addition to using drugs to escape affects that threaten one's sense of self, individuals also use drugs as a means of producing identity-bearing affective–physiological states. Thus, some individuals use drugs to provide a rush, just as other individuals seek a rush from risk-taking behaviours such as gambling, crime, and extreme sports. Khantzian finds that abusers of stimulants, such as cocaine, seek higher states of arousal, either to overcome listlessness, inner emptiness, or depression or to attain a preferred state of hyper-arousal (*ibid.*, pp. 191–192). Sedative–hypnotic substances such as alcohol are used to enable the experience of affective states that have been inhibited by rigid defences against them (*ibid.*, p. 194). Part of the affective–physiological effect of illegal drug use for some people is also the risk and excitement that come with it (Lockley, 1995, pp. 19, 23). For others, the social interaction that is facilitated in various ways by substance abuse provides significant evocation of certain vitality affects. Other people turn to nicotine and caffeine to supply energy and alertness, to alcohol for disinhibition and spontaneity, and to food—and consumerism (the most widespread of addictions)—to provide a sense of greater substance, fullness, fulfilment.

Addictions can also provide significant support for one's body–imagistic identity. As Paul Lockley observes, addiction is really of two types: physiological addiction, in which "the user's body has been so altered by the drug that it needs the drug" (ibid., p. 5) and "psychological addiction, the formation of a habit which is difficult or uncomfortable to break. Any constant behaviour pattern can become a habit and the person finds comfort in its continuance and discomfort in its ending" (ibid., pp. 4–5). Such behavioural habits are comforting because they sustain one's body–imagistic and linguistic identities. The bodily acts of procuring, preparing (measuring, mixing, wrapping, cooking), and ingesting (inhaling, injecting, sucking, chewing, swallowing) an addictive substance all enact a certain identity-bearing script as well as bodily agency and efficacy and thus allay anxiety by enhancing one's sense of self. Drug use also involves the development of new identity-bearing knowledge and skills, and thus "for users who have never seen themselves as having any or many skills, the illegal activities bring a positive sense of worth" (ibid., pp. 50–51; see also Khantzian, 1999, pp. 24–26;) and may also "bolster group identity" (Thombs, 1999, p. 253). Even the simple act of smoking, as many smokers will attest, by giving one something to do with one's hands, helps relieve the awkwardness or self-consciousness that one may otherwise experience, thus helping to maintain one's sense of bodily integrity and agency. The heightened vitality or disinhibition produced at the affective–physiological level also results in behaviours that more adequately perform bodily agency and efficacy. And, finally, drugs that produce distortions of perception offer a more direct and immediate transformation of one's sense of one's body (Krystal & Raskin, 1970, p. 92).

Addictions also enact various identity-supporting signifiers (in the form of roles, ideals, and values) and involve inhabiting certain identity-supporting systems (of knowledge, of procedures, and of relationships). Simply being an "addict" is itself a significant linguistic identity: it establishes a connection with other addicts and it positions one in relation to the social order, various moral codes, and, in some cases, the criminal justice system. "To heroin users", Lockley says,

the identity as a junkie might be a positive term, and this might well be the case for those who are either trying to find some identity or have a very low opinion of themselves. . . . The very term "junkie" is significant as it encapsulates for users the different, anti-authority, minority group feeling, and legitimizes the feeling of being an outsider. [Lockley, 1995, pp. 49, 117; see also Zinberg, 1997, p. 151]

In addition, supporting one's addiction often involves the establishment and maintenance of social relationships—a key form of recognition and belonging—with those from whom one buys or to whom one sells the addictive substance. Lockley notes that the reason many people begin using drugs is for the purpose of fitting in with peers who are using, as well as for the purpose of rebellion (Lockley, 1995, pp. 24–25). Both of these factors serve to support the user's linguistic–conceptual identity. Observing that a drug subculture "can provide a second family", Lockley states:

Apart from just meeting others, the user can become part of the subculture, part of a local group of young people. There is the comforting feeling of belonging. . . . The user's identity is affected by being part of the subculture. Belonging to any group is likely to have an effect on its members and a person's identity is largely determined through personal interaction, through the reactions of others. [ibid., pp. 48–49]

Drug use also produces identity-bearing knowledge. One type of knowledge is of the various ways of consuming a drug. For example, heroin can be consumed by various methods, including multiple ways of injecting it. Among heroin users, "injecting is a skill and status that is given in the subculture to those who learn to inject themselves with a degree of expertise" (ibid., p. 52). In addition, value is also placed on "a knowledge about the whole injecting way of life" (ibid., p. 53). Thus "sometimes injecting is important not because of the action in itself but its relation to the local subculture, and to the user's identity" (ibid., p. 55).

It is the cumulative power of these multiple identity-supporting functions of substance abuse, rather than physiological dependency alone, that makes using so difficult to give up even in face of its considerable costs and its often destructive consequences. As Lockley puts it,

Drugs are merely a means to an end, a way of helping users achieve some desired state. And this can go far beyond mere chemical

effects. Drug use might be [for example] one of several quite different symptoms of difficulties in family functioning, and a relatively
late arrival in a line of symptoms. [*ibid.*, p. 29]

As a result, stopping drug use can threaten one's identity in all
three registers. "Coming off", Lockley notes, "can be an indirect
attack not just on user ideology but on user identity" (*ibid.*, p. 104).
Consequently, in order to free oneself from drug addiction, "the
individual has to engage in a search for personal identity" (*ibid.*,
p. 116). This means that for a society to reduce substance abuse, it
must provide alternative means of identity support and development for individuals who are currently supporting their vulnerable
identities through substance abuse, as well as for all other individuals who have significant identity vulnerabilities and are therefore
at risk for future substance abuse.

Crime and delinquency

Crime and delinquency, including violence, comprise variegated
behaviours that are all efforts to maintain identity by enacting
certain (often malignant) identity components and/or achieving
recognition—by whatever means may be available. Erich Fromm
noted that crime provides a ready source of recognition, which is
often in short supply for members of marginalized groups (Fromm,
1931, pp. 138–139). In addition to providing general recognition for
malnourished identities, crime also provides an opportunity to
enact and be recognized for more specific identity contents. Polly
Radosh observes that most crimes committed by men and women,
respectively, enact key contents of culturally defined masculine and
feminine identity:

> [M]en who commit crimes behave in ways that are consistent with
> male social character. . . . Whether men commit index offenses such
> as robbery, illegal business transactions for profit or greed, viola-
> tions of environmental laws to increase industrial production, or
> territorial aggression related to gang activities, underlying values
> reflecting male social character are emphasized. In each type of
> crime, competition, aggressive usurpation of economic rewards,
> and pursuit of power, authority, and control prevail among the

individual motivations for the illegal behavior. ... [W]omen's crime [in contrast] is closely tied to the social character of women. Women's crime is limited and highly circumscribed. It is generally associated with economic need, rarely predatory, often pressured by inadequate resources for child support, and when violent, it is increasingly associated with patterns of abuse and mistreatment by men. ... Most women's crime is concentrated among low-level property offenses (shoplifting, check fraud, fraudulent theft of services), drug offenses, and defensive violence against male abusers. [Radosh, 2000, pp. 65–67]

Since "over 90 percent of those accused, convicted, and incarcerated for crimes in the United States are men" (*ibid.*, p. 59), this means that the vast majority of crime is an effort to enact and/or be recognized for elements of masculine identity. These elements, as Radosh notes, include competition, aggression, control, power, and domination. Social and cultural forces promote male violence when they construct masculine identity in terms of such contents, but then fail to provide the resources and opportunities for all men to enact and be recognized for these qualities through non-criminal behaviours. Thus, when patriarchy defines masculinity in terms of independence but social institutions and economic realities make many men more dependent and insecure, some men are left with only one apparent recourse for maintaining their masculine identity: crime (Chancer, 2000, p. 35).

The research of UCLA sociologist Jack Katz also points to the need to construct and maintain a viable identity as the fundamental motivation giving rise to all sorts of criminal activity, ranging from the misdemeanours of juvenile delinquents and the aggression of gangs to the felonious acts of robbery and murder (Katz, 1988, pp. 78–79). Amateur criminals, such as juvenile shoplifters, vandals, burglars, and joy-riders, enact several identity components through committing their property crimes. Such acts involve what Katz calls "a public staging of the self" (*ibid.*, p. 75), which elicits recognition from the official, adult world of authority and power. Shoplifters, Katz found, often experience an intense sense of recognition from those they imagine are watching them and trying to prevent their crime. One girl recalled, "What kept running through my mind was this idea of a self-centeredness. I felt like everyone was watching me, following me and like the whole store was at a stand still just concentrating on my next move" (*ibid.*, p. 72). Such public staging of the self through crime also enacts the identity factor of distinction, by engaging in socially deviant behaviour (*ibid.*, pp. 56–58), and a sense of agency, by planning and executing acts of stealth and deception, winning the game of cat-and-mouse against more powerful authorities (*ibid.*, 1988, pp. 58ff.).

Amateur property crimes also enact affective–physiological identity contents such as a rush or an excitement of sometimes orgasmic intensity. One student shoplifter stated, "Every time I would drop something into my bag, my heart would be pounding and I could feel this tremendous excitement, a sort of 'rush' go through me." Another recalled, "The experience was almost orgasmic for me. There was a build-up of tension as I contemplated the danger of a forbidden act, then a rush of excitement at the moment of committing the crime, and finally a delicious sense of release" (*ibid.*, p. 71).

Katz also found that male and female shoplifters tend to steal items that signify masculinity and femininity, respectively, which is additional evidence that the theft is an attempt to bolster their gender identities: "Females take symbols of adult female identity— cosmetics, jewellery, and sexy underwear—while males take gadgets, cigarette lighters, and wallets" (*ibid.*, p. 71).

Some youthful criminals pursue a more intense masculine identity, in the form of the "badass". This identity, Katz explains, is a more extreme form of the deviant identity pursued by those engaging in property crimes. It is enacted substantially in the body–imagistic register, through unusual ways of walking, such as "the ghetto bop and the barrio stroll", tattoos, distinctive postures and ways of talking, and accoutrements establishing an impenetrability of self, including leather, metal, sunglasses, and silence (*ibid.*, pp. 88–89). This resistance to penetration by the other's gaze is enacted not only through wearing sunglasses, but also by active confrontation of a person who may be looking at one. "A badass", Katz says, "may at any moment treat another's glancing perception of him as an attempt to bring him symbolically into the other's world, for this other's private purposes, perhaps to 'fuck with' him" (*ibid.*, p. 110). Katz finds the effort to enact hypermasculine autonomy, control, and dominance epitomized in the badass's exclamation, "Fuck you!" This assertion, Katz argues, claims a penetration of the other "in his most vulnerable, sensitive centre, in his moral and spiritual essence, without revealing oneself to the other" (*ibid.*, p. 107). Like the individual badass, street gangs, too, attempt to enact an identity of deviance and hypermasculinity, often via body images and insignia. Hence, the importance of postures, parading, and uniforms, which are designed to invoke recognition in the form of dread (*ibid.*, pp. 128, 138).

What is ultimately attractive about the life of a street criminal, Katz concludes, is the opportunity it offers to enact "some version of caste or castelike identity" (*ibid.*, p. 273). In examining the lives of robbers, Katz found that such men made a career of robbery in order to enact the identity of a "hardman" (*ibid.*, p. 196), a "formally evil identity" (*ibid.*, p. 227), which is a quintessential instance of Erikson's "negative identity". "Being a hardman", Katz discovered, "is not simply lived as a dispensable tool; rather, it is an organizing theme in the lives of those who stick with stickup" (*ibid.*, p. 227). The hardman, like the badass adolescent, aims for recognition: "stickup men find local audiences who enthusiastically celebrate the hardman's identity. . . . [A]ll eye movements are either toward or away from him. For everyone his identity becomes what the moment is about" (*ibid.*, pp. 231–234). Stickup men seek "spiritual integrity achieved through illicit means. . . . Here 'survival' implies being deviant, and being deviant, or 'bad,' takes on the meaning of *being* in general" (*ibid.*, p. 271). Hardmen often indulge in drugs, sex, and gambling as ways of sustaining the linguistic, imagistic, and affective–physiological contents of their identity between robberies (*ibid.*, p. 207). Moreover, they attempt to extend illicitness to all moments of their lives, by approaching the "innocent" moments of their lives as either times of preparation or periods of resolution of the illicit moments, such that their identity as deviant is continuous rather than episodic (*ibid.*, p. 209).

Violence

The most serious crime, violence in its various forms, occurs primarily when maintaining identity cannot be accomplished by other means. As John Burton observes:

[P]roblems of violence can be traced to the pursuit of human needs of recognition and identity. . . . Empirical evidence suggests that a paramount need being satisfied by the violent is the need for recognition as an individual or group. Individuals in society have always employed whatever means are currently available to them to attain recognition and identity. These means include the now widespread frustration responses of young people who have no ordinary means of attaining a role in society. Typical responses include leaving home and school, joining street gangs, and enacting roles of violence at community and ethnic levels that attract attention and provide some individual recognition. Membership [in] a street gang and carrying a gun, where one is available, as in the United States, is a practical solution to a lack of personal identity. . . . Specific problems, such as family violence, aggressive street gangs, ethnic conflict, secession movements and others, are merely symptoms of this underlying condition. . . . Denial by society of personal recognition and identity leads, at all social levels, to alternative behaviours ranging from participation in street gangs, to dictatorial leadership, to terrorism. [Burton, 1997, pp. 31, 10, 19–20]

Violence as the response of a vulnerable identity

That violence is motivated by the need to maintain one's identity can be inferred from the fact that it is engaged in primarily by individuals (and groups) who (a) have a chronically vulnerable or damaged identity, and/or (b) experience their present situation as embodying an imminent threat to their identity. Psychiatrist James Gilligan found in his work with violent offenders in Massachusetts prisons that these men invariably committed their violent acts in order to defend or enhance a sense of self that they experienced as seriously deficient or threatened. Gilligan reports that, in virtually all instances, these offenders turned to violence as a last resort in order to prevent the destruction of their identity, the annihilation of their sense of self. Murderers, Gilligan found, "do not perceive themselves as having non-violent means by which to maintain or restore their self-esteem or self-respect. . . . Violence is their last resort in the literal sense that it is their last resource" (Gilligan, 2001, p. 37). "A man only kills another when he is, as he sees it, fighting to save himself, his own self" (Gilligan, 1996, p. 112). "Murder", Gilligan says, "represents (for the murderer) the ultimate act of self-defence, a last resort against being overwhelmed by shame" (*ibid.*, p. 76), the sense that one's self is worthless, one's identity destroyed.

Lichtenstein agrees that violence is a means of last resort to maintain identity. "If the more advanced, more cognition-based modes of confirming [one's identity] are poorly developed or break down," he states, "the archaic forms are regressively revived, and the conviction of one's existence becomes dependent on orgastic experiences" (Lichtenstein, 1977, p. 267). If such orgastic experiences also fail to produce an adequate sense of self, then aggression is activated: aggression is used to maintain identity "only if the affirmative function of pregenital and genital libidinal satisfaction fails" (*ibid.*, p. 275). In the same vein, Strean and Freeman point out that

> the more we feel threatened in any way, the more we resort to primitive forms of aggression that include shouting, screaming, and striking or actual destruction of objects and people. The murderer feels the most threatened of all, otherwise he would not be driven to kill. [Strean & Freeman, 1991, p. 27]

Strean and Freeman remind us that "what appears of little consequence to one person may be dangerous and threatening to another" (*ibid.*). Thus if you "call a man who aspires to be macho effeminate . . . he will want to kill" (*ibid.*, p. 35). Damage to identity, which manifests itself as shame, is thus the ultimate cause of all violence:

> The emotion of shame is the primary or ultimate cause of all violence. . . . I have yet to see a serious act of violence that was not provoked by the experience of feeling shamed and humiliated, disrespected and ridiculed, and that did not represent the attempt to prevent or undo this "loss of face" . . . [which] is experienced subjectively as the death of the self. People will sacrifice anything to prevent the death and disintegration of their individual or group identity. [Gilligan, 1996, pp. 110, 97]

Most criminally violent men have severely damaged identities as the result of traumatization during their childhood. James Garbarino, a Cornell developmental psychologist who studies violent youth, reports that his investigations show "that inside most of the adolescent and adult perpetrators of violence are traumatized children" (Garbarino, 1999, p. 86). This conclusion is supported by the fact "that acts of actual and extreme physical violence, such as beatings and attempted murders, are regular experiences in the childhoods of those who grow up to become violent" (Gilligan, 1996, p. 49; see also Gilligan, 2001, p. 35). Gilligan reports that the violent offenders he worked with

> had been subjected to a degree of child abuse that was off the scale of anything I had previously thought of describing with that term. Many had been beaten nearly to death, raped repeatedly or prostituted, or neglected to a life-threatening degree by parents too disabled themselves to care for their child. [Gilligan, 2001, p. 36]

One study of rapists found that eighty per cent of them had been abused as children (Strean & Freeman, 1991, p. 19).

Nor does one have to suffer physical injury in order to be traumatized; severe deprivation of recognition can be sufficient, as Gilligan explains:

> . . . actions that do not directly cause physical injury or death can constitute the kind of psychological torture that can destroy a human personality in ways that are likely to lead to violent behavior in later life—such as locking a child in a closet, verbally threatening him or her with death or mutilation, ridiculing and taunting the child, and so on. Such actions constitute a form of psychological violence which, even in the absence of physical injury, can kill the self. Thus, people do not need to have been physically attacked in order to become violent. [Gilligan, 1996, p. 49]

Gilligan reports that he "never met a group of people who had been so profoundly neglected and deprived, and who had received so little of either attention or respect, as the prison inmates" he worked with (Gilligan, 2001, p. 122). Such traumatization during one's developmental years can leave one with an identity so fragile that later in life even the slightest deficiencies in recognition—the seemingly most trivial instances of being disrespected—provoke recourse to violence as the only effective way to restore or sustain identity.

As explained in Chapter One, inadequately inclusive identity structures render identity vulnerable, and, in doing so, they enable violence. Much violence is the product of an impulsive identity structure, in which one's sense of self is captive to the present moment. As Hans Toch observes,

> The perspective of violence is short-term and impulsive, rather than calculated and future-oriented. The Violent Man measures his worth by the distorted criterion of his physical impact, rather than by his ability to pursue a life plan. [Toch, 1969, p. 221]

This is why, Toch points out, the threat of future punishment is no deterrence: for violent men in the throes of their violent impulses, the future does not exist, because their sense of self does not have such temporal extension.

When they are not in the grip of their violent impulses, many violent men operate with an imperial sense of self. Although this identity structure includes past and future identity states, it does not include other people as ends in themselves, and, as a result, such an individual "sees other people as tools designed to serve his needs" (*ibid.*, p. 183). One type of imperially structured person, which Toch refers to as the "self-indulger", inadvertently precipitates violence through his callous disregard for others:

> The self-indulger . . . proceeds good-naturedly on the assumption that his own welfare must be of primary concern to others. He deals with acquaintances and relations on the basis of this assumption. There is no concern here with the needs of other people, because these are irrelevant to the basic scheme. Information about the views and desires of others is not perceived. Their discontent is never noted until it has blossomed into full rebellion. . . . When the moment of truth arrives, the self-indulger sees people suddenly and mysteriously turning on him and feels compelled to deal with unprovoked aggression. [*ibid.*, p. 166]

While some bullies may be operating with imperial identity structures, others are apparently enacting a perverse form of interpersonal identity, in which the other person's presence and response is an essential part of the bully's sense of self. The same logic holds for sadistic violence in general. Toch states, "The bully is really the man who enjoys the experience of exercising effective violence. . . . What is wanted is the physical and psychological effect of violence on other persons" (*ibid.*, p. 161).

Finally, some individuals, whom Toch labels "norm-enforcing" (*ibid.*, p. 135), engage in violence on the basis of an institutional or systemic identity. Such individuals have identified with a certain system of rules, or a specific organization or group, to a degree that they experience any attack on, or disregard for, this system as a threat to their own identity and respond with violence. Such an individual, "whose violence is ostensibly in the public interest and in the service of society", is actually a

> self-image promoter, who feeds his self-esteem by drawing attention to himself. When he interferes in the affairs of others he advertises his role rather than their problems. "Justice" serves as a convenient excuse for ostentatious interference. [*ibid.*, pp. 167–168]

Toch notes that such individuals "define themselves as policemen, prosecutors, judges, and executioners" (*ibid.*, p. 168), and we may speculate that many individuals who officially occupy these positions in society operate from an institutional identity structure that sanctions violence against anyone who has broken the law or disrupted any of the other institutions one has identified with.

Thus, while individuals operating with an institutional identity structure might be less likely to engage in impulsive, imperial, and interpersonal forms of criminal violence, they are quite capable of doing great harm to other people, and on a much greater scale than that of violent criminals. For their violence takes the form of mass collective violence, such as war and terrorism (the topic of the next chapter), the structural violence of poverty and inequality perpetrated through public policies and institutions, and the cultural violence produced by the lack of recognition for large groups of people in the dominant cultural artefacts, processes, and institutions. It is only the interindividual structure of identity that militates against all forms of violence. For such an identity, any harm done to anyone else is experienced as harm done to oneself, and, as a consequence, engaging in violence is experienced as doing violence to oneself.

Identity enactment through violence

In addition to defending one's identity against further damage, violence can also serve to enact or repair one's identity. Violence is a powerful means for many men to maintain their masculine identity components in all three registers. Since violence is strongly coded as masculine, a man's violent behaviour functions not only as an attempt to destroy that which threatens his claim to this identity, but also as an enactment and reclaiming of this identity. Gilligan provides an example in the case of a twenty-one-year-old man, Ross, who murdered and mutilated a woman who had given him a ride in her car. Gilligan reports that Ross killed the woman at a time when his identity as a man was threatened by the fact that his car was not working, that he lacked both the money and the expertise to fix it, and that he thus had to rely upon a woman for transportation (Gilligan, 1996, p. 63). Through his horrendous act, Ross was attempting to reclaim the identity content "man", which his lack of a car and consequent dependence on a woman who had a car threatened to deprive him of. Gilligan's account of Ross's history reveals that much of his past behaviour had also functioned to enact the identity content "man", an enactment motivated by a chronic fear that he did not really embody that content. Gilligan explains,

> His character—his habits and behavior patterns, the moral value system in terms of which he justified his behavior and goals— served as a defence against the threat . . . of being perceived as a weakling, not a "real man" . . . [*ibid.*]

Ross's chronic sense of imminent deprivation of the identity "man" was itself the result of a social situation that repeatedly conveyed to him the message that he was not really a "man":

> . . . before puberty he was regularly beaten up and teased by other boys, who taunted him as a "wimp," a "punk," and a "pussy," . . . [s]o he was being called an inadequate man, or non-man, in every possible way. [*ibid.*]

Thus, the tenuousness of Ross's claim to the identity "man"—a condition produced in large part by his social situation—was a crucial factor in his aggressivity, or chronic potential for violence, and the situation in which he committed his brutal murder precipitated this violent act by threatening to deprive him completely of his (already terribly insecure) identity as a man.

Another mutilator and murderer, Dennis, used the act of murder as a means to deny his passive desire to stay home with his mother and allow her to care for him, a desire that made him seem "unmanly and weak" (*ibid.*, p. 82). Committing the murder, Gilligan explains, engaged Dennis in ". . . behaving in a way that was active, independent, powerful, and aggressive . . . [thus wiping] out the opposite image of himself as passive, dependent, impotent, and needing love and care—i.e., as not a 'man'" (*ibid.*, p. 82).

In addition to enacting identity-bearing signifiers such as man, violence can also enact identity-bearing systems and scripts. As Toch observes, there exist "subcultures of violence" in which there is "a code which prescribes violent conduct and which is passed on—through word and deed—from one generation to the next" (Toch, 1969, p. 190). Such subcultures inculcate what amounts to a doctrine of violence, and, for some individuals, this doctrine becomes the dominant paradigm through which they interact with the world. Such individuals "do not merely espouse violence as a doctrine or philosophy, but . . . tend to see the world in violent terms and respond to it accordingly" (*ibid.*, p. 191). These violent systems of belief, in turn, often contain or entail identity-bearing scripts of violence, or "stereotyped violence-prone games", such as playing the dozens, duelling, or medieval jousting (*ibid.*, pp. 191–192). In addition, individuals may be socialized to adopt identity-bearing violence scripts through exposure to repeated action sequences in which family arguments, gang rivalries, and retaliation for a wrong all culminate in some form of violence. For many violent men, such scripts of violence may be the only ones in their repertoire for dealing with certain types of situations (*ibid.*, p. 234), such as resolving a conflict, a circumstance in which other people would activate scripts of verbal negotiation rather than violent behaviour (*ibid.*, p. 154). Such scripts can lead a man to look for, and even manufacture, violent situations that call for their enactment (*ibid.*, p. 138), such as "put[ting] the other person in a position where he can justify viciously attacking him" (*ibid.*, p. 141). Violence scripts that are associated with masculine identity are particularly prominent and powerful, including those concerning gender relations, which dictate actions of male dominance and female submission (see Mahalik, Englar-Carlson, & Good, 2003, p. 124; Vandello & Cohen, 2003, pp. 999ff.).

In addition to enacting and being recognized for certain identity-bearing signifiers, beliefs, and scripts, violence also enacts certain identity-bearing affects and body images. Violent behaviour offers a means of quickly establishing identity in the body–imagistic register. For this reason it is an attractive and frequently utilized resource for people with no other means of retaining or recovering identity, despite the fact that it also entails major risks of damaging one's bodily identity by provoking counter-violence. Engaging in— and also watching and even merely acquiescing in—physical violence is a privileged way of protecting and re-establishing one's body image and agency, especially when one's bodily form, integrity, or agency is itself insecure or threatened. Physical violence enacts an immediate reversal of one's bodily position from passive victim to active agent of bodily disintegration. This sense of bodily agency is often amplified by the tools of violence—weapons such as clubs, knives, guns, and explosives—which function as prosthetic devices that dramatically enhance one's bodily agency. And the sense of bodily integrity is often secured by the damage done to the other's body, in comparison with which one's own body appears impenetrable, invincible, omnipotent: the damaged body of another with whom one is not identified provides an ideal receptacle into which one can externalize one's own feared bodily disintegration, thus securing a sense of bodily integrity for oneself. This sense is also supported by damage done to the various surrogate bodies or prostheses of one's opponent, such as the opponent's weapons, vehicles, buildings, and land. Both the destruction and the seizure of the opponent's surrogate bodies and prostheses reinforce one's sense of one's own body's integrity, as is abundantly evident in violence perpetrated by adolescents with the aim of procuring another person's shoes, jacket, or other body-image prostheses such as jewellery.

Violence is also a sure-fire way of activating certain identity-bearing affective–physiological states. Toch notes that some people use violence as a means either of escaping from an undesirable affective state or of activating a desired mood or affect (Toch, 1969, pp. 136, 170–171), and a number of laboratory studies have confirmed "that many people may engage in aggression to regulate (improve) their own affective states" (Bushman, Baumeister, & Phillips, 2001, p. 17). A person whose core, affective–physiological identity comprises anger or intense excitement can get a quick identity fix when needed by turning to violence, in the same way as (and for the same basic reason that) some people turn to drugs. Thus, many men, when they begin to feel the identity-depleted affective states of shame, sadness, anxiety, or depression, either seek out or produce violent situations or manipulate their perceptions of the situation they are in to turn these feelings into the identity-supporting affect of anger or rage, which in turn predisposes them to violent behaviour. A similar heart-pounding, adrenalin-pumping state of intense aliveness can be evoked by the dangers that are attendant upon enacting a violent identity, and, for some violent individuals, this is no doubt a crucial benefit. In such cases, not only the act of violence itself but also the process of planning it (if it is premeditated) and, in its aftermath, the danger of being apprehended or retaliated against keep them in a vigilant state of heightened awareness and sensitivity that is experienced not as anxiety (the signal of a threatened identity), but as heightened being. For many men, whose identities have been constructed in opposition to virtually all intense feelings except anger, orgasm, and triumph, the anger that both produces and is reinforced by violent behaviour may be one of the least inhibited expressions they have of their affective–physiological core. Because we all have had the subjective experience of being endangered, we have all experienced powerful rage and destructive feelings, which means that for all of us aggression plays "a crucial role in the shaping and vitalization of the self" (Mitchell, 1993, p. 368). For many people, this destructive self is peripheral to their habitual self, one component "among multiple self-organizations". For others, however, aggression is an integral part of identity: their "sense of self and connection with others is vitalized through hatred" (*ibid.*, p. 374; see also Glasser, 1998, pp. 890–891; Fonagy, Moran, & Target, 1993, pp. 474–475).

Violence as a source of recognition

Violence also supports identity by eliciting recognition. In fact, virtually all violence may be seen as a form of what Emmanuel

Renault calls "extorted recognition" (Renault, 2004b, p. 65). When a person commits violence against you, it is impossible to ignore him any longer, and much so-called "senseless violence", including vandalism, tagging, and wilding, is an attempt (sometimes quite desperate) to gain the attention and grudging respect of an individual, a group, or an entire society. Some men with fragile identities walk around with chips on their shoulders, looking for an opportunity to commit violence as a means of gaining respect (Toch, 1969, p. 103). Concerning a man who feels that people lack respect for him, Toch comments: "He wants to do something to try to handle this lack of respect, and the *one* thing that he does is to resort to violence" (*ibid.*, p. 148).

People who are ignored by—who are invisible to—the dominant individuals and groups in their society often see no means other than violence to elicit the identity-sustaining recognition that they so desperately need. As Renault observes,

> When identities perceive themselves as disregarded by society, the desire for recognition can lead to revolt—that is, to a behaviour on the road to politicization—or to pure violence, that is, to a behaviour whose political meaning is at best implicit and unclear. [*ibid.*, p. 116]

The turf wars of gangs, Renault suggests, are efforts to defend a location that gang members experience as the only place in which they are assured recognition (Renault, 2004a, p. 386). The violence of soccer hooligans serves a similar function: it is a way of reclaiming recognition in response to the loss of gender, geographical, and class identities produced by degrading social conditions (*ibid.*, p. 387).

* * *

Since such forms of violence, as well as other types of crime and delinquency, are, at bottom, efforts to maintain or restore a threatened or damaged identity, it follows that the most effective means of reducing these social problems is to either prevent damage and threats to identity or provide more benign, prosocial means to develop, maintain, and repair vulnerable identities. The first approach requires policies and programmes that remove or mitigate the traumatizing social and cultural forces examined in Part III, and the second approach requires the provision of social and cultural resources that enable the development and maintenance of more secure, prosocial identities, an approach that is laid out in Part IV.

CHAPTER THREE

Terrorism and war

"Most of the killings in large-group conflict occur because of large-group identity issues"

(Volkan, 1998, p. 78)

The root causes of intergroup violence all relate, like those of individual violence, to identity needs. Vamik Volkan states, "When we study large-group processes, we learn that most of the killings in large-group conflict occur because of large-group identity issues" (*ibid.*). "People kill for the sake of protecting and maintaining their large-group identities" (Volkan, 1997, p. 17). John Burton reaches the same conclusion, criticizing the assumption that international conflicts are concerned fundamentally with territory: "In all cases there are non-material needs to be satisfied that provoke such aggression, particularly the needs of personal status, recognition and identity" (Burton, 1997, p. 17). Although people are usually not preoccupied with their large-group identity, it can become very important to them if either it or their personal identity is threatened:

> When a group is in continuing conflict or even at war with a neigh-
> bour group, members become acutely aware of their large-group
> identity to the point where it may far outweigh any concern for
> individual needs, even survival. [Volkan, 1997, p. 25]

Similarly, if individuals' personal identities are fragile or vulnerable, they may seek compensation by investing more heavily in their
large-group identity and attempting to enhance its stature.

Terrorism

That identity maintenance is the fundamental motivation of terrorism is supported by several facts revealed by research and analysis.

1. Most terrorists have significant vulnerabilities in their personal
    and/or collective identity.
2. Most terrorists have few alternative ways of establishing and
    maintaining a substantial sense of self.
3. Many terrorists are heavily invested in identity contents that
    entail violence.
4. Being a terrorist and engaging in terrorist activities provides
    numerous opportunities for enacting and being recognized for
    key identity contents in all three registers.
5. Terrorists' ideation and actions embody numerous identity-
    supporting defences.

Terrorists' identity vulnerability

"Personal identity problems are common among [terrorist leaders]",
Volkan reports. Many terrorist leaders, Volkan has found,

> experience[d] violations of their personal boundaries in the form of
> beatings by parents, incest, or other such events . . . [or] being aban-
> doned by a mother at an early age, disappointment over being let
> down by loved ones, a deep sense of personal failure following
> parental divorce, or rejection by peer groups. [Volkan, 1997, p. 161]

Terrorist violence is a way of compensating for their wounded
personal identities:

Because of flawed personal identities, those who become leaders of terrorist cells use their shared ethnic identity as their primary identity. In other words, the tent canvas serves as both personal garment and ethnic tent. In their ethnic identity, they find a second layer of clothing that compensates for the inadequacy of the first layer. [*ibid.*, p. 163]

Volkan emphasizes that terrorism can be both preventive and reparative of damage to identity:

[The terrorist's] conversion to terrorism comes when he believes that passivity will bring further trauma and when he identifies the ethnic garment as his principal tool for dealing with anxiety. . . . Those who become terrorist leaders or their lieutenants have a psychological need to "kill" the victimized aspects of themselves and the victimizing aspects of their aggressors that they have externalized and projected onto innocent others. [*ibid.*, p. 162]

A similar identity vulnerability is characteristic of the followers of these terrorist leaders, Volkan reports. Many are young and are in one way or another alienated or outcast from mainstream society, and terrorist leaders do various things to intensify their identity vulnerability to the point where these individuals seek refuge and recognition by joining the terrorist group (*ibid.*, p. 164). Volkan finds that this profile holds for suicide bombers as well, who are typically unmarried males in their adolescence or early adulthood (a time of maximum identity insecurity and crisis), whose prospects under current economic and political conditions are dim (i.e., who receive little structural recognition), and who have been directly traumatized in some way by ethnic conflict (e.g., have suffered physical injury or lost a loved one in the conflict) (*ibid.*, p. 165).

Many American terrorists have been victims of unresolved trauma caused by poverty, bullying, parental abuse or neglect, or parental conflict and divorce. One neo-Nazi group in Detroit was formed by young white males who had been bullied by blacks in school and on the streets, lived in poverty, had lost a parent, or been subjected to parental violence (Gallimore, 2002, p. 155). Ted Kaczynski, the Unabomber, was traumatized as a child by an illness and by severe psychological abuse at the hands of his parents and peers (*ibid.*, p. 156). Timothy McVeigh was humiliated by bullies as a child, suffered through three parental separations and finally a divorce, and suffered war trauma in the Persian Gulf War when he deliberately crushed living Iraqi soldiers with his tank and then reportedly had to scrape their body parts off the tanks' tracks (*ibid.*, pp. 157–159). Many school shooters in the USA, including Dylan Klebold and Eric Harris at Columbine High School, were victims of bullying at school and abuse or neglect at home (*ibid.*, pp. 159–162).

Jerrold Post's research corroborates the conclusion that the major motive for terrorism is identity maintenance necessitated by some sort of trauma or identity disruption. The terrorist's attempt to destroy the establishment, Post has found, "is driven by the terrorist's search for identity". Post reports that "a great deal has gone wrong in the lives of people who are drawn to the path of terrorism" (such as loss of, or conflict with, parents), and that many terrorists are driven to terrorism in an effort to heal the "narcissistic wounds" of an "injured self": "the act of joining the terrorist group represents an attempt to consolidate a fragmented psychological identity" (Post, 1998, pp. 26–31).

But Post and others warn that it is a mistake to see terrorists as psychologically abnormal and to view their identity vulnerability solely in terms of their personal traumas. As Fabick suggests, "Overall, cultural and political factors may weigh more heavily in the development of a terrorist than individual personality" (Fabick, 2002, p. 228). More specifically, as McCauley argues, for many terrorists, it is damage to their group identity more than their personal identity that is the major cause of their terrorist activity: "The mistake is to imagine that self-sacrifice must come from personal problems, rather than identification with group problems" (McCauley, 2002, p. 9). Michael Wessells, noting that threats to collective identity increase the likelihood of violence, observes:

> Western ascendancy and hegemony, coupled with the rise of transnational corporations and the spread of Western culture by movies, television, computers, and other media, have provided enormous threats to Islamic identities. Externally, the threat is one of economic imperialism, which creates dependency while relegating one's own culture and practices to secondary status. . . . Internally, the threat is that Western values will be internalized.
> [Wessells, 2002, p. 67]

Richard Rubenstein makes a similar observation, stating that "the rapid and pervasive spread of Western (especially American) political, economic, military, and cultural influence around the globe since the end of World War II" has been experienced by many people around the world as "invasion" that "threatens people's core identities" (Rubenstein, 2003, p. 146; see also McCauley, 2002, pp. 10ff.). Rubenstein mentions, in particular, things such as "Coca-Cola, freedom of expression, Beverly Hills fashions, gender equality, Internet pornography, parliamentary democracy, gangsta rap, religious pluralism, TV satellite dishes, and the whole panoply of American and European lifestyles and politico-cultural values" (Rubenstein, 2003, p. 146). Taken together, the things in this list embody alternatives, and hence threats, to virtually all types of identity contents in each register of many people in other cultures. Like Wessells, Rubenstein sees the threat as twofold; it comes both in the form of a challenge to the supremacy or social currency of traditional, indigenous contents and in the form of a temptation to embrace the alien contents and abandon the traditional ones (*ibid.*, p. 146).

Of particular significance is the lack of status and recognition accorded by the Western secular world to identity-bearing Islamic beliefs, values, ways of life, and political power. As Bernard Lewis points out, during the past three or four centuries, the political power of Islam has been in continuous decline, beginning with "loss of domination in the world", extending to "the undermining of [the Muslim man's] authority in his own country through an invasion of foreign ideas and laws and ways of life and sometimes even foreign rulers or settlers" (Lewis 2003, p. 196), and culminating in "the challenge to his mastery in his own house, from emancipated women and rebellious children" resulting from Western "forces that have devalued their traditional values and loyalties and, in the final analysis, robbed them of their beliefs, their aspirations, their dignity, and to an increasing extent even their livelihood" (*ibid.*, p. 200).

Volkan explains that such collective traumatizing conditions can result in what he calls the "transgenerational transmission of chosen traumas", through which individuals are traumatized by the still unresolved traumatic experiences of past generations. A "chosen trauma" is the enduring impact of a calamity suffered by the group's ancestors, which the group now uses unconsciously as a central identity content, thus transferring from one generation to the next a wounded identity embodying the memory of the trauma. A chosen trauma is not just a recollection; "it is a shared mental representation of the event, which includes realistic information, fantasized expectations, intense feelings, and defences against unacceptable thoughts" (Volkan, 1997, p. 48). Additonally, the transmission occurs not just through stories of the trauma that are told to the young, but also through non-verbal messages and patterns of behaviour through which members of elder generations unconsciously externalize their wounded identities on to members of later generations during their formative years, making the young into receptacles for the unhealed identity wounds of their elders. As a result, "it becomes the child's task to mourn, to reverse the humiliation and feelings of helplessness pertaining to the trauma of his forbears" (ibid., p. 43). In this process,

> the transmissions of traumatized self-images occur almost as if psychological DNA were planted in the personality of the younger generation through its relationships with the previous one. The transmitted psychological DNA affects both individual identity and later adult behaviour. [ibid., p. 44]

Lack of resources for identity maintenance

Other researchers have emphasized that terrorists lack the resources for identity construction and maintenance that most non-terrorists have. As Martha Crenshaw points out, one prominent cause of terrorism is "lack of opportunity for political participation" (Crenshaw, 2003, p. 95), which is a significant source of identity support for many people. Post observes that some terrorists' "only sense of significance comes from being terrorists" and that "to give up terrorism . . . would be to lose their very reason for being" (Post, 1998, p. 38). Taylor and Louis argue that the disruption of collective identity discussed in the previous section has made it impossible for many terrorists even to form, much less to maintain, an adequate personal identity. They emphasize not how Western influences have disrupted traditional Islamic identity, but, rather, how the Islamic fundamentalist reaction to Western influence is itself disruptive of more or less stable collective identities:

[T]he sudden implementation of a fundamentalist religious collective identity as a reaction to a more secular collective identity would produce a chaotic collective identity for most. All of a sudden, established norms, values, and goals are replaced with new ones that are often totally at odds with the previous collective identity. [Taylor & Louis, 2004, p. 176]

Even worse, many "young people who languish in refugee camps live out their life with not merely confused collective identity, but an empty collective identity", and these individuals are most likely to embrace the collective identity offered by a terrorist organization (*ibid.*, p. 179). The more difficult it is to affirm a collective identity, the more likely it is that young people will "be drawn to the comparatively uncomplicated identity paradigm of defining themselves as 'not the out-group'" (*ibid.*, pp. 182–183).

Burton makes a similar point about terrorists in Northern Ireland:

Many of their more active followers were also ordinary citizens who in due course had a vested interest in the continuation of the conflict in that without it they would have no social role or identity, and no job or income. The perception we have of "terrorists" is that of persons who are abnormal and disturbed and who need to be removed from society. Yet in fact they have, typically, more than average intelligence, but frequently have been deprived of educational and career opportunities. The role their [terrorist] activities provide gives them an identity. [Burton, 1997, p. 27]

Burton concludes that if terrorists and other violent leaders had been given opportunities and resources for constructing and maintaining alternative, benign identities, most of them would have been normal citizens condemning the violent actions they now engage in (*ibid.*, p. 28).

Violence-entailing identity contents

Another significant motivational factor in some terrorists is violence-entailing identity contents that they have acquired through either socialization or trauma. Each of the three registers of identity can either entail or incline toward violence. Identity-bearing values and ideals such as masculinity, toughness, and domination have significant force in the lives of some terrorists (Long, 1990, p. 23; Piven, 2002, p. 126). The identity contents of hero and martyr are also prominent in the identities of some terrorists, especially those whose terrorist acts are suicidal (see Kfir, 2002, pp. 145–147). The identity of victim, too, can motivate terrorist acts, including suicidal ones (see Piven, 2002, pp. 132–133). As Olweean explains,

> Taking on the identity of victim places us in the role of someone wronged who deserves justice, and allows for a self-righteous perspective that can eventually rationalize inhumane treatment of others identified as the perpetrators of our victimization. . . . If we select any society or culture in recent history that has been identified as a perpetrator against another, . . . invariably that group carries a deeply held myth of itself as victim, martyr, or even champion of a higher good—sometimes the good of all. . . . Entire cultures can take on the identity of tragic victim and unwittingly use this energy of fear to become the perpetrators. [Olweean, 2002, pp. 119–120]

Certain identity-bearing beliefs of all types—including religious beliefs, other mythic world views, and political ideologies—also motivate terrorism. One of the most significant beliefs is a corollary of the victim identity: the conviction that one's own group is innocent and good and that its problems derive from the aggressive or oppressive actions of another group, which is guilty of egregious transgressions against it. This identity-bearing ideology and its violent entailments can be found in the rhetoric of most terrorist groups, which Post describes as follows:

> [T]he uniformity of their rhetoric is striking. Polarizing and absolutist, it is a rhetoric of "us versus them." It is a rhetoric without nuance, without shades of gray. "They," the establishment, are the source of all evil, in vivid contrast to "us," the freedom fighters, consumed by righteous rage. And if "they" are the source of our problems, it follows ineluctably, in the special psycho-logic of the terrorist, that "they" must be destroyed. It is the only just and moral thing to do. Once the basic premises are accepted, the logical reasoning is flawless. [Post, 1998, pp. 25–26]

In the case of many Islamic terrorists, this polarized belief combines with an identity of "cosmic specialness" (Kfir, 2002, p. 144) in an apocalyptic world view that sees the relation between Islamic civilization and Western civilization as a cosmic struggle between good and evil (Juergensmeyer, 2001; Mack, 2002, pp. 177ff.; McCauley, 2002, p. 14). The identity structure operating here is clearly quite restrictive, admitting no contents with even the hint of a negative valence.

Terrorist violence is also motivated by certain identity-bearing scripts and narratives of violence. These can originate in traumatic childhood experiences of abuse by care-givers, in response to which children develop non-verbal, behaviour scripts of hostile, abusive, and violent interactions with others (Piven, 2002, pp. 126ff.), but such scripts can also be produced by enculturation that results in the internalization of stories in which violent behaviour constitutes a laudable response and successful solution to problems (Ellens, 2002, pp. 154ff.). One of the most potent violence-entailing scripts operating in terrorism is revenge ideology (Ardila, 2002, p. 12), which functions synergistically with the identity of victim and the identity-bearing belief in a world polarized by good and evil. As McCarthy points out, adolescents are particularly susceptible to the internalization of scripts that support terrorist activities (McCarthy, 2002, p. 131), and such scripts can be internalized from films, television, video games, and music (ibid., p. 133). The intergenerational transmission of stories of a group's chosen traumas is perhaps an even more effective means of internalization than the new media, however, for such stories do not merely transmit information about past events, but also introject into the identities of the young certain "valued paradigms for action" (Tololyan, 2001, p. 221), which "plot out how ideal selves must live lives . . . [and] dictate biographies and autobiographies to come" (ibid., p. 218). Thus, Tololyan argues that

> in cultures like the Armenian, terrorism is not the product of a particular individual's alienation, but the manifestation of a desire to give one's individual life an iconic centrality in the eyes of the community, which professes to value certain forms of behavior articulated in narratives. [ibid., p. 227]

Religion plays a major role in constructing the sorts of identity-bearing scripts that can motivate terrorist violence. The major religions all have stories in which revenge is presented as the ultimate solution. In the Christian doctrine of atonement, for example, a vengeful, bloodthirsty god is dissuaded from killing all humanity only by the death of his son (Ellens, 2002, p. 155). In Islam, there is the identity-bearing script of *jihad*, the struggle against evil, which, despite efforts by progressive Muslims to explain it as a metaphor for inner struggle, has clear historical roots in Mohammed's own military struggle and has been internalized as such by many Islamic terrorists (*ibid.*, p. 160).

Imagistic identity contents no doubt also play a powerful, though less evident and more unconscious, role in the motives of many terrorists. Individuals who have been physically traumatized or neglected are often overly invested in, and hypersensitive to, their bodily integrity and autonomy. Many terrorist behaviours, including preoccupation with weapons and geographical territory, can be seen as functioning to protect and assert the integrity, autonomy, and power of one's own vulnerable body by means of bodily prosthetics (weapons, armour, vehicles) and/or surrogate bodies (buildings, vehicles, geographical territory). Blowing up planes, buildings, and other people is a way of asserting one's own bodily integrity, by contrast with the bodies of one's victims. At the same time, making oneself vulnerable, through such actions, to retaliatory bullets and bombs can function as a counterphobic defence of one's bodily vulnerability. And all these actions, including suicide bombing, work to defend a vulnerable bodily identity through the passive-into-active defence, whereby one gains a sense of agency, control, and power by enacting what one has previously been forced to endure—or has feared having to endure—passively. Thus, by engaging in suicide bombing, one can put an end to anxiety concerning one's body's vulnerability to penetration, dismemberment, and fragmentation by oneself producing the utter fragmentation of one's body.

Affective-physiological identity contents that entail or at least potentiate violence include anger, rage, hatred, excitement, and anxiety. A number of researchers have noted that many terrorists seem to be stimulus hungry and seek out risky situations as ways of producing an optimal sense of self (see, for example, Post, 1998, p. 27). Long suggests "that the dangers of risk-taking [in terrorism] serve as a stimulus for those who are otherwise lacking in personal feeling" (Long, 1990, p. 19).

Identity-maintaining features of terrorism

That terrorism is motivated by efforts to maintain identity is also supported by the fact that being a terrorist, belonging to a terrorist organization, and engaging in terrorist activities can serve not just to enact malignant identity contents but also to support "normal", benign identity elements through processes that are also normally benign. One powerful way terrorism supports the identities of many terrorists is by providing ongoing recognition in multiple modes. The most obvious is the public attention that terrorists garner, particularly in the form of the terror that their actions produce (Crenshaw, 2003, p. 96). Whereas prior to their terrorist actions many terrorists are invisible, ignored by the powers that be, after their terrorist actions they become the focal point of those in power, who in some cases become obsessed with identifying, finding, and capturing or killing them. As Taylor and Louis observe, "the powerful out-group's attention may become the reinforcement that terrorist behaviour attempts to elicit, so that outrage may be seen as preferable to being ignored by the powerful out-group" (Taylor & Louis, 2004, p. 184). Indeed, one fundamental aim of much terrorist activity may be to elicit in the target group the deepest form of recognition, empathy, by eliciting the profound despair, humiliation, and helplessness that the terrorists themselves feel but to which the target group has remained complacently oblivious. As Diane Perlman explains,

> Terrorism can be thought of as a perversion of the desire for empathy. After September 11, 2001, everyone from bin Laden to America's allies said in one form or another, "Now you know how we feel," with a sense of grim satisfaction. It is a universal human experience to want others to know how we feel when we are suffering. Perhaps the desire for empathy is an unrelenting nonnegotiable requirement . . .: if empathy is not naturally forthcoming it will be extracted in a pathological manner. [Perlman, 2002, p. 30]

Sue Grand has observed a similar motive operating in some of the most brutal and horrific acts of interpersonal violence (see Grand, 2000).

Another important form of recognition comes from membership in a group. As a number of researchers have reported, the need to belong is often an important motive in the decision to join a terrorist group (Crenshaw, 2003, p. 101; Post, 1998, p. 31; Rubenstein, 2003, p. 140). The very fact of being accepted by the group constitutes a powerful form of recognition, implying the group's approval of one's identity (values, beliefs, goals, affective states, and so on), and the interchanges and interactions with group members enact further forms of recognition.

In addition to eliciting recognition, being a terrorist also enacts benign identity contents. These include identity-bearing signifiers such as righteous, courageous, strong, and loyal, as well as identity-bearing roles and social categories (nationality, ethnicity, gender) that are often in and of themselves benign rather than malignant. Non-malignant identity-bearing beliefs and knowledge can also be enacted by terrorism. Particularly significant is the expertise or know-how that is necessary to carry out terrorist acts, provide for the group's material needs, maintain invisibility, and so on. Such identity-bearing knowledge and skills can include bomb-making, the procurement, maintenance, and operation of weapons, surveillance, espionage, sabotage, and other clandestine operations.

Terrorism also provides numerous opportunities to enact benign body images, integrity, agency, and efficacy through various prosthetics and surrogates such as weapons and vehicles, as well as through the feats of stealth, strength, and agility that are required by some terrorist activities. Somewhat ironically and paradoxically, suicidal terrorist missions can be one of the most powerful enactments of bodily agency and efficacy, transforming an individual from an invisible nobody, a nothing having no significance for the powers that be, into a force that overpowers and even destroys those powers. Acts of "destructive suicide" such as those of 9/11 can thus "elevat[e] one from an inferior to a superior position" (Kfir, 2002, p. 147).

In addition to enacting malignant, violence-entailing affective–physiological identity contents, terrorism also provides opportunity for the enactment of identity-bearing affective states that are, in and of themselves, basically benign. Belonging to a terrorist group can lead to intense emotional bonds; successfully executed terrorist missions can result in calmness, relief, happiness, or joy; and acts of killing and destruction can produce ecstasy of an orgasmic intensity. Piven reports that terrorists' accounts of their actions often reveal an intense pleasure in the act of killing. There is an orgasmic relief expressed in descriptions of their violence. . . . Stomping the guts of others can be an ecstatic triumph over mortality itself, and such ecstasy can be so orgasmically fulfilling that it becomes seductive and addictive. [Piven, 2002, p. 130]

Ernst Becker agrees, noting that "men spill blood because it makes their hearts glad and fills out their organisms with a sense of vital power" (quoted in Piven, 2002, p. 130).

Violence-enabling defences

Harmful identity defences also play a significant role in enabling terrorist violence. Dissociative and externalizing defences are quite prominent in terrorist identities (Fabick, 2002, p. 228; Post, 1998, pp. 27, 29) and are produced and enabled by some of the identity-bearing belief systems considered above, as well as by the absence of more complex and inclusive identity structures. The polarized world views promote the dissociation of good from bad and the externalization of all things bad on to another group. Dissociation of actions from their consequences is also a crucial defence in terrorism, facilitating the perpetration of great human suffering with a clear conscience. As Bandura observes,

It is relatively easy to hurt others when their suffering is not visible and when causal actions are physically and temporally remote from their effects. . . . Even a high sense of personal responsibility is a weak restrainer when aggressors do not know the harm they inflict on their victims. [Bandura, 1998, p. 177]

Displacement can also facilitate terrorism, in so far as some of the anger and hatred directed against the enemy may be displaced from earlier, childhood targets such as the parents (Piven, 2002, p. 128). And, as noted above, the passive-into-active defence may be involved in some terrorist suicides (Fabick, 2002, p. 232).

Terrorist violence is also facilitated by the minimizing defences. One prominent defence of this type is euphemistic labelling, of which four types have been identified (Bandura, 1998, p. 170). Palliative expressions such as "freedom fighters" and "servants of God" rather than "killers" (Fabick, 2002, p. 233), and legitimizing locutions such as "team players" and "game plans", "make the reprehensible respectable, while the agentless passive construction is used to obscure the perpetrators of evil acts, and metaphors are used to obscure the nature of such acts" (Bandura, 1998, p. 170). Another minimizing defence is rationalization, which reconstrues violence, brutality, and killing in such a way that moral individuals can kill without inhibition from their conscience. Such rationalizations involve visions of oneself "as fighting ruthless oppressors who have an unquenchable appetite for conquest, protecting their cherished values and way of life, preserving world peace, saving humanity from subjugation to evil ideology," and so on (Bandura, 1998, p. 164).

Finally, in addition to being facilitated by various identity defences, terrorism actually constructs and enacts certain defences. For one, it functions as a kind of reaction formation, facilitating the repression of, and displacement of attention from, the identity-threatening psychological and social conflicts, frustrations, and failures of everyday life. The intense affects produced by terrorist activities can effectively defend against identity-threatening affects: "people may thrive on violence as a means of overcoming feelings of rage, humiliation, helplessness, impotence, and the dread of death" (Piven, 2002, p. 130). Minimization also results from terrorist activity: in comparison with the life and death events terrorists are involved in, most other concerns become rather insignificant.

Terrorist acts also facilitate various dissociations, severing links that could threaten one's sense of self. The danger and excitement of terrorist activity, as well as the isolation of the individual within a terrorist group, can effectively break off thinking about the causes and consequences of one's actions. And, while terrorism is facilitated by splitting, dissociating the good from the bad, it also reinforces the splitting of the world into good and evil, us and them: research has revealed that when one individual or group does harm to another, the guilty party will attempt to view its victim as deserving the aggression and thus begin to obscure the victim's positive and innocent attributes and amplify the victim's negative qualities (Staub, 1989). Similarly, while terrorism is greatly facilitated by externalizing defences, it also enables such defences, by rendering its victims in various ways inferior, more hateful, and more aggressive, and thus making them even more suitable targets for the externalization of one's own negative qualities.

War

Threats to identity

Like terrorism, war is also motivated by identity needs, not only of military personnel, but also of the general populace that supports war. War-entailing identity factors include:

1. Threats to the integrity of certain identity contents, especially threats seen as coming from another nation.
2. The embodiment of malignant identity contents—contents entailing war, violence, conflict, or competition.
3. The opportunity to enact benign identity contents by participating in war.
4. Recognition through engaging in war.
5. The embodiment of malignant identity defences (individual and collective) that enable scapegoating—that is, absolving oneself and blaming another party for one's predicament.

In the first place, most wars occur not primarily because of disputes over material interests, but, rather, because of threats to identity. Ervin Staub states that mass killing such as war and genocide is triggered when "difficult life conditions and certain cultural characteristics ... generate psychological processes and motives that lead a group to turn against another group" (Staub, 1989, p. 13). Both the difficult life conditions and the cultural characteristics that Staub identifies as facilitating mass killing constitute one form of identity threat or another. Difficult life conditions include starvation, severe deprivation of food and shelter, decline in material well-being, or "the frustration of expectations for improved well-being", as well as hostility or violence of various types (war, crime) and the disruption of established patterns of work and other social relations (ibid., p. 14). Such material deprivations threaten identity in all three registers. One's affective–physiological state is directly altered by inadequate nourishment or shelter, and, of course, by physical violence as well. One's sense of bodily self is also profoundly altered by material deprivation and physical violence: one's agency and efficacy are severely impaired by hunger or exposure to the elements, which can also profoundly alter one's bodily appearance and one's confidence in the integrity of one's bodily boundary. Being subjected to violence can produce even greater damage to these identity components. These same difficult life conditions can also deprive one of one's linguistic identity contents. Master signifiers such as important, strong, independent, good parent, successful, and so on are hard to sustain in the face of hunger, poverty, unemployment, or physical violence. So are identity-sustaining beliefs that justice ultimately prevails, that freedom reigns, that opportunity exists, or that there is a future worth waiting and working for. Identity-bearing narratives of progress can also be destroyed by such life conditions, as can smaller identity-bearing action scripts through which one conducts one's day-to-day and moment-to-moment social relations.

Such threats to identity quite naturally evoke identity-maintaining responses from people. Staub observes:

> Difficult conditions threaten the self concept as people cannot care for themselves and their families or control the circumstances of their lives. . . . Powerful self-protective motives then arise: the motive to defend the physical self (one's life and safety) and the motive to defend the psychological self (one's self-concept, values, and ways of life). There is a need both to protect self-esteem and to protect values and traditions. There is also a need to elevate a diminished self. [*ibid.*, p. 15]

Other groups can threaten and damage the integrity or status of one's identity contents in multiple ways. Denigration of a society's master signifiers, master narratives, or identity-bearing beliefs threatens the identities of its members. The same is true of denigrations of body-image identity contents, such as criticizing or satirizing distinguishing facial features (eyes, lips, nose), hair, skin colour, body shape, body size, or clothing. Incursions into, or challenges to, a nation's surrogate bodies—such as its territory, buildings (e.g., embassies), ships, and planes—are experienced not just as material losses but as much more serious losses of identity security. The same result is produced by attacks on affective–physiological identity contents, such as expressions of amusement, disbelief, or disgust regarding the particular modes of enjoyment associated with a culture's food, music, games, and other forms of entertainment, examples of which can be found in Americans' expression of disgust for food such as dogs, insects, or internal organs, as well as befuddlement or amusement regarding Indian music or African dance. A nation's identity contents can also be damaged or threatened by the promotion of competing identity contents through cultural imperialism. People all over the world today have suffered identity damage from American cultural imperialism, through the dissemination of hegemonic American values, ideals, beliefs, knowledge, scripts, narratives, body images, and modes of affective–physiological enjoyment. Similarly, many Americans experience identity threats from the alternative identity contents of groups within the USA, including various immigrant groups, as well as other groups practising lifestyles significantly different from their own.

Malignant identity contents

Malignant identity contents inclining towards war include master signifiers such as man, warrior, patriot, hero, tough, aggressive, and brave. Many such identity-bearing signifiers are derived from cultural ideals. As Staub notes, "Some cultures (and individuals) idealize aggression" (Staub, 1989, p. 54). The Nazis and the Bolsheviks did, Staub observes, and so does America, as evidenced by its movies and television programmes, as well as the prominence of groups such as the National Rifle Association (*ibid.*). Staub also points out the malignancy of certain identity-bearing roles, such as those of soldier and prison guard, in so far as "the devaluation of some other people" is inherent in them (Staub, 1989, p. 69).

Identity-bearing beliefs that incline people towards war include convictions that one's own country is, or should be, dominant, that defeating the other country is decreed by a god, evolution, or the march of history, and that might makes right. Such beliefs can be found behind European colonialist and imperialist wars; in the doctrine of manifest destiny, which validated and motivated the Euro-American genocidal wars against the indigenous peoples of the Americas; in Hitler's belief in Aryan supremacy, which motivated and validated the Holocaust and Germany's invasion and occupation of other European countries; in Soviet imperialism; and in American imperialism and unilateralism of the twentieth and twenty-first centuries. An identity-defining belief in the current or historical victimization of one's own nation can also be a significant factor, as demonstrated by the role of chosen traumas in inclining a nation towards war (Volkan, 1988).

Related identity-bearing narratives include those in which war or some other form of violence is the proper and honourable response to a challenge, an insult, or a sign of disrespect, or simply the most effective solution to intergroup conflicts and other problems. Scripts of heroic actions in battle and narratives of military campaigns and victories are internalized by many individuals as part of their sense of self, and these identity contents predispose them towards supporting a war, if not actually fighting in it, when the opportunity for war presents itself. As Staub observes, "Some researchers believe that aggression becomes self-perpetuating because children learn aggressive 'scripts' or cognitive schemas, representations of reality that serve as blueprints for aggressive behavior" (Staub, 1989, p. 71). Television programmes and films provide countless narratives and scripts of this sort, as do some types of video games and popular music. But one of the most powerful sources of identity-bearing violence narratives may be religion. Harold Ellens points out that the Bible is replete with narratives of God's violence, beginning with the expulsion of Adam and Eve from the Garden of Eden, including Noah's flood and the exiles of the Israelites, and culminating in the crucifixion of Jesus, which, Ellens argues, predisposes individuals in the Western, Christian world to solve problems through violence, in blatant contradiction to the ostensible message of Christianity:

> The crucifixion of Jesus of Nazareth is an image and a metaphor right at the center of the Master Story of the Western world for the last two thousand years, which radically contradicts the grace ethic it purports to express, and cuts the ethic's taproot by means of the dominant model of solving ultimate problems by resorting to the worst kind of violence. With that kind of metaphor at our center— and associated with the essential behavior of God—how could we possibly hold, in the deep structure of our own unconscious, any notion of ultimate solutions to ultimate questions or crises other than violence? How can we not opt for human solutions that are equivalent to God's kind of violence? . . . Until we are ready to analyze those Master Stories and eradicate from them their violent core metaphors, it is impossible for us to develop at the unconscious level—where the action is—warrantable nonviolent alternatives for our strategies in conflict resolution. [Ellens, 2002, pp. 155, 161]

Body–imagistic identity contents that incline people towards war include massive size, power, and impenetrability, which predispose people to various actions of defensiveness regarding their various surrogate bodies (homeland) and bodily prosthetics (weapons) and towards belligerence and aggression in relation to the surrogate bodies of other nations. One of the appeals of military membership is the tremendous enhancement of bodily power it offers an individual, including not only the enhanced physical strength and endurance often produced by basic training, but also the possession and use of firearms, combat vehicles (boats, planes, tanks, etc.) that function as surrogate bodies, and the use of sophisticated electronic equipment (radar, sonar, night vision goggles, laser technology) that dramatically extends and intensifies the powers of the senses. Even many civilians who only observe, and do not actually use, these devices become giddy with enthusiasm at their power and effectiveness, as the USA's national anthem itself indicates, with its (scandalous) celebration of "the rockets' red glare, the bombs bursting in air". Without the existence of such prosthetics and surrogates of violence, and, more fundamentally, without the widespread attraction of many people to such prosthetics and surrogates as a means of maintaining their own vulnerable sense of bodily agency and efficacy, war would no doubt still exist, but it would not have quite the same attraction that it has for many people today.

It must be acknowledged that many of the malignant identity contents that incline individuals to embrace war are those that are inculcated through military training. Basic military training systematically decommissions many of the individual identity contents of recruits—including gentleness, calmness, kindness, independence, spontaneity, and aversion to suffering, fighting, and killing—and replaces them with their opposites: the identity contents of a warrior, for which war and battle are the ultimate—and really the only—means of enacting and being recognized. New identity contents are produced in recruits through multiple means. The presence of a rigid authoritarian structure that ruthlessly proscribes and prescribes specific modes of interaction and other behaviours, together with the forceful and repeated articulation of military ideals, values, and codes, induces the formation and enactment of new identity-bearing roles such as "soldier", new values such as toughness, insensitivity, and aggression, and new belief and knowledge systems such as those of military organization and codes of conduct. The constant repetition, in the form of drills and protocols, of various body postures, body movements, facial expressions, and eye control, and of certain behavioural and interaction scripts, produces new identity-bearing know-how regarding the weapons, machines, and instruments of war and new identity-bearing action scripts such as those of hand-to-hand combat, patrol, surveillance, fortification, and interaction with comrades. In addition, military uniforms and haircuts provide recruits with a (sometimes dramatically) different body image, and various weapons, weapons systems, vehicles, and tracking and surveillance systems (including radar, sonar, laser scopes, and night vision goggles) offer them exciting new surrogate bodies and body prosthetics, which can marvellously enhance their sense of agency and efficacy. Military training also reworks affective–physiological contents, using the force of emotional contagion produced by immersion in a group to induce in recruits, and habituate them to, affective–physiological states involving or inclining towards hyperarousal and aggression. Combat obviously provides the optimal scene for enacting these identity contents, which include roles such as soldier and warrior and identity-bearing values such as brave, ferocious, and fearless. The same is true concerning identity-bearing systems of military belief and knowledge and the various action scripts concerning battlefield behaviour. Bodily agency and efficacy can also be optimally enacted on the battlefield through the effective and successful employment of the various instruments of war that function as body prosthetics or surrogate bodies. In addition, combat has also been experienced by some individuals as providing the most powerful support of one's affective–physiological register of identity, in the form of a vitality, excitement, or ecstasy as intense as that of any orgasm or drug-induced rush (Hedges, 2002, pp. 84–89, 101, 161–163).

Opportunities for identity maintenance in war

War is also motivated by the opportunity individuals find in wartime to enact and be recognized for their various benign identity contents. This is true for civilians as well as military personnel. Civilians who identify with a war effort find countless opportunities to make their lives matter, which is the essence of the sense of self. Whether it be working in a factory that manufactures war materiel, filling in for individuals who have joined the military, giving up certain material goods and creature comforts to aid the war effort, or working to boost troop morale, such activities can produce a powerful sense of purpose, of making a difference, of mattering. In addition, such activities also provide heretofore unavailable opportunities to enact various identity contents, including identity-bearing signifiers such as patriot, identity-bearing knowledge such as that required to perform one's various tasks, and the various scripts enacted in performing the tasks. Some tasks also involve the performance of—and possibly the development of new—body-image identity contents, producing a greater sense of bodily agency, efficacy, integrity, and/or appearance.

Recognition

The recognition provided for fighting in war is also a major motivating force. Such recognition takes multiple forms. Holidays, parades, and ceremonies celebrating military service and victories provide powerful recognition for soldiers, as do news reports of military service and accomplishments, individual and collective. Military personnel are also given direct and express recognition in the form of praise from government officials and civilians alike, and via military citations, commendations, decorations, medals, and promotions. Another form of recognition occurs in the provision of military uniforms and insignias of rank, which in turn elicit recognition from the public. In principle, institutions such as departments of veterans affairs and organizations such as the American Legion and Veterans of Foreign Wars also provide identity-supporting recognition, though these forms of recognition operate primarily after the fact rather than as motivation for fighting in the first place.

Malignant identity defences

War is also facilitated and motivated by multiple defence mechanisms, which are powerfully enacted and reinforced by public discourse about one's own nation, the adversary nation, and the interactions between the two. Denial of the terrible consequences of war is a crucial defence enabling its prosecution. When people confront the horrible suffering of those injured and killed in war—in the form of visual images of disfigured and mutilated bodies (living as well as dead) and the sounds of the wounded (civilians as well as soldiers, children as well adults) shrieking, screaming, and moaning in agony—they become significantly less enthusiastic in their support for the war, as the televised coverage of the Vietnam war demonstrated. As a result, the American government and media now collude to prevent these brutal realities of war from reaching the American public and thereby enable the denial of the most real and most important truths about war: the unspeakable things it does to the bodies of real, living and breathing human beings.

In the relatively rare instances when these facts are actually acknowledged, euphemistic, intellectualizing language is used to minimize the truest and most real elements of these facts—for example, the obscene use of abstractions such as "collateral damage" to refer to children decapitated, dismembered, mutilated, or disfigured by one's own military actions. Accounts of the Iraq war are saturated with such euphemisms, including "casualties", "blood and treasure", and even "dead" and "wounded", which are abstractions that block from our awareness the horrible suffering that was endured by most of the "dead" and "wounded" as their bodies were ripped open or torn apart, or as they lay bleeding to death or slowly choking on their own blood. The description of the American invasion of a country that posed no imminent threat to us as "bringing democracy to the Iraqi people", rather than as killing and maiming hundreds of thousands of innocent men, women, and children (Burnham, Lafta, Doocy, & Roberts, 2006, p. 1421) and wasting three trillion dollars that could have brought life and comfort to hundreds of millions of suffering people is an even more obscene instance. In the absence of such publicly shared and validated minimizing defences, our leaders and their support- ers would be more likely to recognize their own murderous impulses and deal with them in a less destructive way.

Rationalization, which concocts a (spurious) logical justification for behaviours that are driven by impulses, wishes, or feelings that contradict key identity contents, is also powerfully enabling of war. American rationalization of the motives behind the invasion of Iraq has been massive and is perhaps most obvious in the Bush administration's offering of numerous shifting reasons for the invasion, none of which has been able to withstand scrutiny: preventing Saddam from attacking us with nuclear, biological, or chemical weapons of mass destruction (such weapons did not exist); destroying a haven for terrorists (Saddam's supposed collaboration with terrorists was a fabrication); getting rid of an evil dictator (forgetting about all the evil dictators, including Saddam himself, that we have not only not attacked but actually supported); and so on. That rationalization is at work here is clear from the interchangeability of these various "reasons". That this rationalization was serving as a cover for the irrational, murderous impulses of Bush and many of his followers is indicated by, among other things, Colin Powell's observation that after the 9/11 attacks, "the president wanted to kill someone" (Woodward, 2003). If Bush and company had been aware of their own murderous (and other unconscious) impulses and owned them, they would have been less apt to act them out in such a terribly destructive way.

Repression is also essential for war. Specifically, the repression of fear, shame, and grief enables individuals to put their lives and those of others at risk in waging war. Such repression can be inferred from the statements and policies of figures such as George W. Bush, Saddam Hussein, Dick Cheney, Osama bin Laden, Donald Rumsfeld, Yassar Arafat, and Ariel Sharon, which are totally devoid of any reference to "painful feelings of weakness, shame, humiliation, grief, and fear" (Retzinger & Scheff, 2006, p. 243) and full of professions and displays of power, pride, triumphalism ("Mission accomplished!"), courage and optimism ("Stay the course!"), and fearlessness and bravado ("Bring it on!"), all of which are reaction formations against the painful feelings. Given the events that these public figures have presided over, it is impossible for them not to have such painful feelings. No one who recalls George W. Bush's facial expression, gestures, and body language as he descended from his helicopter and walked toward the White House upon his return to Washington following the 9/11 attacks can doubt that he experienced feelings of pain, fear, and shame, which are feelings that most other Americans had as well. Retzinger and Scheff articulate what Bush might have said if his repressive defences against these feelings had not been operating:

I am truly sorry that the 9/11 attack occurred. Since I was in charge when it happened, I feel partly responsible for allowing it to occur.

I feel violated, weak, helpless, impotent, humiliated. I am ashamed of my own helplessness. I am ashamed that I cannot protect my own people. I am ashamed that I lacked the foresight to see this coming.

I am sad beyond reckoning at all the losses that we have suffered. I need to cry bitter tears forever.

I am afraid. I am afraid to die. I fear for my loved ones and the citizens of this country and the world. [*ibid.*, pp. 243–244]

Rather than expressing these feelings, however, Bush repressed them and "attacked Afghanistan and Iraq instead" (*ibid.*, p. 244).

Repression of hostile, belligerent impulses and aggressive and provocative actions of one's own nation also promotes warfare, by allowing individuals to perceive any hint of unfriendliness or aggression on the part of the adversary as an unwarranted provocation deserving retaliation. The discourse of politicians and the reporting of the news media facilitate this repression by directing attention away from individuals' own hostile feelings and their nation's less than friendly policies and actions, and instead scrutinizing the adversary's discourse and behaviour and seizing on anything that can be construed as a sign of aggression.

This repression of one's own hostile impulses and aggressive actions enables and precipitates, in turn, the externalization of these impulses on to the other nation. Abundant examples of externalization can be found in American characterizations of Islamic fundamentalist terrorists as fanatic, dogmatic, morally blind, and indifferent to human life. While such characterizations may be true of many of these terrorists, they are also true of many Americans, including President George W. Bush, whose fanatical pursuit of Saddam Hussein and dogmatic opposition to stem cell research, to name but two actions, have demonstrated considerable indifference to human life. But most Americans, even those who are critical of Bush, roundly condemn the terrorists as evil and ignore the presence of quite similar qualities in themselves and their president. Such externalization is facilitated by the production in political discourse and the media of caricatures of other nations as "evil"—

as in Bush's infamous proclamation of the "axis of evil"—which make the other nations into what Volkan refers to as a suitable targets for externalization (see Volkan, 1988).

War and genocide are also enabled by various forms of dissociation among motives, actions, and consequences, which "enables people to focus and act on goals that conflict with important [i.e., identity-bearing] values" (Staub, 1989, p. 83). One form of such dissociation involves focusing on one's actions *per se* as a way of blocking awareness of their consequences. The Holocaust, for example, was enabled by the German bureaucracy's diffusion of responsibility through having individuals focus only on their own job and ignore its contribution to genocide:

> A person could schedule trains transporting Jews to extermination camps and keep the relationship of this activity to the genocide out of awareness; . . . the same division of functions and compartmentalization characterized officers in the Pentagon during the Vietnam War. [*ibid.*, p. 29]

Another form of this dissociation sequesters one's identity contents that are contradicted by one's actions. An example of this form can be seen in the recession of George W. Bush's self-proclaimed Christian identity—an identity that presumably takes as its model Jesus, whom Bush once declared to be his favourite philosopher and who admonished his followers to love their enemies—as soon as Mr. Bush decided he wanted to be a "War President", which he proclaimed himself to be on NBC's *Meet the Press*.

A third form of dissociation of motives, actions, and consequences involves focusing exclusively on the effects of one's actions and delinking them from the motives and actions that caused them: in those infrequent instances when the terrible consequences of war are confronted, we focus on their occurrence *per se* and not on the fact that we are responsible for their occurrence. Even less do we link the terrible events with terrible impulses in our own hearts. Our true motives are thus dissociated from our actions, and these actions are dissociated from their terrible results, enabling us to "stay the course" of war without struggling with a guilty conscience or the shameful realization that we ourselves are the enemy—and our own worst nightmare.

A similar distracting function is performed by affectualization: when people suffer the loss of a loved one in war, or sympathize with those who do, they often immerse themselves in grief, sorrow, or pity and thus prevent cognitive acknowledgement that their own actions—such as supporting a war, or voting for war-mongering politicians—are indirectly responsible for the suffering they are experiencing or commiserating with. Displacement of attention is also operating when Bush trumpets the fact that an evil dictator is gone but remains utterly silent about the fact that hundreds of thousands of innocent people are also dead, trillions of dollars have been wasted, much of the USA's international political capital has been destroyed, hundreds if not thousands of new terrorists have been recruited, and the Middle East has been further destabilized.

Multiple additional defence mechanisms operate for combatants. Fighting and other wartime tasks, by compelling full attention and engagement, enable the avoidance of identity-depleting realities of civilian existence, including boredom and meaninglessness. War can also serve a repressive function, enacting, for example, reaction formation by replacing depression, boredom, or anxiety with powerful feelings of anxiety, terror, or excitement. These intense emotions, as well as physical exhaustion and pain, also produce dissociation, by immersing individuals in the present and preventing significant attention to the past or the future, thus relieving individuals of the need to interpret the past or plan for the future. The authoritarian structure of the military also promotes dissociation, absolving combatants not only of the need for thinking about the ends, strategies, or tactics of war, but also of taking responsibility for their actions (as the Nazi war trials demonstrated). Finally, war also promotes the same externalizing defences that enable it in the first place. While the prelude to war is often characterized by an escalation of externalization, in which individuals can evade their own negative qualities by finding them in the adversary, war makes this process infinitely easier and more intense, by providing people with an indisputably violent and dangerous enemy and a self that is undeniably required to defend itself. Taken together, these defences also amount to a de-structuring or disorganizing of identity, at times reducing the boundaries of one's sense of self to physical survival in the immediate moment. Especially when, in mortal danger during combat, one's sense of self, which may ordinarily encompass other people as well as the past and future, constricts to the immediate here and now, the polar opposite of the interindividual structure, which is the optimal identity structure for both individual and collective well-being.

* * *

War and terrorism are, therefore, symptoms of multiple types of identity problems, including the presence of malignant identity contents and defences and the lack of adequate identity structure, benign contents, and opportunities for their enactment and recognition. What this means is, first, that any attempt to prevent war or terrorism that exacerbates these identity problems—and this would include most aspects of George W. Bush's War on Terrorism—will only increase the problem and, second, that any programme or policy we can devise to reduce any of these identity problems will contribute to the prevention of war and terrorism. What programmes and policies might accomplish this task will be made evident in later chapters.

PART III

THE ROLE OF IDENTITY IN THE FAILURE TO SOLVE SOCIAL PROBLEMS

CHAPTER FOUR

Phobic objects, subalterns, and enemies as resources for identity maintenance

"Most of the social problems we face . . . are not the result of 'human nature' or fate or inevitable economic or technological processes. More often than not, they involve choices that we make or fail to make about our priorities as a society. . . . Very often, social problems 'are not solved because people do not want to solve them'"

(Currie & Skolnick, 1997, pp. 12, 16)

The existence of most subaltern groups—including criminals, addicts, and terrorists, as well as ethnic, racial, sexual, economic, and political Others—is usually assumed to be the consequence of historical contingencies ("fate", "fortune") and different levels of innate ability and moral fibre, or at the very most, of the economic interests of the elite. Rarely is it acknowledged that (1) the existence these subaltern groups is the result of political choices made by the masses of "normal" people, and (2) that such subalterns serve crucial psychological needs for most "normal", privileged citizens. In order to solve the social problems "produced" by these subalterns, it is essential that we recognize that they—and, more important, the pursuit of ineffective and even counterproductive responses to them—are largely the result of attempts by policy makers and the general public to address their own identity problems by designating certain people as the causes of these problems and then working to exclude or eliminate these people, on the assumption that such action will resolve these (individual or collective) identity problems. The establishment of such subaltern groups helps people to maintain their own sense of self primarily by enabling the operation of major defences against threats to their identity.

One defence facilitated by subalterns is the minimization of one's own lack of status and recognition. By identifying another group as inferior to themselves, people can have recourse at any time to "downward social comparison", the process by which one selectively measures one's own status only against that of perceived inferiors, in order to arrive at a more positive sense of self. Sociologist Michael Lewis has argued that the major reason we have failed to eliminate poverty, racial inequality, educational failure, and crime is that the presence of poor people, a black underclass, poorly educated people, and criminals is necessary for the majority of Americans to feel successful. Because of the American Dream's promise of success to all who work hard, many Americans are

> haunted by a sense that they are inadequate no matter what they have actually achieved, dissatisfied with what they are because they believe they should be more than they are, terribly insecure about the meaning and value of the lives they lead. [Lewis, 1993, p. 40]

The presence of various subaltern groups, however, ensures that

> if people are not the successes they hoped to be, they may nevertheless take comfort in the belief that they are not the failures that they might have been and that others—for want of effort and competence—are. [ibid., p. 43]

Thus, "in our desperate need for reassurance, many of us in fact have an investment in those social and economic conditions which insure apparent failure among others" (ibid., p. 45). Lewis concludes that "if some people victimize others, denying them opportunity and treating them as pariahs, they do so, more often than not, because they are driven to do so" (*ibid.*). That is,

the victimizers act as they do because they themselves are victims, because their innocent faith in the "American Way" engenders in them a need for reassurance which only the visible and presumably personal failures of others can assuage. [*ibid.*]

Lewis warns that this production of subaltern groups will persist as long as the "threat to self" that is motivating it persists (*ibid.*, p. 47). A second powerful defence enabled by subalterns is externalization, including projection and projective identification. Subalterns constitute what Vamik Volkan calls a suitable target for externalization: a group that people have constructed as possessing certain powerful negative characteristics that they are unable to recognize and own in themselves. Volkan argues that we unconsciously cultivate enemies in order to supply ourselves with such targets for externalizing our own negative qualities (Volkan, 1988). My argument is that we unconsciously cultivate not only our enemies, but also other subalterns and stigmatized Others as targets for externalization. The presence of a subaltern group that apparently possesses these negative qualities distracts the attention of the externalizers (and also those who observe them) away from their own less visible flaws and redirects it, along with derogation, hatred, aggression, and violence, towards the subaltern group, thus enabling the externalizers to maintain their idealized sense of self while at the same time acting out their own repressed qualities and impulses—including laziness, ignorance, self-indulgence, and aggression—in relation to the subaltern.

A third defence enabled by subalterns is displacement, a process by which people redirect their feelings and actions from their legitimate target on to a substitute that is less threatening and/or more accessible. Subalterns enable people to redirect their anger over social and material deficiencies in their lives away from the true causes of these conditions—including bad luck, an unfair economic system, and the plutocrats who maintain that system—and on to scapegoats who have little or nothing to do with these conditions but who are relatively defenceless and ready-to-hand. As objects of displaced fear and anger, subalterns, or their conditions or behaviours, function as a type of phobic object for the more privileged majority. Focusing on the phobic objects or events and the individuals supposedly responsible for them enables people to ignore other objects, circumstances, and individuals that actually cause much greater suffering and death but in which people are themselves implicated and hence need to ignore in order to protect their identities. Focusing on and attacking the phobic object rather than the really dangerous forces or phenomena thus protects their identities while leaving them objectively just as vulnerable.

In his book *The Culture of Fear: Why Americans Are Afraid of the Wrong Things*, sociologist Barry Glassner documents numerous phenomena that function as phobic objects for many Americans. Some of these phobic objects are individuals who harm children, such as strangers who abduct them, day-care workers who sexually abuse them, internet pornographers who traumatize and corrupt them, Halloween sadists who poison or booby-trap their candy, and drug-addicted mothers whose drug use abuses their children and damages their brains. While all of these dangers are real, public concern over them is out of proportion to their actual rate of occurrence and harm. Such excessive concern, Glassner notes, allows parents and the public at large to ignore or minimize, and thus evade feeling guilty for, conditions that actually cause much greater harm to children and for which they are at least partly responsible and could themselves help to change. Thus "anonymous Halloween sadists . . . were a useful diversion from some truly frightening realities, such as the fact that far more children are seriously injured and killed by family members than by strangers" (Glassner, 1999, p. 31). Concerning the dangers of the sexual predators on the internet, Glassner comments:

> For those children most at risk of sexual abuse, to be left alone in their rooms with a computer would be a godsend. It is poor children—few of whom have America Online connections—who are disproportionately abused, and it is in children's own homes and those of close relatives that sexual abuse commonly occurs. In focusing on creeps in cyberspace, reporters neatly skirt these vital facts and the discomforting issues they raise. [*ibid.*, p. 35]

Anguishing over addicted and abusive mothers serves a similar function. Stories about such mothers constitute a form of minimization or displacement: they say that we—or our wives, sisters, daughters, or friends—are good mothers by comparison. They invite us to redirect (more accurately, misdirect) our self-doubts. When we lose our temper or strike out at our children we may secretly worry about our potential for child abuse. But at least we know we could never do the things [such mothers] did. [*ibid.*, pp. 98–99]

Our guilt about our individual and collective neglect and abuse of our (individual and collective) children is so great that it drives us to (indirectly) attack even our children themselves through economic policies that leave millions of them unprotected against hunger, poverty, illness, neglect, and ignorance. Our increasing eagerness to punish child offenders is an expression of the degree to which our guilt over this neglect and abuse threatens our identities. When children commit crimes, they demonstrate to us that we as a society have failed in their upbringing. We resent them for this identity-threatening reminder, so we respond with violence. As Glassner explains,

By failing to provide adequate education, nutrition, housing, parenting, medical services, and child care over the past couple of decades we have done the nation's children immense harm. . . . Our fear grows . . . proportionate to our unacknowledged guilt. By slashing spending on educational, medical, and antipoverty programs for youths we adults have committed great violence against them. Yet rather than face up to our collective responsibility we project our violence onto young people themselves, and onto strangers we imagine will attack them. [Glassner, 1999, pp. xxvi, 72]

We experience a similar guilt over our failure to provide for our elderly—a failure that exposes as cheap hypocrisy our laudation of them as "the greatest generation"—and we respond to this identity threat with a similar externalizing, phobic defence. In this case it is concern over the elder abuse perpetrated by wicked nursing home care-takers. News stories of elder abuse enable "the root problems of lack of funding and inadequate oversight [to] disappear amid overdrawn images of evil caretakers . . . [thus letting] the individual reader or viewer off the hook by focusing on particularly evil people" (*ibid.*, p. 48).

The most powerful phobic objects for most white Americans, however, are black men. Focusing on the very real dangers posed by a small percentage of black men allows white Americans to ignore—and thus avoid feeling guilty over—their own responsibility for the much greater vulnerability and suffering of black men in general, who are much more likely than white people to be victims of homicide, as well as of AIDS, suicide, heart disease, prostate cancer, and unemployment. Glassner reports,

> A black man is about eighteen times more likely to be murdered than is a white woman. All told, the murder rate for black men is double that of American soldiers in World War II. And for black men between the ages of fifteen and thirty, violence is the leading cause of death. [ibid., p. 112]

Our need for such subalterns as means to defend and maintain our own identity is one of the main reasons we have not solved our major social problems, including crime, violence, addiction, and terrorism, as well as poverty, homelessness, unemployment, and inadequate education and health care. These social problems are produced or at least perpetuated in large measure because they serve as an important means for the relatively privileged individuals who collectively control social and economic policy to defend their own identities against threatening realizations concerning the nature and consequences of their identities. Figure 4 provides a graphic representation of this process by which privileged individuals in our society indirectly maintain their (restricted) identities by enacting social and economic policies that establish or maintain various subaltern groups. These policies traumatize—that is, damage the identities of—the subalterns, which leads them to extreme, "abnormal", and/or antisocial behaviours to repair their (damaged or vulnerable) identities. Such behaviours, in turn, make these individuals ideal targets for minimization, displacement, and externalization, thus enabling the privileged individuals who are ultimately responsible for these damaged identities and consequent negative behaviours to escape detection, responsibility, and guilt at the expense of these subalterns—whom they have created precisely, it would seem, for this purpose.

Prejudice and group hatreds

The most obvious and widespread instance of the creation of subalterns for identity maintenance is found in prejudice and group

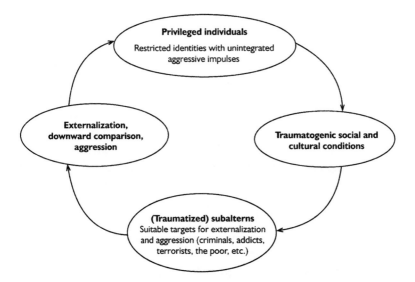

Figure 4. The use of subalterns for identity maintenance.

hatred. Empirical studies have demonstrated that prejudice functions as a way to maintain identity. These studies have shown that, when one's sense of self is threatened, one is more likely to engage in negative evaluation of subaltern groups, and also that such negative evaluations can enhance one's sense of self. Prejudice is thus "an attractive way for many individuals to feel better about themselves in the absence of more readily available means of alleviating self-image threats or of affirming oneself" (Fein & Spencer, 1997, p. 41). It allows individuals "to reclaim for themselves a feeling of mastery and self-worth, often saving themselves from having to confront the real sources of self-image threat" (*ibid.*).

Prejudices such as racism, sexism, and homophobia support vulnerable identities in several ways. One way is through protecting one's identity-supporting world view by derogating those who subscribe to different world views, the very existence of which poses a threat to one's own world view (Pyszczynski, Greenberg, & Solomon, 1997, p. 16; Schimel et al., 1999, p. 922) and hence to one's identity. In addition, when people's identities are threatened, they often prefer outgroup individuals who appear to conform to their stereotypes because the existence of such individuals supports their (identity-bearing) world view (Schimel et al., 1999, pp. 923–924). Prejudices also support identity more directly, through splitting and projection. This phobic response—the attribution of one's individual and/or collective deficiencies to a delimitable, external object—provides several identity benefits. First, it allows one to ignore the internal, systemic threats to one's identity: namely, the threats posed by those qualities and impulses of one's own that one has had to reject in order to assume and maintain one's identity as "man", "woman", "civilized", "human", "kind", "compassionate", and so on. Second, this phobic strategy provides reassurance that, if one can only avoid or destroy the phobic object, one will have eliminated all significant threats to one's identity, which will therefore be secure again. Third, by blinding people to their own destructive impulses, which they have projected into the phobic object, and convincing them of the unmitigated evil of this object, the phobic strategy makes it possible for people to enact their own most despised and destructive impulses on the phobic object with a clear conscience and without even being aware that they are enacting impulses and embodying qualities that contradict their own identities.

Thus, in racism one projects on to the racial other one's own bestial, "uncivilized", and "perverse" libidinal and aggressive qualities and impulses (i.e., vitality affects and body images) which the socialization process caused one to split off and repress in order to assume a conceptual–linguistic identity as human rather than beast, refined instead of crude, good rather than evil, and so on. The superego aggression, together with reaction formation, that would normally operate against these rejected impulses and qualities within oneself can then be diverted from this internal target towards the external other, which is perceived as being crude, unclean, violent, over-sexed, and sexually perverse—"evil". By avoiding this phobic object (as in segregation), excluding it (as is done through immigration restrictions), or eliminating it (as in genocide or war), one creates the illusion that one has maintained one's ideal linguistic, imagistic, and affective identity. One is oblivious to the bestial and perverse impulses that one has enacted in the very process of demonizing and persecuting the racial other and in voyeuristically scrutinizing and fantasizing about this other's vitality affects and bodily agency and behaviour. The racial other as phobic object thus provides one with a receptacle for one's own rejected qualities and impulses that allows one to (a) vicariously gratify these impulses by observing/fantasizing the other's gratification of them and (b) actually to enact some of these impulses in the process of judging, condemning, and punishing the other.

Racism also reinforces identity-bearing signifiers, in a number of ways. First, it provides racists with immediate, direct recognition that they embody certain signifiers. While non-racists have to perform in order to demonstrate that they embody signifiers like human, intelligent, good, important, and powerful, a white person in a white racist society embodies these signifiers not by doing anything but simply by being white. Second, a racist linguistic system enhances one's claim to these signifiers by linking their antitheses with "black". Third, racism protects one's claims to one's identity-bearing signifiers by eliminating, through projection on to the racial subaltern, those impulses and qualities that contradict these signifiers.

Through these resources for identity stability in the linguistic register, racism provides a powerful incentive for people to embrace it. Furthermore, to the extent that a society deprives its members (socially, economically, or culturally) of alternative, non-racial ways of enacting these signifiers, or to the extent that it fails to offer its members identity-bearing signifiers that are not racially coded, it increases the likelihood that people will seek to claim their identity-bearing signifiers through the racist means of enactment. One reason racism is sometimes more explicit and virulent among lower social and economic classes is that such individuals lack the material, economic, social, and cultural resources that other individuals have for enacting and being recognized for their more benign identity-bearing signifiers.

Racism also reinforces body–imagistic identity, in several ways. First, it constructs an ideal body image that is composed of physical traits that are generally possessed by the racist group but not the racial Other. Thus white racism has portrayed lighter skin, straighter hair, narrower nose, and thinner lips as being attractive, and the opposites as being unattractive. Such racist ideals of beauty allow white people to reinforce their body–imagistic identities simply by contrasting their bodies with those of black people. Identity-enhancing contrasts can be especially welcomed by people who fail in almost all other ways to measure up to their culture's ideal of physical beauty. This visual racism not only enhances racists' opinions of their bodies, it also reinforces their imagistic identity at a deep level.

This same dynamic of identity maintenance operates in sexism. Here, men reject those attributes, desires, impulses, and enjoyments of their own that have been coded feminine. These include the desire to be passive or subordinate and to be taken care of rather than to always be active and dominant, as well as the enjoyment of being tender or receptive rather than tough and imposing. At the same time, these men deny that the qualities they code as masculine and claim for themselves are possessed to any significant degree by women. Through a range of social and cultural practices ranging from the most overt and blatant to the most subtle, covert, and unconscious, patriarchy establishes masculine and feminine identity by splitting each gender in two and acknowledging one half of its attributes while attributing the other half exclusively to the other gender. It also reinforces masculine identity by denigrating in women the elements that this masculine identity has rejected.

The identity-supporting dynamic of the phobic object is also powerfully evident in homophobia, where the most severe hatred and violence towards homosexual men is often enacted precisely by those men and boys who have the greatest difficulty repressing and controlling their own homoerotic impulses and fantasies. The only way they can prove to themselves that they are "real men" and not "sissies"—that is, gay—is to disparage, ridicule, attack, and in some cases even kill other men whom they (correctly or incorrectly) perceive as gay. The degree of hatred and violence they express is a direct indicator of the level of anxiety they are experiencing, which itself indicates the degree of vulnerability of their identity in the face of their own homoerotic urges: research has shown that the most homophobic men are those who become most aroused when watching homoerotic films of gay men (see Adams, Wright, & Lohr, 1996). Gay-bashing protects their identity from the intrapsychic threat constituted by their own homoerotic impulses through externalizing these impulses and enacting a reaction formation against them, in the form of the attitude, "I don't love gay men, I hate them." And, in so far as aggression and violence are coded as masculine, violence against this phobic object is a way of enacting certain masculine identity-bearing vitality affects, body images, and signifiers. One reason that group hatreds are so intractable is that they provide phobic objects not only for their perpetrators but also for the rest of us. In fact, identity benefits for the non-prejudiced or "innocent" members of society are identical in kind to those derived by prejudiced people from their hatred and discrimination: we, too, support our identity by demonizing an Other—in this case, racists, sexists, and homophobes—in essentially the same way as they demonize their subalterns. That is, we label bigots as "low-life", "pigs", "assholes", "white trash", and so on, and thus use them as receptacles for our own bestial and inhuman impulses, which we externalize on to them and allow ourselves free rein to attack there, while we ourselves bask in the approval of our individual and collective superegos, performing our own identity-bearing signifiers such as good, civilized, humane, egalitarian, and unprejudiced, and vicariously enacting our own individual and collective bodily agency and integrity through excluding and rejecting the physically threatening other body. Such demonization of bigots, while serving to support our identities, does little to undermine their prejudice and advance equality and respect. In fact, it often does the opposite, forcing the bigots, because their identities are being threatened by our contempt, to embrace their own phobic strategies all the more passionately, thus undermining the chances of reducing their bigotry. By attacking bigots, anti-bigotry often exacerbates the identity vulnerability that drove bigots to their bigotry in the first place, thereby contributing to the production of more bigotry. But while such an outcome is counterproductive in relation to our conscious intentions, it may be exactly what we are unconsciously seeking in order to maintain our identity as "good": a subaltern on to which we can externalize our own unacknowledged, rejected "bad" parts and at the same time unconsciously enact some of those parts (e.g., aggression), while also using the subaltern—in this case, the bigot—as an object of downward social comparison in relation to which we ourselves appear superior.

The War on Drugs

This same unconscious strategy of identity maintenance motivates the War on Drugs. The symptomatic nature of this policy—the fact that it is more about supporting identity (through creating and attacking a phobic object and a subaltern group) than about solving a social problem—is indicated first of all by the policy's irrational, even self-contradictory, nature. As Michael Pollan observes,

> [We] would be hard-pressed to explain the taxonomy of chemicals underpinning the drug war to an extraterrestrial. Is it, for example, addictiveness that causes this society to condemn a drug? (No; nicotine is legal, and millions of Americans have battled addictions to prescription drugs.) So then, our inquisitive alien might ask, is safety the decisive factor? (Not really; over-the-counter and prescription drugs kill [many] Americans every year while, according to *The New England Journal of Medicine*, "There is no risk of death from smoking marijuana.") Is it drugs associated with violent behavior that your society condemns? (If so, alcohol would still be illegal.) Perhaps, then, it is the promise of pleasure that puts a drug beyond the pale? (That would once again rule out alcohol, as well as Viagra.) Then maybe the molecules you despise are the ones that alter the texture of consciousness, or even a human's personality? (Tell that to someone who has been saved from depression by Prozac.). . . . Historians of the future will wonder how a people possessed of such a deep faith in the power of drugs also found themselves fighting a war against certain other drugs with not-dissimilar powers. [Pollan, 1999, p. 28]

In addition to the illogic involved in categorizing some drugs as legal and others as illegal, the symptomatic quality of the War on Drugs is also demonstrated by its cost-ineffectiveness. As Dan Baum observes,

> While we argue about whether the country can afford foreign aid, the Environmental Protection Agency, public broadcasting, or the National Endowments for the Arts and the Humanities, the federal drug budget quietly exceeds all of them combined. [Baum, 1996, p. viii]

This might be justified if the expenditures were effective. However, a RAND study in 1994 found that treatment is much more cost effective: seven times more cost-effective than arresting and imprisoning buyers and sellers, ten times more cost-effective than stopping drugs at the border, and twenty-three times more cost-effective than attacking the production of drugs in other countries (Massing, 1999, p. 14). Clearly, if reduction of drug use were the true motive behind the War on Drugs, the expenditures for treatment would be greatest and those for law enforcement, interdiction, and source-control considerably less—precisely the opposite of current policy.

In addition to its monumental direct cost of hundreds of billions of dollars, the War on Drugs has also produced extreme indirect costs, in terms not only of dollars but also of human lives:

> The Drug War clogs the courts to the point of breakdown. It keeps more Americans in federal prison for drug crime than were in *for all crimes put together* in 1980. It criminalizes a generation of African-American men, being the main reason a third of all black males in their twenties are under correctional control—jail, prison, probation, or parole. [Baum, 1996, p. viii]

And, ironically, the War on Drugs often results in drug use, distribution, and procurement practices that are considerably worse than those it tries to eliminate (*ibid.*; see also Wurmser, 1995, p. 31).

In spite of its counterproductivity, however, our society continues to prosecute the War on Drugs, largely because, as Baum notes, drugs have come to function for our society as a phobic object:

> Costly, destructive, and failing in its stated mission, the War on Drugs is government lunacy beyond the wildest waste-fraud-and-abuse accusations of Rush Limbaugh and Ross Perot. Yet we soldier on, speaking the language of war, writing the budgets of war, carrying the weapons of war, and suffering the casualties of war, . . . [all because of] our belief that drugs radiate a supernatural evil, like Kryptonite. [Baum, 1996, p. viii]

Wurmser is even more explicit. The war on drugs, he says, is "a mass phobia . . . , where the drug is treated as the concretized evil, a demon to be exorcized by the most concrete, brute measures of persecution" (Wurmser, 1995, p. 19).

That drugs function as a phobic object, and drug users as subalterns, is clear from the demonizing characterizations of drugs and drug users by public officials, in contrast to the actual damage drugs do. In 1970, Justice Hugo Black declared:

Commercial traffic in *deadly mind-soul-and-body-destroying drugs* is beyond a doubt *one of the greatest evils of our time.* It cripples intellects, dwarfs bodies, paralyzes the progress of a substantial segment of our society, and frequently makes hopeless and sometimes violent and murderous criminals of persons of all ages who become its victims. Such consequences call for the most vigorous laws to suppress the traffic as well as the most powerful efforts to put these vigorous laws into effect. [quoted in Baum, 1996, p. 29; my emphasis]

During the year prior to Black's dire warning, however, the total number of people who had died from drugs, legal and illegal, was 1,601, as compared with 1,824 who had died from falling down stairs, 2,641 who had died from choking on food, and 29,866 who had died from alcohol-related cirrhosis of the liver (*ibid.*, p. 28).

Similar demonization has been directed against drug users and traffickers. A former director of Richard Nixon's Office of Drug Abuse Law Enforcement declared: "Drug people are the very vermin of humanity" (quoted in Baum, 1996, p. 83). Nixon himself referred to drug traffickers as "the slave traders of our time" and declared, "They must be hunted to the end of the earth" (quoted in Baum, 1996, p. 72). The demonization of drug users is so intense in the USA that, Baum reports, a survey done in 1967 indicated that "almost half of Americans said they'd turn in their own kids to the police if they found them using drugs" (*ibid.*, p. 8).

Nowhere is the dynamic of the phobic object more evident than in the demonization of marijuana. Although this drug actually has medical benefits (Pollan, 1999, p. 27) and has not been responsible for a single recorded death (Baum, 1996, p. 265), it has none the less been characterized as a "gateway" drug that leads to use of more addictive drugs and a life of crime, when, in fact, "if anything, smoking marijuana *inhibits* criminal behavior" (*ibid.*, p. 71). The discrepancy between the public image of marijuana and the reality of the drug's effects was so great that even the National Commission on Marihuana and Drug Abuse appointed by Nixon recognized its phobic status and concluded, in their report that also recommended that the drug be legalized:

Many see the drug as fostering a counter-culture which conflicts with basic moral precepts as well as with the operating functions of our society. . . . "Dropping out" or rejection of the established value system is viewed with alarm. Marihuana becomes more than a drug: it becomes a symbol of the rejection of cherished values. [quoted in Baum, 1996, p. 71]

The identity-supporting function of drugs as a phobic object is the same as that of other phobic objects: it allows one to disavow the deficiencies of one's (individual and collective) identity by focusing one's anxiety and aggression on a single, isolatable object and attacking it. The demonization of drugs as a phobic object performs this function for both one's collective, national identity and one's individual, personal identity. Concerning the Drug War's function to protect our national identity, Baum writes:

The War on Drugs has walked point for a national retreat from handling crime and drug abuse as symptoms of larger problems— racism, exclusion, injustice, and poverty—for which all Americans bear some responsibility. [*ibid.*, p. ix]

Blaming drugs for these problems allows us to avoid the self-blame that would threaten our identities as good citizens. Baum's history of the War on Drugs recounts numerous instances in which focusing on drug use as the putative cause of a problem enabled government officials and the general public to avoid recognizing and dealing with the actual causes, which were multiple, complex, and often systemic—and in which, moreover, the government, and hence the general populace as well, were themselves implicated. Thus, the Senate Commerce Committee responded to a growing number of near mid-air plane crashes in the early 1980s by approving random drug tests for airline pilots, ignoring the fact that the drastically reduced number of air traffic controllers produced by their mass firing by Ronald Reagan in 1981 might have played a role in the near disasters (*ibid.*, pp. 237–238). *U. S. News* similarly suggested that drugs were the reason that growth in the USA's productivity was lagging behind that of Japan and other nations in the early 1980s, thus displacing attention from the more systemic problems of Reaganomics and multi-national capitalism (*ibid.*, pp. 187–188).

Thus, as Pollan observes, the phobic War on Drugs is only incidentally about a social problem. It is first and foremost about

maintaining the drug warriors' own identities by means of minimization, displacement, and especially externalization:

> In this war there is no Them. The enemy in the drug war is Us—
> our faith in the power of drugs to bring us pleasure, to alter the
> given textures of consciousness, even to gratify the (unspeakable)
> wish to get high. These are qualities hard to accept in oneself.
> [Pollan, 1999, p. 28]

Wurmser reaches a similar conclusion and observes, moreover, that
the phobic efforts of the war on drugs manifest the same anti-intel-
lectualism and avoidance of reflection—supported by defences of
denial and externalization and the search "for external solutions to
internal problems . . . magical answers to complex inner questions"—that characterize drug users themselves (Wurmser, 1995,
p. 387).

By creating phobic objects out of drugs and their users, the war
on drugs enables mainstream Americans to minimize or ignore the
more fundamental, systemic threats to their identities and externalize their own harmful impulses and destructive addictions, chief
among which are their addiction to television fantasies and the
commodities of capitalism (*ibid.*, p. 433). This second addiction, by
consuming an inordinate proportion of the world's resources, is
responsible for the suffering and death of millions of innocent
people around the world, and, thus, ultimately entails a much
greater culpability than does drug addiction. By focusing their
attention and condemnation on drug users, the War on Drugs
allows mainstream Americans to avoid the guilt that confronting
their own commodity addiction would produce and thus protect an
identity that would be severely shaken if it were to confront this
and other truths about itself.

The War on Crime

Another extremely important, but even less recognized, production
of subaltern targets for externalization, displacement, and minimization is the War on Crime, which has established the USA as the
most punitive of all developed nations except Russia, and without

significantly reducing violent crime. Between 1971 and 1996, the prison population in the USA increased nearly sixfold, and the rate of incarceration increased more than fourfold. As of 1995, the USA's rate of incarceration was 600 per 100,000 population, compared to about 100 in Spain and the UK, 60 in Holland and the Scandinavian countries, and 36 in Japan (Currie, 1998, p. 15). By 2008, that rate had increased to one per cent of all adults in the USA, and the 2.3 million prisoners is the largest number of any country, including China (Aizenman, 2008, p. A1). As criminologist Elliott Currie observes, "An incarceration rate that is many times higher than that of comparable countries is a signal that something is very wrong" (Currie, 1998, p. 20).

The War on Crime has consumed a tremendous amount of financial and human resources that could be used much more productively. Between 1980 and 1993, a period when federal funding on jobs programmes was cut, federal spending on prisons increased more than fivefold (Mauer, 1999, p. 68), and by 2008, the total of the USA's expenditures on corrections was around $55 billion a year (Aizenman, 2008, p. A1). Several states now spend more on incarceration than on higher education (*ibid.*). Incarceration also has significant hidden costs. For example, when inmates serving life sentences get older, their medical care becomes more expensive (Currie, 1998, p. 73). In addition, when, as is increasingly the case, mothers are imprisoned because of drug possession or related property crimes, society incurs the expense not only of caring for their children but also of dealing with the greater delinquency, welfare dependency, and drug abuse of children deprived of their mothers (*ibid.*). Among the most significant hidden costs of the War on Crime is its foreclosure of other possibilities for preventing crime, such as education, jobs programmes, and drug rehabilitation programmes (Mauer, 1999, p. 116).

Despite its tremendous costs, the War on Crime has been largely ineffective and even counterproductive. An index of its counterproductivity is found in the fact that "our imprisonment rates are five to ten times higher than those of any other developed nation, and our death rates from murder are also five to ten times higher" (Gilligan, 2001, p. 24). As these statistics suggest, rather than decreasing criminal activity, imprisonment often increases the likelihood that a person will commit more crimes. One reason is that imprisonment reduces one's chances of getting a job (Currie, 1998, p. 74), but the more fundamental reason is that incarceration often damages identity and enhances malignant identity contents in individuals, especially in those incarcerated for non-violent offences like drug possession, and thus increases the likelihood that they will commit more aggressive and even violent crimes. As Currie comments, "the tendency for incarceration to make some criminals worse is one of the best-established findings in criminology" (ibid.). Thus, as Gilligan declares,

> The criminal justice and penal systems have been operating on the basis of a huge mistake, namely, the belief that punishment will deter, prevent, or inhibit violence, when in fact it is the most powerful stimulus of violence that we have yet discovered. [Gilligan, 2001, p. 116]

Persisting in the belief that punishment deters crime and that the harsher the punishment the greater the deterrence, we have increased the identity damage of offenders by subjecting them more frequently, and for longer periods of time, to the identity-damaging conditions of prison life.

The symptomatic nature of the War on Crime is most evident in the perpetuation of capital punishment in the face of compelling evidence of its ineffectiveness and even counterproductivity. Research has shown that virtually all the reasons put forth in support of capital punishment are invalid, including the claim that it is cheaper to execute murderers than to imprison them for life (it is not; see Milburn and Conrad, 1996, p. 61, and Costanzo, 1997, pp. 60–61) and the belief that executions serve as a deterrent (they do not; see Costanzo, 1997, pp. 98–101). In addition to its cost and counterproductivity, the death penalty is also extremely vulnerable on the grounds of fairness: individuals who are poor and/or black are much more likely to be put to death than those who are wealthy and/or white (Costanzo, 1997, pp. 75–80). Most unfair of all, of course, is the fact that hundreds of innocent people have been sentenced to death, and many of them have actually been executed (Milburn & Conrad, 1996, p. 2; Strean & Freeman, 1991, p. 245).

Why are we pursuing such costly, inhumane, unfair, and counterproductive strategies and disdaining cheaper, fairer, more humane strategies whose effectiveness in reducing violence has been demonstrated? "We have relied on the jails and prisons as our first defence against crime; yet we still maintain the developed world's worst level of violence," Currie laments (Currie, 1998, p. 37). Why? Why do we "spend incomparably more money on police, prisons, punishments and criminal courts than we do on providing the kinds of community services that have been demonstrated to achieve equal reductions in criminal violence for one-fifth of the price" (Gilligan, 2001, p. 23)? Why have we "systematically depleted other public institutions in order to pay for our incarceration binge—a self-defeating course that helps to insure that violent crime will remain high despite ever more drastic efforts to contain it" (Currie, 1998, p. 37)? Why, when it comes to issues like education and poverty, do we decrease funding on the principle that "throwing money at a problem" will not fix it, but then throw more and more money into building and operating prisons, which not only do not fix violence but actually make it worse (*ibid.*, p. 76)?

Various plausible explanations have been offered for this self-contradictory, self-defeating social policy. Currie identifies four factors: (1) the failure of political leaders to engage the problem of violence in an honest and responsible manner, (2) the ignorance and misinformation that permeate the layperson's views of the nature of violence, its causes, and its cures, (3) the benefit such policies provide to special interest groups that profit from high rates of crime and incarceration, and (4) the convergence of these policies with the ideology of the American Dream, which asserts that one's behaviour and circumstances in life are determined solely by one's individual worth and responsibility and not by any conditions beyond one's control (*ibid.*, pp. 6–7). Each of these factors no doubt plays a role in the promulgation of our self-defeating strategies of crime prevention. But political leaders and special interests do not carry the day unless they find broad public support; public ignorance about violence in the information age is not involuntary, but motivated; and the ideal of individual responsibility can be abandoned by most Americans when they find it to their advantage to do so. The question, then, is why the vast majority of Americans still support massive expenditures for a policy that not only has failed mightily, but actually makes things worse.

Currie's observation that "the present drift of national policy . . . reflects a stunning degree of collective denial" (*ibid.*, p. 159) points to a deeper reason than the four he identified: the need of most Americans to maintain their identities through simultaneously externalizing and enacting their own sadistic and violent impulses on a subaltern. "What emotional gratification are people seeking", Gilligan asks, "when they advocate punishing other people harshly, as opposed to quarantining them in order to restrain them?" (Gilligan, 1996, p. 182). His answer is pride and power: the

> . . . wish or need to dominate and humiliate others is in the service of gaining a swelled sense of pride and power by having dominion over others, including the power to inflict pain on them, punish them. . . [*ibid.*]

What this means, Gilligan points out, is that the thirst to punish violent offenders is motivated by the same psychological need that motivates the violent behaviour of the offenders themselves:

> interestingly, the motive behind such punitive attitudes turns out to be identical to the motive behind the very crimes that many of us are eager to punish—namely, the fear that one will be laughed at, held in contempt, or made a fool of (i.e., shamed), unless one is sufficiently sadistic. [*ibid.*, p. 184]

This fear, and the feeling of shame, as we have seen, are manifestations of a damaged, vulnerable identity.

Strean and Freeman reach the same conclusion about capital punishment. If the death penalty is expensive, inequitable, and counterproductive, why does our society perpetuate it and even celebrate it (as demonstrated most blatantly by the spectators who gather at the scene of executions)? Because, Strean and Freeman conclude, of the murderous wish in all our hearts:

> The vengefulness we feel toward a murderer, which drives us to champion execution, is identical to the wish for revenge the murderer feels for what he believes to be the horrendous injustices in his life. . . . We feel as murderous toward them as they do toward those they have killed. We wish either to kill or torture them. [Strean & Freeman, 1991, p. 244]

The War on Crime is externalization at its purest: punishing criminals allows the rest of us to deny our own transgressive and murderous impulses by focusing on more severe and obvious instances of these impulses in another. As Sandra Bloom and Michael Reichert explain,

> We need criminals to be criminals. They are playing a social role that we cannot presently do without. ... They are acting out our submerged conflicts and if we dare to decide that they do still belong to the human race, we are in danger of having to deal with our conflicts ourselves. [Bloom & Reichert, 1998, p. 240]

Arguing along the same lines, Kevin Anderson declares,

> The intense desire by some members of society to punish criminals masks the fact that these "respectable" members of society themselves have criminal inclinations. ... "[T]he louder a man calls for punishment of the lawbreaker," [Alexander and Staub write], "the less he has to fight his own repressed impulses". [Anderson, 2000, p. 90]

Punishment of criminals is also a way for non-criminals to enact on to an object of displacement the aggression they feel as a result of the damage their own identities have suffered. As Erich Fromm observed,

> Punishing the criminal provides a form of gratification for the aggressive and sadistic drives of the masses, which are thereby compensated for the many renunciations forced upon them. Punishment makes it possible for them to transfer their natural aggression against the oppressive ruling class onto the criminal, and thereby to find release for their aggression. [Fromm, 1931, p. 146]

After making much the same point, legal scholar Martha Grace Duncan concludes: "From this perspective, criminals are far from being an unequivocal evil: they are, in fact, necessary for us to be what we are" (Duncan, 1999, p. 117). That is, we need excessive, expensive, counterproductive punishment, including capital punishment, in order to maintain our own identities—a conclusion also supported by empirical evidence (Cohen, Aronson, & Steele, 2000; Judges, 2000). To have such punishment, we need criminals, which our current traumatogenic culture and society produce in abundance, through means that will be explored in the next chapter.

The War on Terrorism

This same identity need, and the same strategy for maintaining it, can be found motivating the USA's War on Terrorism. In fact, the primary purpose for the War on Terrorism was to provide identity support for George W. Bush and his supporters. If its primary objective were really to prevent future terrorist attacks, the USA's response to terrorism would have been to identify, understand, and finally address the root causes of terrorism. Michael Wessells states this rather self-evident but crucial principle quite bluntly: "To prevent terrorism, one must first understand it" (Wessells, 2002, p. 62). John Mack, in turn, points out that

> the proper place to begin our effort to understand [terrorism] . . . is with the question of causation, [f]or no matter how loathsome we may find the acts of "fanatics," without understanding what breeds them and drives them to do what they do in a particular time and place, we have little chance of preventing further such actions, let alone of "eradicating terrorism." . . . It is inconceivable that terrorism can be checked, much less eradicated, if these causes are not addressed. [Mack, 2002, pp. 174–175]

Diane Perlman and Richard Rubenstein make essentially the same point. Rubenstein observes that "without identifying the underlying causes of a conflict, one cannot begin to resolve it" (Rubenstein, 2003, p. 144), and Perlman explains that our entire future "depends on whether we focus only on superficial eradication of *terrorists* or deep eradication of *terrorism*—the psychological, political, economic, social, and spiritual conditions that clearly foster terror" (Perlman, 2002, p. 18).

Instead of pursuing this logical path to the prevention of terrorism, however, Bush and his followers took a path leading in the opposite direction. In the first place, rather than enquiring into the causes of terrorism (causes that, as we saw in Chapter Three, are not hard to identify), Bush and his people *a priori* rejected the very idea that there could be any causes other than the evil nature of the terrorists. As Mack observes, the statements made by Bush and his crew after 9/11 give the impression that terrorism "arises from a kind of void, unconnected with history, without causation other than pure evil fueled by jealousy" (Mack, 2002, p. 175). As Rubenstein explains, Bush's characterization of terrorists as "evil" foregrounds the supposition that the sole cause of terrorism is the evil acts of the terrorists themselves and thus forecloses all possible enquiry into other possible causes, such as "the socioeconomic or geopolitical factors that make terrorism seem an attractive or even a necessary activity to hundreds of thousands of young militants around the world" (Mack, 2002, p. 144).

This refusal to enquire into the root causes of terrorism bespeaks a desire for war that is stronger than the desire for an end to terrorism, and Bush and his followers desired war because they perceived it as offering them the optimal means of protecting and maintaining their vulnerable individual and collective identities. The most direct and explicit evidence that the War on Terror functioned as a way for Bush to strengthen his sense of self came during a moment of self-labelling (itself an indicator of identity insecurity), when Bush declared to Tim Russert on *Meet the Press*, "I'm a war president."

That the primary goal of Bush and his supporters was not to prevent terrorism, but to shore up their vulnerable identities, is also demonstrated by the fact that, from the outset, this war was more likely to intensify terrorism than to reduce it and that Bush and company adamantly refused to acknowledge this likelihood. These negative consequences have become abundantly clear regarding the invasion of Iraq, where the primary results predicted by the Bush administration were that American soldiers would be greeted by the Iraqis as liberators, that the war would be over in a few months, and that Iraqi oil would pay the cost of the military operation. Now, following the rejuvenation of al-Qaeda (and hundreds of thousands of deaths, three trillion dollars, and one civil war later), the utter irrationality of this prediction is abundantly clear. That the larger War on Terror is unlikely to produce positive results is also clear to many who have analysed its likely consequences. As Mack states, the War on Terror

> may result mainly in provoking still greater antagonism, spawning
> more terrorism, and, in the long run, bringing about a widening

war, without doing anything about what gave rise to the hatred and aggression in the first place. [Mack, 2002, p. 175]

Warning that "efforts to suppress a symptom without addressing the causes will create more problems", Perlman predicts that, by attacking the symptoms of the terrorists' anger rather than its root causes, the War on Terror is likely to "actually make things worse by provoking untended consequences (blowback). . . . No amount of counterterrorism can make the United States secure", she declares, "and may ultimately make it less secure" (Perlman, 2002, pp. 35, 20). In a similar vein, noting that "there is no evidence that a get-tough policy yields anything other than increased levels of violence", Sharif Abdullah concludes that the War on Terrorism

has done nothing that will reduce the threat of terrorism in the future, and everything to guarantee that terrorist attacks will expand and increase in the future. Yes, we have significantly hurt al-Qaeda—and that hurt will be the launchpad for the next waves of violence. [Abdullah, 2002, p. 136]

This is the case because the War on Terrorism exacerbates in multiple ways the very identity vulnerability that motivates terrorism in the first place, whereas an effective response needs to eliminate the conditions that have damaged and threatened the identities of those who engage in and support terrorism and to provide resources and opportunities for these people to develop, maintain, and receive recognition for more benign, non-violent identity elements. Taking such counterproductive actions in the face of considerable countervailing expert knowledge indicates that the overriding function of Bush's policy was to maintain his and his supporters' individual and collective identities rather than to prevent terrorism.

That the primary goal of launching the War on Terrorism was to maintain the individual and collective identities of its perpetrators is also indicated by the fact that, in addition to refusing to recognize that terrorism has causes other than "evil" terrorists, or any serious negative effects, these perpetrators also assumed that there was only one feasible response to the 9/11 attacks: counter-attacking terrorists, verbally, economically, politically, and militarily. Wessells points out that "the president's choice of a label—'war on terrorism'—prescribed military action" (Wessells, 2002, p. 58), and

Perlman recalls,

> There was widespread acceptance of the idea that the United States had no choice but to attack, even though it would provoke reprisals. . . . It seemed to be implicitly assumed that no other options existed. [Perlman, 2002, p. 35]

This presupposition, together with the refusal to consider either the root causes of the 9/11 attacks or the counterproductive consequences of military action, paved the way for Bush to mount his War on Terrorism and thus become a "War President", thereby stabilizing the shaken identities of himself and his followers.

Declaring terrorists to be irrational and evil people and embarking on a "crusade" to exterminate them defends the crusaders' identities in a number of powerful ways. In the first place, it enables them to avoid the identity-damaging acknowledgement of all the ways in which their own collective impulses and actions (such as American military action, economic hegemony, and cultural imperialism) not only contradict many of their most celebrated identity-bearing values and ideals (such as equality and liberty and justice for all) but also play a significant role, as we saw in Chapter Three, in producing the very acts of terrorism they say they want to prevent. This belligerent and bellicose response to terrorism mobilizes multiple defences. The declaration "We are a peaceful, freedom-loving people", uttered to help justify the War on Terrorism, functions to repress awareness of the very impulses—rage and bloodlust—that the utterer's eagerness and enthusiasm for war betray but that contradict key identity contents such as fair and peaceful. This rage and bloodlust are themselves a reaction formation against the prior terror and shame originally evoked in the utterer by the terrorist attacks.

Dissociation and externalization are also enacted by the War on Terrorism. The first "splits the world into right and wrong, good and evil, us against them, and winning or losing in a zero sum game" (Perlman, 2002, p. 17). Such splitting enables the externalization of all one's own bad qualities on to the terrorists, their supporters, and in some cases an entire country, region, or culture, resulting in declarations that "we are peaceful and freedom-loving" but they are part of an "axis of evil", and "If you're not with us, you're against us". Such defences protect a vulnerable identity from a truth that is otherwise abundantly clear—namely, that "we" are, at bottom, in the depths of our hearts, the same as the terrorists, no better and no worse:

> The seeds of terrorism lie within each of us. . . . To stare terrorism in the face is to look in the mirror. The perpetrators of violence around the world all believe that their brand of violence is good, just, and necessary. The perpetrators of violence all believe that they oppose evil people, and that the only way they can stop that evil is to perpetrate violence. Each violent person, for the "other," is a terrorist. So George Bush believes that Osama bin Laden is evil. Bush is willing to kill to stop bin Laden's actions. He is willing to risk the lives of innocent civilians in his efforts to stop bin Laden. It can't be helped. And, Osama bin Laden believes that George Bush is evil. Bin Laden is willing to kill to stop the actions of Bush. He is willing to risk and expend the lives of innocent civilians to stop Bush. It can't be helped. [Abdullah, 2002, p. 135; see also Rubenstein, 2003, pp. 142–143]

This externalization not only protects us from our own identity-threatening impulses and qualities, it also blinds us to the collective identity-threatening fact that we have American terrorists in our midst, such as Timothy McVeigh and the Unabomber, Theodore Kaczynski, as well as the Taliban-like Christian Identity movement (Abdullah, 2002, pp. 135–136).

In addition, this externalization, which allows us to perceive ourselves as good and pure and the other as evil and bearing sole responsibility for the attacks of 9/11, works in concert with, and partially enables, a second type of dissociation: an erasure of causal connections linking American policies and actions to the living conditions (material, economic, social, political, and cultural) of the terrorists and thence to the terrorist attacks themselves. Such dissociation permeated the thinking and discourse of Bush and his followers. It is a thinking "that cannot see, or chooses not to see, the interconnections among various conditions and events", and it produces a "blindness to diversity, obliviousness to the effects of inequalities of resources, and a lack of concern for the vast suffering that prevails on this planet, [which] have given rise to the present dangerous crisis" (Mack, 2002, p. 177). Operating together, such dissociation and externalization rendered Bush and his followers invulnerable to the identity-threatening realization of just how implicated, and even complicit, we Americans are in the attacks of 9/11, thus enabling this country to continue blindly down its path of self- and other-destruction.

* * *

Clearly, the identity needs of the powerful and privileged are at the root of our major social problems, for they produce the identity damage, vulnerability, and lack of development and support in subalterns that cause these individuals to engage in the behaviours that are the immediate causes of these social problems. The following chapter will explain how these identity conditions, as well as many of the identity needs of the privileged class itself, are produced by traumatogenic social and cultural conditions that are themselves the result of the political, social, economic, and cultural decisions and activities engaged in by these same privileged individuals.

CHAPTER FIVE

Identity-damaging social and cultural forces

"Social conditions can either directly traumatize people or make it more likely that they will be traumatized"

(Bloom & Reichert, 1998, p. 18)

"Trauma destroys identity"

(Gallimore, 2002, p. 144)

I n the preceding chapters we have seen that social problems have their roots in, and are symptoms of, identity needs. The perpetrators of social problems, we have seen, are motivated by their need to enact, be recognized for, and/or defend their identity contents in ways that are harmful to others. This means that the best way of solving social problems is to address the identity needs that give rise to them. There are two basic ways to do this. The first way is preventive. It involves eliminating, reducing, avoiding, or counteracting social and cultural forces that damage, threaten, or deplete identity or that promote the development of malignant identity contents and defences. The second way is supportive and developmental. It involves providing opportunities to develop, enact, and be recognized for multiple benign, prosocial identity contents and integrated, inclusive identity structures. We will consider first the social and cultural forces that prevent the development of secure, prosocial identities and instead produce fragile, antisocial identities. This will reveal what social and cultural changes need to be made—through the reform of social policies and institutions—in order to nurture rather than impede prosocial identity development.

According to Sandra Bloom and Michael Reichert, a fundamental reason for our most serious social problems is that ours is a trauma-organized society, one in which the psychic integrity—the identity—of virtually every individual is subjected to significant damage. "Virtually all of our human systems", they assert, "are organized around trauma and the prolonged, transgenerational, and often permanent, effects of traumatic experience" (Bloom & Reichert, 1998, p. 2). One reason this trauma is so pervasive and so damaging is that we are generally aware of only a small portion of it.

> [T]he effects of multigenerational trauma lie like an iceberg in our social awareness. All we see is the tip of the iceberg that is above the surface—crime, community deterioration, family disintegration, ecological degradation. What lies below the surface of our social consciousness is the basis of the problem—the ways in which unhealed trauma and loss have infiltrated and helped determine every one of our social institutions. [ibid., p. 9]

Our lack of awareness, Bloom and Reichert explain, is itself one of the effects of trauma. Just as individuals who are repeatedly abused come to see the abuser's behaviour and the abuse suffered as more or less natural and normal, so we have been constructed and conditioned by the traumas endemic in our society to see these conditions and the behaviours that produce them as simply indefeasible aspects, respectively, of the human condition and human nature (see Bloom & Reichert, 1998, p. 99). As a result, we have become increasingly fatalistic about our most serious social problems, such as war, terrorism, and criminal violence, attributing them either to human nature in general, as in the case of war, or to the particular (evil) natures of individuals, as in the cases of terrorism and criminal violence. Our failure to recognize and understand the traumatic, identity-damaging root causes of social problems is thus itself both an effect of these causes and a major impediment to ameliorating the problems.

However, the presence of numerous traumatogenic forces in our society is not due simply to our failure to recognize them. Rather, the major cause of our failure to eliminate these traumatogenic forces, as well as our failure even to recognize them as traumatogenic, is the same as the cause of our pursuit of counterproductive "solutions" such as the War on Crime, the War on Drugs, and the War on Terrorism: these failures are motivated by our need for subalterns on to whom we can externalize and enact our own rejected qualities and on to whom we can displace responsibility for the frustrations and disappointments of our lives. Like these counterproductive "wars" against various social problems, the traumatogenic elements of society are also identity-supporting for many members of society—most notably the power elite, but also many middle-class individuals and, in certain instances, working-class individuals as well. The traumatogenic social conditions and cultural forces that are the subject of this chapter are the systemic instantiation of the same subaltern dynamic discussed in the previous chapter.

This claim is supported by a number of facts. First is the fact that we could greatly reduce the traumatogenic conditions, but choose not to. This suggests that we must be getting some benefits from them. Many people would agree, but would argue that the benefits are economic rather than psychological: we fail to eliminate poverty, homelessness, and other traumatogenic conditions, they would claim, because doing so would cost us money that we would rather keep for ourselves. Such an argument, however, is undermined by several facts. First, these conditions actually cost most individuals more in the long run than preventing or reducing them would. Second, as should be quite evident by now, people are motivated not primarily by economic considerations, but by identity needs. This means that economic motivations have whatever force they possess by virtue of their implications for identity. This fact is made abundantly clear by studies in minimal group theory, demonstrating that, when given a choice between (a) distributing a given amount of money equally among all members of one's own group and another group, and (b) distributing a lesser amount of money to members of one's own group and an even smaller amount to the other group, many individuals choose the latter option, because it enhances their collective sense of self by elevating their group above the other group. People will literally pay money in order to make another group in some way inferior to their own, because having a subaltern enhances their sense of self. As explained at the beginning of Chapter Four, subalterns enhance our identities in three basic ways.

1. Subalterns provide an opportunity for downward social comparison, which defends against the awareness of our own deficiencies by directing attention to individuals or groups whose deficiencies we perceive to be even greater than our own. When we are feeling depressed or inadequate, we can often feel better by thinking of people who are worse, or worse off, than we are.

2. The subalterns produced by poverty, unemployment, homelessness, and other traumatogenic conditions also support the identities of the power elite (including many middle- and working-class individuals) by functioning as suitable objects for externalization, thus helping us remain oblivious to our own negative qualities. That such subalterns are used for externalization is evident from the derogatory remarks made about them.

3. These subalterns function, like prisoners, drug addicts, and terrorists, as socially acceptable objects of the displaced aggression of "good, law-abiding citizens", enabling them to unconsciously enact, through various forms of institutional, structural, and cultural violence, the very qualities that they fear and condemn in these subalterns.

Traumatic experiences

War traumas

The best recognized instance of trauma is probably that suffered by military personnel in combat, which is often taken as a prototype for trauma. Roughly half of the USA's military personnel who served in Vietnam have suffered from post traumatic stress disorder (PTSD), and some reports indicate that as many as one-third of the veterans of the Iraq War have already shown PTSD symptoms. In addition, the trauma suffered by war veterans can produce behaviours that in turn traumatize the veterans' children, spouses, other family members, friends, and associates.

It is often assumed that war trauma occurs only as a result of being wounded or placed in life-threatening situations. In fact, however, soldiers are sometimes more deeply traumatized when they kill others, particularly if the killing occurs at close range so that the victim's agony and terror are observed. And when one kills non-combatants, the trauma can be even greater. "Killing comes at a price", Dave Grossman concludes, "and societies must learn that their soldiers will have to spend the rest of their lives with what they have done" (Grossman, 1996, p. 191).

In addition to the acute traumas suffered on the battlefield, military training is often, in and of itself, traumatogenic, before soldiers ever experience combat. Milburn and Conrad state that

> an important element, perhaps the key to creating a torturer, as well as a Marine, has to do with the systematic destruction of personal identity and self-esteem and their replacement by a new, heightened sense of self-esteem based on toughness. Recruits are, in effect, first broken and then offered a "better" self as a Marine or an ESA officer in exchange for their former identity. . . . Exactly the same process was used to produce SS officers in the Third Reich. . . . These examples of military training have parallels with the [traumatic] experiences of children in physically or mentally abusive families. [Milburn & Conrad, 1996, p. 185]

As a result of these several sources of trauma, it is not surprising that over one third of all war veterans may suffer long-term identity damage. One study found that "35.8 percent of male Vietnam combat veterans met the full American Psychiatric Association diagnostic criteria for PTSD at the time of the study in the late 1980s . . . almost twenty years after their war experience" (Shay, quoted in Hillman, 2004, p. 65). Americans have long been aware of the phenomenon of post traumatic stress disorder in the form of "battle fatigue" or "shell shock", going back at least to the Civil War. But, even today, when the public awareness of the nature and symptoms of PTSD is probably higher than it has ever been, and when its frequency is increasing as a result of the war in Iraq, politicians and the general public have, for the most part, failed to recognize the frequency, severity, and long-term consequences of this identity damage, which, if not adequately treated, will also produce identity damage in other individuals, beginning with the veterans' family, friends, and co-workers.

Child abuse and neglect

Interpersonal traumas suffered by children are also widespread, and the identity vulnerabilities of many violent individuals can be traced to traumatizing interpersonal experiences and relationships they suffered as children. Bloom and Reichert state:

> The root cause, the lowest common denominator for violence, is that perpetrated against children. And this includes all forms of violence—allowing children to go hungry in the midst of plenty, permitting homelessness, lack of medical care, lack of other sustaining adults to support overwhelmed families, and oppressive policies that make good parenting virtually impossible. [Bloom & Reichert, 1998, p. 3]

The most obvious type of child abuse is physical abuse, which each year produces about 5,000 deaths, 18,000 permanent disabilities, and 150,000 severe injuries (Currie, 1998, p. 82). In addition, such abuse makes its victims much more likely to become violent when they get older. James Gilligan reports that the violent men he treated and studied in prisons had been subjected to childhood abuse that was ". . . so extreme and so unusual that it gives a whole new meaning to the term 'child abuse'" (Gilligan, 1996, p. 43), with hundreds of them having been beaten almost to death (*ibid.*, p. 47). One study of fourteen inmates on death row for heinous juvenile crimes found that thirteen of them had suffered severe abuse as children. One was hit on his head with a hammer by his stepfather; another was hit in the face with a board by his father; a third was kicked in the head by a relative and stamped on and beaten by his older brother; a fourth was set on a hot burner by his stepfather; and a fifth was sodomized by his stepfather and the stepfather's friends (Currie, 1998, p. 83).

Such abuse undermines identity by sending the resounding message that a child is worthless, or worse than worthless, thus not only depriving the child of necessary positive recognition, but actively counteracting whatever recognition he might be getting in other situations. Moreover, in repeatedly eliciting terror and rage, abuse establishes these affects as key contents of the victim's affective–physiological identity. At the same time, it establishes a malignant identity schema or script based on the categories of domination and abjection, either explicitly, through the utterance of derogatory labels, or implicitly, through the enactment of these positions in the body–imagistic register, in which the traumatizer is physically dominant and the traumatized person is physically subjected. Abuse thus establishes identity in all three registers along the axis of dominance and submission, with dominance embodying the most secure identity. As a result, interactions with other people, even of the most mundane and insignificant nature, are often experienced in terms of dominance and submission, their corresponding body images, and the affects of terror, shame, guilt, and rage.

Neglect, while not as dramatic as physical abuse, can be even more devastating to identity. For physical abuse, although it is traumatizing and destructive of identity on many levels, does none the less constitute a form of recognition that functions to establish and support an identity, albeit a malignant identity of dominance and subjugation, whereas "to be ignored gives us the feeling we are being annihilated" (Todorov, 2001, pp. 82–83). The devastating effects of neglect were made clear by the cases of hospitalism reported by René Spitz, in which a significant number of infants died if they were not held and talked to, even though all of their physical needs were being met. It is, thus, no surprise that some studies have found that neglect might be an even greater risk factor for violence than abuse (Hawkins, Farrington, & Catalano, 1998) and that most violent criminals are victims of childhood neglect. "I have never met a group of people who had been so profoundly neglected and deprived", Gilligan states, "and who had received so little of either attention or respect, as the prison inmates" (Gilligan, 2001, p. 122).

Dysfunctional families

Membership of a dysfunctional family can traumatize children by subjecting them to toxic group dynamic forces involving splitting, projection, identification, projective identification, and displacement, as well as various identity-deforming rituals and other group defences. Such forces not only fail to recognize the child's own affective, imagistic, and linguistic identity components, they also powerfully summon the child to embrace particular functions for the family—such as scapegoat or redeemer—that may entail violence and that in any case inhibit the growth of other, more productive identity components by depriving these of the recognition and enactment opportunities that they need in order to develop. Garbarino points out that the reversal of roles between parents and children—"where the child is the protector and the parent is needy—is common in the lives of violent boys" (Garbarino, 1999, p. 56). A child whose family's failures and frustrations are sources of family shame or humiliation will often be burdened with the task of restoring the family's fortunes or serving as the excuse for the family's misfortune, each of which can in itself entail aggression and violence, in addition to the constriction and dissociation it produces in identity. And if he escapes such a summons to right (as redeemer) or excuse (as scapegoat) the family's wrongs, he may simply incorporate the introjects of his family's destructive identity components into his own identity or develop other destructive identity components as a means to survive within the toxic system of the dysfunctional family.

Traumatogenic institutions

Prisons

The severe, acute traumas that occur during the formative years of most violent criminals are reinforced and exacerbated by various forms of institutional violence. The most traumatogenic institution is, no doubt, the prison. "Prisons are hotbeds of trauma", Bloom and Reichert declare.

> It would difficult to create environments more brutalizing than many of our present prisons. . . . We have set about creating environments that are as traumatogenic as possible, short of reinstituting the use of torture devices and the methods of the Inquisition. [Bloom & Reichert, 1998, pp. 230–232]

Prisons traumatize prisoners—damage their identities—in countless ways. Their body–imagistic identities are assaulted by their
being deprived of their own distinctive clothing, living spaces, and
freedom of movement, as well as by searches of their cells, their
bodies, and at times even their body cavities, which constitutes a
form of "digital rape" (Gilligan, 1996, p. 154). Even more traumatic
is the constant fear of, and frequent subjection to, actual rape by
other inmates, which Gilligan estimates occurs at the rate of
millions per year (ibid., p. 175). Homosexual rape not only violates
bodily integrity, but also shatters one's conceptual identity as a man
and produces identity-dystonic affective–physiological states. Men
who are raped by other men are put in the position of a female and
are called galboys, whores, wives, punks, and bitches, and they
"almost universally report that they feel emasculated, castrated,
and deprived of their masculinity" (ibid., p. 173)—an identity situation that, as we saw in Chapter Two, is responsible for much of the
violence that lands men in prison to begin with.

Heterosexual deprivation can also be traumatic, constituting "a
symbolic castration or emasculation of those men who are heterosexual" (ibid., p. 164) by depriving them of identity-defining behaviours, body images, and affective–physiological experiences. As
Gilligan explains, "Since one's sexual identity is such a central con-
stituent of a person's sense of self, if it is destroyed, so is the self"
(ibid., p. 152).

More generally, life in prison traumatizes by depriving inmates
of identity-sustaining agency and efficacy, not only through rapes
and beatings but also through the enforced passivity, powerless-
ness, and helplessness, together with the crowding, lack of privacy,
and constant noise to which prisoners are subjected (see Bloom &
Reichert, 1998, pp. 232–234). As a result of such conditions, "many
inmates leave prison in worse shape than when they entered"
(Bloom & Reichert, 1998, p. 87). "If the purpose of imprisonment
were to socialize men to become as violent as possible", Gilligan
declares, "we could hardly find a more effective way to accomplish
it" (ibid., p. 155).

Schools

While schools are by no means as brutal as prisons, they, too, traumatize many individuals. Many students and teachers are subjected

to bullying and/or are constantly in fear of being attacked or humiliated. As Bloom and Reichert report, statistics from the National Education Association show that, on any given school day, at least 100,000 students bring a gun to school and as many as forty students are hurt or killed. The chance of an American teenager being murdered is at least four times as great as in other industrialized countries. One study found that one fifth of eighth-grade students surveyed reported having seen a weapon at school. Each day 160,000 students skip classes because they are afraid of being physically attacked. Many students are also subjected to traumatizing experiences of shame, humiliation, and disrespect by teachers and school authorities. In addition, over 6,000 teachers are threatened with physical harm, and between 200 and 300 teachers are actually assaulted each day. In any given month, over 5,000 high school teachers are physically assaulted, with about 1,000 of them requiring medical attention. Teachers also report 130,000 thefts each month, as well as habitual behaviour problems on the part of seven per cent of their students (Bloom & Reichert, 1998, pp. 56–58).

Schools can also be structurally traumatogenic, by virtue of their differential dispensation of recognition and enactment opportunities for different identity contents. For example, in most schools competition receives greater recognition (in the form of praise, awards, and dedicated spaces and periods for engaging in it) than does co-operation, which is often seen merely as a means to greater competitive success (e.g., the best teamwork wins). As a result, everyone who does not win the prize is left feeling somewhat wounded and deficient. And violent activities and competitions—such as football, hockey, wrestling, and other (primarily male) sports—draw much greater recognition and rewards than non-violent and non-competitive ones, such as painting, sculpture, writing, choir, orchestra, band, and dance. Indeed, the latter activities often have to insert themselves into the margins (i.e., the sidelines) of the violent and competitive activities in order to get any recognition at all. Hence the relegation of bands and dance squads (cheerleaders, flag teams) to the sidelines and intermissions of high school football and basketball games. Every high school—even those with losing teams—has football heroes, but high schools (outside of the movies) rarely have marching band heroes or dance heroes. As a result of this structure, kind, sensitive, and gentle

students can be subjected to a form of neglect that can be traumatizing in the same way that familial neglect is.

The church

A third prominent traumatogenic institution in American society is
the church, particularly in its Protestant fundamentalist and Roman
Catholic forms. One way in which Protestant fundamentalism
promotes trauma is through its support of corporal punishment of
children, which is still a widespread practice, with over 80 per cent
of adults reporting that they were spanked and 65 per cent of adults
today approving of the practice, the assumption being that "physical discipline communicates a positive spiritual lesson to children
that can ultimately save their souls" (Bloom & Reichert, 1998, p. 61).
More generally, the religious belief in a clear and absolute distinction between good and evil is used to justify not only corporal
punishment, but also other traumatizing actions. These include
brutalizing and even deadly practices, such as imprisonment, capital punishment, and war.

Also traumatogenic is the church's strict policing of sexual
behaviour, most notable in the Catholic Church's condemnation of
birth control, abortion, and homosexuality. The ban on birth control
clearly produces significant trauma for the Catholic women who
suffer unwanted pregnancies as a result, and it undoubtedly produces a different sort of trauma for the faithful women who prac-
tise birth control in opposition to their church's teaching. The
condemnation of abortion produces even greater traumas, not only
for the women who are forced to bear and care for children they do
not want and whom they are often unprepared for and incapable of
raising, but also for the unwanted children themselves, as well as
for others in the household and extended family. Still further traumas are produced when these unwanted children, who are subjected to greater traumatization in the form of abuse and neglect,
themselves engage in various forms of violent behaviour. Empirical
support of this distant effect of the Catholic Church's ban on abortion could be found in the possibility that, as some social analysts
have recently argued, the rise in abortions in the 1970s resulting
from its legalization might have been a factor in the decrease in
violent crime in the 1990s (Levitt & Dubner, 2006).

The fundamentalist and Catholic churches' condemnation of homosexuality is also traumatizing, in several ways. Most immediately, it constitutes a devastating attack on core identity components of gay, lesbian, and queer individuals who believe in the church's authority, often causing them to experience profound inner conflict and even self-loathing. In addition, the church's pronouncement of homosexuality as evil serves to legitimize the various sorts of violence that other institutions and individuals perpetrate against gays, including the most brutal of physical attacks. When Catholic cardinals declare homosexuality to be evil, when fundamentalist believers quote the Old Testament in pronouncing it to be an abomination, and when fundamentalist ministers assert that the AIDS epidemic, the attacks of 9/11, and Hurricane Katrina are God's punishments for homosexuality, they are providing supreme justification for all forms of traumatizing violence against gays and lesbians.

The Catholic Church, in particular, has also perpetrated severe trauma on thousands of children who have been sexually abused by its priests. First by admitting paedophiles into the priesthood and later by retaining many of them in positions of authority over children after their abusive behaviour became known, the church not only enabled their sexual abuse but also sent the tacit but powerful message that the church's authority and financial interests are more important than the psychological well-being—and even the lives and souls—of the abused children, all while preaching "the sanctity of human life" in its opposition to abortion and espousing a "culture of life" as one of its deepest principles.

Traumatizing social conditions and structures

Poverty and inequality

In addition to interpersonal and institutional causes of trauma, there are also ongoing social and cultural conditions that produce a chronic, lower-grade form of trauma that often goes unrecognized but that, none the less, produces significant identity damage, which in turn has profound social consequences. One such instance of chronic trauma occurs when the economic structure and taxation policies of a society with an overabundance of material resources and a substantial reserve of logistical, technological, informational, and administrative capacity allow tens of millions of its citizens, including children, to subsist without adequate food, shelter, health care, education, or personal attention. As Gilligan observes, "It is not lack of material things as such—but rather, relative deprivation, which really comes down to a form of psychological rather than material deprivation, of dignity, self-respect, and pride" (Gilligan, 2001, p. 201).

The lack of recognition embodied in relative deprivation is reinforced when government officials and their policies give greater priority to dozens of other issues than to eliminating the poverty of children, or when a president who proclaims himself compassionate demonstrates greater sympathy for the wealthy stockholders of corrupt corporations than for these millions of innocent, suffering children. Perhaps even more damaging to the identities of the deprived are the blatant contradictions between their condition, on the one hand, and their country's egalitarian ideals and norms of affluence, on the other. Norms of affluence, Bloom and Reichert point out, heighten the humiliation of poverty and contradict egalitarian ideals "that are the bedrock of the American identity" (Bloom & Reichert, 1998, p. 255).

Poverty in a nation, and indeed a world as a whole, where scarcity is no longer insurmountable traumatizes the poor by sending them a tacit but unmistakable message of non-recognition by authorities, society, or the cosmos itself. If one is impoverished while most other people are not, it must be for one of two reasons: either the system is unfair or one is oneself in some way deficient or unworthy. Whichever explanation one chooses, the implications for one's identity are negative. If one views the system as unfair, then the conclusion one inevitably draws (whether conscious or not) is that the powers that be do not care enough about people like oneself either to recognize one's plight or to change the system in order to prevent one's suffering. If one assumes that the poverty is one's own fault, then one must draw the even more identity-damaging conclusion that one is in some way profoundly deficient or unworthy.

Such lack of recognition embodied in poverty produces (often beneath the alienation, anxiety, and depression that are more accessible to consciousness) a profound experience of shame and humiliation, the emotional sense that one's being is without value or significance. "The poor", Todorov says, "are those no one notices, who never manage to exist in the eyes of their fellow citizens" (Todorov, 2001, p. 58). One of the USA's founding fathers, John Adams, described how poverty damages one's identity by directly depriving one of the generalized Other's recognition: Adams says,

> Mankind takes no notice of [the poor man]. He rambles and wanders unheeded. In the midst of a crowd; at church; in the market. . . . [H]e is in as much obscurity as he would be in a garret or a cellar. He is not disapproved, censured, or reproached; he is only not seen. . . . To be wholly overlooked, and to know it, are intolerable. [quoted in Gilligan, 1996, p. 198]

Poverty damages identity because it deprives one of even the most basic recognition by the generalized Other, the recognition that one exists, that one is a human being, a recognition without which it is impossible for a person to go on living. The fact that "the joint wealth of the three richest individuals is equal to the combined wealth of 600 million of the poorest" (Eagleton, 2000, p. 51) sends a deafening message to the 600 million that their existence is not worth serious concern. The structural non-recognition of a global economic system that allows the 225 richest individuals to accumulate and keep as much combined wealth as almost half of the people on the planet (Gilligan, 2001, p. 82) is overwhelming and powerfully depleting of the identities of these three billion people, even if they do not verbalize this fact or even consciously experience it.

Unemployment

Unemployment can also be traumatic, particularly for men, for whom work is perhaps the most important arena for enacting their identities. As Thomas Cottle puts it,

> A man's job is . . . essential to his identity and self-conception. . . . [W]ork provides the structure and substance of a man's life as well as his thinking. It is the activity causing him to feel sane and whole. It is the activity assuring him he is who he is, whatever his

deficiencies, whatever his broken dreams and seemingly wasted efforts. [Cottle, 2001, pp. 10, 253]

In addition to providing a major forum for enacting various aspects of one's identity, work is also a very important source of recognition: the fact that others desire and use the fruits of one's labours constitutes a tacit but powerful recognition of one's worth (Honneth, 1995, pp. 147–148). Conversely, lack of work implies that one is not needed and constitutes a powerful tacit non-recognition. "When a man loses his job . . . he loses face, status, position" (Cottle, 2001, p. 27). Losing a job destroys a significant degree of a person's social position and status and deprives a person of one of the most important opportunities available for demonstrating competence and agency and eliciting recognition. It also disrupts one's position and action within various identity-constituting systems, including interpersonal networks, professional networks, and knowledge systems (Breakwell, 1986, p. 52).

Because work is such a central factor in identity maintenance for most men, unemployment is often traumatic, damaging and disintegrating identity. As Cottle concludes,

a man is what he does. . . . Take the job away and a man loses his soul. . . . It is this reason, this natural, seemingly inbred assumption of having a job, that makes the reality of unemployment so drastic and . . . traumatic for men. [Cottle, 2001, pp. 10, 25]

Thus, as Breakwell observes, "The fact that unemployment acts as a threat to identity is undeniable" (Breakwell, 1986, pp. 52–53). Cottle describes the traumatic effects of unemployment as follows:

In truth it is almost impossible to summarize the dynamics of long-term unemployment in terms of the traumatic effects it has on workers. Yet consider the following list of features noted in these workers: psychological numbness or the almost spaced-out manner of acting; the inability, on occasion, to associate the actual events with the feelings one is experiencing; an overriding anxiety and difficulty in self-nurturing; a sense that one is going mad; the perpetual feeling of being upset; a desire to become invisible or the belief that one is a fraud; a fright coupled with rage; moments of agitation mixed with moments of almost eerie calm; the inability to concentrate sufficiently to even read a newspaper; and finally, the commitment one morning to battle unemployment with renewed intensity followed by a morning in which one appears to have succumbed to the status, or relinquished all personal struggles. . . . [T]hese features point to . . . posttraumatic stress. [Cottle, 2001, pp. 2, 274]

The trauma of unemployment plagues many more individuals than one might assume. While unemployment in the USA in recent decades has been below ten per cent, Cottle found that that one third of all American households suffered loss of at least one job between 1975 and 1995 (*ibid.*, p. 11) and that the experience often traumatizes not only the job loser but other family members as well:

[P]eople describe a shock rippling across their bodies and spirits [when they lose their job]. Almost all long-term unemployed men speak of this. So, too, do their wives. Many use the words *trauma* and *traumatic* to describe their reactions, by which they mean deep wound coupled with a lack of preparation. Families recognize that their sense of trauma continues for as long as the man remains unemployed. It is, in other words, chronic, everyday trauma. And although the children in these families may not use these words nor fully comprehend the psychological repercussions of unemployment, surely they feel the impact of the trauma. In fact, research supports their describing the experience of long-term unemployment as traumatic, as studies reveal an association between unemployment and mortality occurring within one year. . . . Research indicates that within two weeks of a man being laid off, medical and psychological problems begin to emerge among family members. [Cottle, 2001, pp. 19, 22]

In addition to the fact of unemployment, a society also traumatizes people by the ways it deals with those who are unemployed. Breakwell notes that current UK representations of the unemployed stigmatize them, branding them as either unfit or undeserving (Breakwell, 1986, pp. 55–56). People's

descriptions of the unemployed are significantly more negative than those of the employed on every possible dimension of comparison, whether it be intelligence or sociability, cleanliness or kindness, laziness or sporting ability. . . . The unemployed are deprecated, demeaned and derogated in every comparison with the employed regardless of the relevance of the descriptive domain to employability or employment status. The negative social representation of the unemployed has thoroughly permeated the attitude of individuals and the stereotype they hold. [Breakwell, 1986, p. 59]

The omnipresence of such a view is quite destructive for the identities of the unemployed, Breakwell concludes:

> The psychological effects for the unemployed person of accepting this negative stereotype cannot be overestimated. To acknowledge it and adhere to it is to strip away personal self-esteem. Even to recognize that others despise and deprecate the unemployed is a shattering blow to the self-concept without going on to concur with them[,] which is what the unemployed do. [*ibid.*, p. 60]

Job insecurity

Because of such traumatogenic positionings and representations of the unemployed, even a slight degree of job insecurity and lack of continuity can be identity-eroding. And, in recent decades, the types of jobs and structures of work in the USA have changed in ways that subject the majority of workers today to such lack of security and continuity. As Richard Sennett points out, careers are being replaced by "short-term, contract, or episodic labor" (Sennett, 1998, p. 23):

> In work, the traditional career progressing step by step through the corridors of one or two institutions is withering; so is the deployment of a single set of skills through the course of a working life. Today, a young American with at least two years of college can expect to change jobs at least eleven times in the course of working, and change his or her skill base at least three times during those forty years of labor. [*ibid.*, p. 22]

Such working conditions deprive work of some of the same identity-sustaining factors as unemployment does. Specifically, short-term and episodic work deprives one of the key identity-bearing and recognition-accruing narrative of a single career spanning one's entire working life. A man with a single career, even a relatively boring one like that of janitor, carved out a clear story for himself in which his experience accumulated materially and psychically; his life thus made sense to him as a linear narrative. Though a snob might dismiss [a janitor's life] as boring, he experienced the years as a dramatic story moving forward repair by repair, interest payment by interest payment. The janitor felt he became the author of his life, and though he was a man low on the social scale, this narrative provided him a sense of self-respect. . . . He got recognition as a distinctive human being from those who knew him long enough to understand his story. [*ibid.*, p. 16]

Moving from job to job, in contrast, deprives one of such a narrative and the identity it supports. The absence of long-term employment produces "a conflict between character and experience, the experience of disjointed time threatening the ability of people to form their characters into sustained narratives" (Sennett, 1998, p. 31).

Whereas fifty years ago an American man could expect to find a blue-collar or white-collar job that he could keep until he retired, that would pay enough to provide a comfortable life for him and his family, and that would also provide for his retirement and health care (Faludi, 1999), today most men and women can expect that they will have not just multiple jobs, but more than one career during the course of their working lives, that their jobs will not adequately provide for their retirement or health care, and that they will lose their jobs without warning, as news reports of corporate downsizing, business failures, and business relocations continually remind them. This new structure of work sends a resounding message of non-recognition to American workers. It tells them, as a book titled *Corporate Executions* unabashedly states: "Employees are interchangeable components that can be plugged in wherever and whenever they are needed. They are disposable as well. When the immediate demand for their services has subsided, they can be discarded" (quoted in Mills, 1997, p. 79). This message constitutes a significant blow to the identities of all working people.

Homelessness

Homelessness is traumatic in many of the same ways that joblessness is, even when one has a job. The mere fact of homelessness undermines identity by being a powerful social stigma. The

humiliation is exacerbated by the countless experiences of derogation that homeless people are subjected to, ranging from looks
of disdain and contempt from ordinary citizens to harassment
by law enforcement officers and denigration by the bureaucrats,
bureaucracies, and charitable organizations to whom they are often
forced to turn for shelter. In addition to the damage to one's social,
linguistic identity contents produced by such experiences, the
absence of a stable, familiar, warm, safe physical place deprives
one's body–imagistic identity of a very significant source of sustenance. Having a house, apartment, or even just a room of one's
own provides one with multiple visual and spatial reference points
in relation to which one establishes a visual and kinaesthetic continuity that is integral to bodily identity.

Immigration and the traumatic roots of American society

Given the multiple interpersonal and structural forms of trauma
discussed so far, it should not be surprising to learn that "recent
studies confirm clinical impressions that a substantial proportion of
Americans—about three-quarters—have experienced some significant traumatic experience in their lives" (Bloom & Reichert, 1998,
p. 149). Much of this trauma, especially of the interpersonal kind, is
the product of the transgenerational transmission of trauma,
whereby parents who were themselves traumatized as children
often inadvertently, unconsciously, and even invisibly re-enact their
traumas with their children, thus traumatizing them. Such transgenerational transmission is particularly significant in a society like
ours, where everyone except relatively small numbers of American
Indians (themselves the victims of transgenerational transmission
of traumas of dislocation and genocide) is either an immigrant or a
descendant of immigrants:

> On a very broad scale, there is not a single American family that is
> absent a history of what for many was a wrenching experience—
> immigration. By definition, immigration is founded on broken
> attachment bonds. For many, the migratory experience itself was
> preceded by persecution, wartime flight, extremes of poverty that
> necessitated the abandonment of home, or forced enslavement.

Given what we are beginning to understand about intergenerational trauma, it should not surprise us that we have become a "trauma-organized society". [*ibid.*]

These traumatogenic conditions are major social problems in their own right, and for that reason alone they should be eliminated. But they are also major causes of other social problems, including all forms of interpersonal and intergroup violence, which is an additional reason that eliminating them is crucial. To eliminate them, however, requires that we also take into account that they are symptoms of the identity deficiencies of the more privileged members of society, who (largely unconsciously) allow these conditions to persist, despite possessing the means to eliminate them, because they rely on the subalterns produced by these conditions to support their own pampered but insecure identities. Thus, addressing in some way the identity needs of the elite may be a prerequisite for eliminating these traumatogenic social conditions.

Traumatogenic cultural elements

Racism

In racism, traumatogenic social forces and structures collaborate with, and are underwritten by, traumatogenic cultural phenomena. Researchers have identified at least four ways in which racial prejudice and discrimination undermine the identities of racial minorities. First, there are racial insults. Delgado states that "speech that communicates low regard for an individual because of race 'tends to create in the victim those very traits of 'inferiority' that it ascribes to him'"(Delgado, 1995, p. 163). By corroding identity, racial insults contribute to alcoholism, drug abuse, antisocial behaviour, mental illness, and psychosomatic illness such as high blood pressure, which blacks suffer and die from at higher rates than whites (*ibid.*, pp. 160–161). In addition, the psychological and physical ailments undermine effective career pursuits, which constitutes a further erosion of identity (*ibid.*, p. 161). Not surprisingly, children are particularly susceptible to traumatization by such insults: "Because they constantly hear racist messages, minority children, not surprisingly, come to question their competence, intelligence, and worth.

Much of the blame for the formation of these attitudes lies squarely on value-laden words, epithets, and racial names" (*ibid.*, pp. 163–164).

Second, prejudice and discrimination make one continuously aware that one's racial identity is devalued by the dominant culture (Jones, 1997, p. 262). Prejudice and discrimination send the message, powerful even though tacit, that the general order of things, the generalized Other—in the form of one's neighbours, fellow citizens, society, humankind, God, nature—does not recognize one's race or ethnicity as being as important or as worthy as advantaged ones are. To this extent, at least, one's racial or ethnic identity becomes a burden rather than an asset, all the more so if one internalizes this negative recognition or lack of recognition. In addition, to the extent that the dominant culture disparages one's physical characteristics (skin, hair, facial features, body type) and one's ethnic modes of affect and expression of affect (music, dance, food, spirituality), one is deprived of considerable support for one's imagistic and affective identity components as well. In order to succeed socially and economically, one must embrace the values of the very culture that denigrates one's identity. But if one chooses to embrace one's identity instead and hold on to the identity contents of one's racial subculture, the result will be another type of damage to identity, in the form of lesser social and economic status and perhaps even unemployment (*ibid.*, p. 264). This is a dilemma that confronts African-Americans on a daily basis in school, where to do well is perceived by some African-Americans as racial treason, the abandonment of one's black identity and submission to the values and other identity qualities of the oppressor's culture (Gilligan, 1996, p. 206).

Third, the presence of racist stereotypes in a culture produces a self-consciousness that undermines one's sense of self, in the form of an ever-present fear that one might unwittingly enact the stereotype. This fear of stereotype validation has been shown to have a significant detrimental effect on academic performance by African-Americans. One study found that black students performed just as well as white students when a test was presented as non-evaluative, but significantly more poorly than white students when the test was said to provide an evaluation of the students' abilities. In a second study, when students were told that the test was non-evaluative but were reminded of their race before taking it, black students performed at a significantly lower level than whites (Jones, 1997, pp. 267–268). The drop in performance caused by the identity anxiety elicited by their awareness of the racist stereotype further undermines their identity by constituting what appears to be objective evidence that they are indeed not as knowledgeable or as intelligent as their white counterparts. In order to avoid this identity threat, some students divest from the identity content of student through "a reduction of the level of effort, or, more tragic, the rejection of academic performance altogether as an indication of self-worth" (Jones, 1997, p. 267). One consequence of this move appears in the fact that, by the tenth grade, most black males show no correlation between self-esteem and GPA (*ibid.*, p. 270): that is, identity is divested from academic performance, with the likely consequence of limiting the students' opportunities for identity maintenance and enhancement in the future (*ibid.*, p. 271).

Finally, a racist culture undermines identity by infusing well deserved identity-supporting recognition with ambiguity, causing one to ask, for example, whether a supervisor's friendly manner is a sincere expression of respect or rather a compensation for racist attitudes (*ibid.*, 1997, p. 262). Thus, when one receives positive feedback from another person, one often wonders whether the feedback is a sincere recognition of one's merit or merely a form of undeserved (personal or institutional) affirmative action. And when one is the object of a negative evaluation, even if one attributes the response to prejudice, one often experiences some concern that the negative response might have some validity (*ibid.*, 1997, p. 273).

As a result of such systematic assault on their identities and the dearth of resources available to maintain them, many black males have no other recourse for psychological survival than to enact an identity of "protest masculinity" through the violent lyrics of gangsta rap or aggressive and violent behaviour of various kinds (Bloom & Reichert, 1998, p. 39).

Sexism and heterosexism

Sexist and heterosexist elements of culture embody similar traumatogenic forces. The most traumatizing forms of sexism and heterosexism are those involving physical violence, such as rape, battery, and even murder, and the frequency of such acts is alarming: a study in the 1980s, for example, found that one in four of 900 randomly chosen women had been raped and that one out of three of these women had been sexually abused as a child (Herman, 1997, p. 30). In light of such findings, it must be concluded "that the most common post-traumatic disorders are those not of men in war but of women in civilian life" (*ibid.*, p. 28).

Underwriting and legitimizing such traumatizing physical violence are cultural embodiments of sexism that are also traumatogenic in their own right, in much the same way as racist cultural elements are. Studies have shown, for example, that women's performances on science and math tests are hampered by their awareness of the cultural stereotype that women are less capable in these fields than men. When experimental subjects were told before taking a test that men generally outperformed women on the test, the women's scores were significantly lower than the men's, but when they were told that there was no difference in performance between men and women, the women performed as well as the men (Jones, 1997, p. 269). Another study found that women are subject to the same sort of attributional ambiguity that afflicts African-Americans. When the women in an experiment were certain that a male evaluator was prejudiced against them, they discounted his negative evaluation and maintained their self-esteem. But when they were not sure that the evaluator was prejudiced, they tended to blame themselves for the poor evaluation and their self-esteem was reduced (*ibid.*, p. 273).

In the cultural domain of literature, which has received intense scrutiny of its sexist aspects, scholars have identified a number of traumatogenic factors whereby sexist literature damages the identities of female readers. One of the most fundamental and widespread of these traumatizing forces is "immasculation", the way many prominent (male authored) literary texts in the traditional canon and curriculum manipulate female readers to identify with male protagonists who experience female characters as obstacles to fulfilment. "As readers and teachers and scholars," Judith Fetterley explains, "women are taught to think as men, to identify with a male point of view, and to accept as normal and legitimate a male system of values, one of whose central principles is misogyny"

(Fetterley, 1978, p. xx). In reading prominent male-authored novels,

> the female reader is co-opted into participation in an experience from which she is explicitly excluded; she is asked to identify with a selfhood that defines itself in opposition to her; she is required to identify against herself. [Fetterley, 1978, p. xii]

The effect of such reading experiences and, more generally, of living in a patriarchal culture, Fetterley argues, is serious identity damage: "Forced in every way to identify with men, yet incessantly reminded of being a woman, [a female reader] undergoes a transformation into an 'it,' the dominion of personhood lost" (*ibid.* p. ix), resulting in "self-hatred and self-doubt" (*ibid.*, p. xxi). Thus, the reading and study of traditional, male-authored works of literature, which was once touted as a central force in a liberal, liberating education, can actually be traumatic for many women, significantly impeding their identity development and often doing damage to the identities they have already achieved (Schweickart, 1986, pp. 40–41).

Since women are (still often largely) defined and recognized for gentleness and passivity rather than for aggressivity and violence, it might be assumed that their socialization promotes peacefulness rather than violence. Such an assumption would be valid, in so far as women engage in far fewer acts of violent behaviour than men and are generally less socially and politically belligerent and bellicose than men. However, women who accept the cultural prohibition of aggressive impulses as part of their identities do not simply lose those impulses any more than men lose their tender and passive impulses; rather, they must either consciously suppress them or unconsciously repress them and then enact them unconsciously and surreptitiously. Many women apparently do the latter. Some women manage to gratify their aggressive urges by insulting or humiliating individuals (including other women) of lesser wealth, status, or power—such as subordinates in the workplace, servers in restaurants, cleaning personnel, clerks, and groundskeepers—or by morally castigating criminals, often including female prostitutes. But one of the surest and most invisible (and hence identity-maintaining) ways for women, like men, to enact their identity-contradicting aggression is by perpetrating institutional, structural, and cultural violence, through voting for and otherwise supporting precisely the sorts of social, political, and economic structures, policies, and institutions that, we have seen, traumatize individuals in ways that damage their identities and thus lead them, in turn, to engage in physical violence. Thus, the cultural traumatization of women also plays an important role in the perpetuation of violence, although since aggression and violence are precisely what is excluded from women's identity, the path from cultural traumatization to violence is usually more circuitous and hidden for women than it is for men.

Just as traumatogenic as sexist literary texts, canons, curricula, and pedagogies have been the heterosexist and homophobic instances of these same phenomena. The traumatogenic effects of these forces have been well documented in other literary texts, among which are E. M. Forster's *Maurice* and Jeanette Winterson's *Oranges Are Not the Only Fruit*. In *Maurice*, Forster reveals the self-loathing that results when the homosexuality of the eponymous protagonist is systematically denied recognition and subjected to derogation by the heterocentrism and homophobia of early twenti-eth-century British culture. The denial of recognition to gay sexual-ity begins with a schoolmaster's presentation of sexuality through a crude diagram of heterosexual coupling, includes a Cambridge's dean's admonition to his class to skip over a textual passage refer-ring to "the unspeakable vice of the Greeks" (Forster, 1971, p. 51), and culminates in Maurice's expulsion from Cambridge after this same dean sees him cutting classes for a motorcycle ride with a male companion. After Maurice's friend Durham, who had suffered a nervous breakdown at the age of sixteen over his own secret homosexuality, renounces and represses his (largely sublimated) homosexual desire, Maurice experiences himself as an outcast with no one to turn to and begins to contemplate suicide (*ibid.*, p. 135). Subsequently, when he feels "lust" (*ibid.*, p. 150) for the nephew of a family friend and then for an old man on a train, he experiences a self-loathing that sends him in search of a "cure" for his homo-sexuality, which his culture allows him to conceive of only as a disease. In broaching his concerns with young Dr Jowitt, Maurice is confronted with the systematic foreclosure of the subject by his culture: "On all other subjects he could command advice, but on this, which touched him daily, civilization was silent" (*ibid.*, p. 156). And when he sobbingly confesses to his family's friend Dr Barry, "I'm an unspeakable of the Oscar Wilde sort", and implores the doctor to help him, the doctor responds, "Rubbish, rubbish!"— another categorical refusal of recognition, with the full authority of science behind it, of a core component of Maurice's identity (*ibid.*, p. 159). After an unsuccessful attempt at "self-cure" by dating a woman, he turns in desperation to a hypnotist, reasoning, "If this new doctor could alter his being, was it not his duty to go, though body and soul would be violated? With the world as it is, one must marry or decay" (*ibid.*, p. 170).

The traumatic, identity-destroying refusal of recognition, together with active denigration, of homosexuality are particularly virulent in fundamentalist Christian culture, as detailed in Winterson's *Oranges Are Not the Only Fruit* (1985). The homophobia is so powerful in the adolescent Jeanette's religious community that it leads her mother to denounce her to the church elders when she discovers Jeanette's relationship with Melanie. There ensues a public outing of the two girls in church, followed by their permanent separation and the brutal attempt to "exorcise" the evil demon of homosexuality. Melanie succumbs to this identity assault, renouncing not only Jeanette, but also the better parts of her own identity and retreating into a bovine conformity, leaving Jeanette alone in her attempt to find recognition and enactment of her lesbian identity contents in a culture hostile to same-sex love. A similar fundamentalism-induced trauma can be seen in the recent efforts of the American evangelical preacher Ted Haggard to deny that he is gay, despite his admitted sexual relations with male prostitutes.

Masculinity as traumatogenic

In addition to these more obviously traumatic cultural forces, masculine socialization is also traumatizing in American culture. All socialization is traumatic in so far as it involves the withholding of recognition and enactment opportunities for certain parts of the self and the imposition on identity, through intensive interpellation and insistent recognition, of qualities that are not actually part of one's self. American socialization into gender and sexual identities is particularly traumatic. Just as girls and women can be traumatized through disempowerment, deprivation of agency, and enforced passivity, boys are often traumatized by being forced to embrace violence, as both victim and perpetrator. "Masculinity", Gilligan observes, ". . . is literally defined as involving the expectation, even the requirement, of violence" (Gilligan, 2001, p. 56). Bloom and Reichert note that

> the social world through which boys must pass on the way to manhood ensures that all males in this culture absorb a healthy dose of masculine, violent conditioning. Practically all males experience interpersonal violence, directly or indirectly; boys push, pull, threaten, bully, and hurt each other normatively, usually under the noses of adults, from the time they are quite young. . . . We expect and permit boys to be violent. . . . Boyhood in the United States, in light of these findings, practically seems a training ground for violence in service to an ethic of proving one's manhood. [Bloom & Reichert, 1998, pp. 34–35]

The allocation of recognition in the socializing process also excludes passive, submissive, and tender impulses and feelings from the identities of men and boys, through, for example, according recognition and honour to boys who perform most violently in violent sports such as football, hockey, boxing, and wrestling and by withholding recognition from, and even shaming, boys who excel intellectually (e.g., "computer geeks") or artistically (e.g., "band nerds" and "fairies" who dance). As Terrence Real explains:

> Just as girls are pressured to yield that half of their human potential consonant with assertive action . . . so are boys pressured to yield attributes of dependency, expressiveness, affiliation—all the self-concepts and skills that belong to the relational, emotive world. These wholesale excisions are equally damaging to the healthy development of both girls and boys. . . . [B]oys "become" men by lopping off, or having lopped off, the most sensitive parts of their psychic and, in some cases, physical selves. The passage from boyhood to manhood is about ritual wounding. It is about giving up those parts of the self that do not fit within the confines of the role. [Real, 1997, pp. 130, 132]

Thus, as Real observes,

> For most boys active trauma is an integral part of life. . . . Such boyhood injury operates like a fault line in troubled men, coloring their emotional lives, ready, given the right circumstance, to emerge. The wounded boy they think they have long left behind acts like a reservoir of hurt and shame. [*ibid.*, pp. 113–116]

But boys do not have to experience physical violence to be traumatized by the masculine socialization process. Even relatively mild forms of neglect, Real argues, can be traumatic for children (*ibid.*, pp. 105–109):

> These emotional amputations can be effected through active or passive injury in transactions severe or seemingly mild. They can occur with extraordinary drama, . . . [or] they can appear as mundane as dinner non-conversation. . . . Some boys lose their "souls" in great chunks, others find it chipped away in small bits, through the most ordinary interactions. [*ibid.*, pp. 135, 128]

Bloom and Reichert describe the trauma of such emotional amputations as follows:

> If we do not respond empathetically to children's emotional needs, then they will cut off their emotional responsiveness to others and grow into adults incapable of empathy. This is particularly true for men, who are culturally brainwashed from a very early age that the expression of any emotion except anger is not entirely acceptable. . . . [O]ur present social norm of disavowing emotional experience is, itself, a traumatogenic force that pervades the entire cultural milieu. [Bloom & Reichert, 1998, pp. 28, 30][

By thus cutting off certain parts of the self from participating in one's identity and imposing on identity some elements not included in the self, such socialization processes produce and sustain a low-grade trauma that harms identity in ways that contribute directly not only to physical violence, but also to institutional, structural, and cultural violence. The very process by which boys are supposedly being toughened up and made into men leaves them wounded and insecure, with a greater need to enact their tough, aggressive masculine identities. And the simplest way to do so, as we have seen, is through violence. Hence, for men, the path from cultural traumatization to violence is quite direct and is paved by the fact that aggression and violence are socially recognized—indeed, insisted upon—in numerous ways as essential components of masculine identity, and violence-suppressing qualities like submissiveness and tenderness are roundly excluded from their identities. Thus "being a boy is inherently traumatic in our culture" (Garbarino, 1999, p. 160), and traumatized boys turn into traumatized men who traumatize their own sons, and so on *ad infinitum.*

Hyperindividualism and social Darwinism

Closely related to, and reinforcing, the traumatization produced by socialization into masculinity is the traumatization resulting from the USA's hyperindividualist ideology, which celebrates almost gangster-like autarchy and shames those who are not self-sufficient. Assured by parents, teachers, and politicians that in the USA one can be whatever one wants to be, and challenged by admonitions such as those of military recruitment ads to "be all that you can be" and to "be an army of one", American children and youth become convinced, especially when they judge others, that any time an individual comes up short, the reason is to be sought primarily in that individual's own character, with no causal significance accorded the circumstance that might have elicited or constrained the individual's behaviour, or the developmental conditions that might be responsible for character flaws and weaknesses. This message is reinforced by stories, real and fictional, of individuals who appear to become rich and famous solely through single-minded and aggressive pursuit of their goals. Whenever people watch television or a film, they encounter living proof, in every actor on the screen, of the truth of the American dream. The same is true whenever they go to a concert or listen to the radio or a CD, and whenever they attend a professional sports event or watch one on TV. As a result of such demonstrations that hard work and perseverance can, in fact, work miracles, many people come to believe that individuals who are not financially successful enough to support themselves and their families simply have not worked hard enough and are themselves to blame for their lack of success. This assumption is powerfully reinforced by the USA's social and economic systems, institutions, and policies: the resounding message of the USA's social practices, policies, institutions, and structures is, "Your health, intelligence, education, wealth, income, job, success, and general welfare are your own responsibility, and if you don't measure up to your own or society's standards in any of these categories, it is entirely your own fault". Such a message can traumatize those who feel they do not measure up.

Underwriting this hyperindividualism, along with most of the other traumatogenic cultural forces discussed above, is a resurgent social Darwinism. One chilling example is the statement by the New York City police captain who was evicting homeless people from Central Park. "We have to cut off the head of the enemy," he declared, "and the enemy is the homeless" (quoted in Mills, 1997, p. 22). Such social Darwinist discourse has also become more prominent in the corporate world, reflecting a revival of the corporate Darwinism that plagued the United States a century earlier, as articulated in John D. Rockefeller's infamous assertion that "the growth of a large business is merely a survival of the fittest, the working out of a law of nature and a law of God" (quoted in Mills, 1997, pp. 64–65), and Andrew Carnegie's declaration that the "best interests of the race" were served by an economic arrangement that "inevitably gives wealth to the few" (quoted in Mills, 1997, p. 72). As Mills observes,

> A century later the defenders of corporate Darwinism don't come so well known or with such impressive credentials, but the corporate culture they have managed to establish is as coherent and ruthless as that of the 1890s, and it has helped create in America the widest gap between rich and poor of any industrialized nation. [Mills, 1997, pp. 72–73]

Rather than eliciting opposition from the workers it traumatizes, this social Darwinism of the political and economic elite replicates itself in them, where it directs them to find their nemesis not in the elite, who dominate, exploit, and traumatize them, but, rather, in those who are below them on the economic ladder and whose needs they perceive as the greater threat to their well being:

Middle-class workers . . . join with business in treating the inner-city poor as if they were strangers from foreign nations whose habits and values put them beyond the reach of help. . . . In contrast to the workers of the 1930s, who believed that solidarity was in their interest, today's workers, especially those who regard themselves as middle class, have no such confidence. Aware of the ease with which they can be replaced, they simply try to get by on their own. The new anxious class has, as a consequence, also become the new angry class, venting its frustrations on those who seem to be getting a free ride on welfare or through affirmative action preferences. [*ibid.*, pp. 6, 25]

The same logic holds for those at the lowest social and economic realms. They, too, have been distracted from demanding their fair share from the system and those who control it by their own social Darwinist opportunities to dominate others. Thus, rather than banding together as had been done with some success in the past, disempowered individuals attempt to heal their traumatized identities by finding their own subalterns and traumatizing them. Whether by participating (immediately or vicariously) in ultimate fighting, professional wrestling matches, or athletic contests, by watching violent films or television programmes, by gambling or playing bloody video games, by producing or consuming brutal music lyrics, or simply by putting each other down in playing the dozens, individuals on the lowest rungs of the social Darwinist ladder embrace and replicate this traumatogenic culture of meanness.

Such social Darwinism is traumatogenic not only in so far as it promotes and legitimizes traumatizing behaviours, institutions, and social structures, but also in as much as it denies the unconditional worth of the individual. In a social Darwinist culture, where one is only as good as one's latest accomplishment, as soon as one ceases to dominate others, one's identity begins to wane. Like capitalism, the social Darwinist individual is in need of continual expansion, in the form of an ever-new supply of subalterns to dominate. This logic of capitalism embodied in individual identity constitutes a powerful chronic traumatogenic force, confronting individuals with an ever-present threat of the annihilation of their identities. But, while the resurgent culture of social Darwinism is traumatogenic in this removal of unconditional, ontological recognition of the worth of all individuals, it is difficult to debunk, because it simultaneously offers immediate recognition via juxtaposition with any subaltern individual or group one can find or produce, as well as an ever present opportunity to enhance one's identity by triumphing over, or enacting one's superiority in relation to, these subalterns (see Lewis, 1993, for a similar argument).

* * *

The identity deficits that underlie all our major social problems are thus themselves the product of multiple layers of trauma. These layers include:

1. The traumas that the perpetrators of physical violence and other forms of antisocial behaviour have suffered, in the form of severe and ongoing physical and emotional abuse and neglect, and that are at the root of their antisocial behaviour.
2. The trauma resulting from institutional violence such as the harsh, punitive treatment of prisoners, including non-violent substance-abusers, by our criminal justice and penal systems, which exacerbates the identity damage done by the original child abuse and neglect sustained by these prisoners and thus fuels rather than subdues their violent tendencies.
3. The lower-grade traumatization produced by institutional and structural violence—including poverty, unemployment, inadequate health care, authoritarian religion, and an impersonal, mass-production system of education—which victimizes the perpetrators of physical violence in numerous ways and is also experienced by many of the non physically violent perpetrators of (i.e., ardent advocates of) institutional violence (e.g., angry white men) who are often themselves also among the principal (political) perpetrators of this very institutional violence that is traumatizing them.
4. The all-pervasive trauma constituted by the cultural violence inflicted in socializing children into American boys, American girls, and American individualists, which harms everyone (though in differing ways and to different degrees) through cutting off certain parts of the self, on the one hand and, on the other hand, thrusting alien attributes (such as toughness for

sensitive boys and passivity for active girls) deep into children's identities.

Each type of traumatogenic force—physical, institutional, structural, and cultural—is the product of an effort to protect or repair an identity that has itself been injured by one or more of these same types of trauma. And, in each instance, the trauma-producing behaviour is pursued because it offers individuals the best opportunity for maintaining their identities, given their particular identity contents and structure and the identity-supporting resources that are available to them. Participating in the perpetration of institutional and structural violence, for example, is an easy, readily available, low-cost way to support one's identity: it is socially approved and hence recognition-garnering (i.e., being a staunch advocate of the "War on Crime", the death penalty, or welfare reduction in American society elicits approval from many people), and it produces an abundance of subalterns ("criminals", "riff-raff", etc.) on to whom righteous, upstanding citizens can simultaneously externalize and unconsciously enact their own unacknowledged violent impulses, while convincing themselves and others that their support of harsh punishments and niggardly public assistance is a virtue.

At the core of our most pressing social problems is thus an unending chain of trauma, whereby those who are traumatized inflict trauma on others (as well as themselves), who repeat the infliction on victims of their own, *ad infinitum*. Those (policymakers and the general public) who could change the circumstances that produce the perpetrators' original traumas fail to do so, in large measure, because maintaining their own less seriously traumatized identities also relies on having these perpetrators to hate and do violence to, albeit in a more covert form.

What this means is that solving our most serious social problems requires breaking this vicious circle of trauma. There are two basic ways to do this. One is by eliminating or reducing the traumatogenic forces identified in this chapter. The other is by reducing the need for traumatized identities to maintain themselves through activities—physical, institutional, structural, or cultural violence—that are themselves traumatogenic. This requires providing alternative, more benign ways for traumatized identities to maintain themselves and/or helping these identities to heal and to develop components and structures that both make the identities more secure and resilient and entail more benign, prosocial, non-traumatogenic activities for their maintenance. It is to this second strategy that we now turn.

PART IV
SOCIAL CHANGE AND IDENTITY DEVELOPMENT

CHAPTER SIX

Promoting benign identity contents

A s one social analyst has observed, most interventions aiming to prevent social problems

> do not create change either in the individuals who exhibit the behavior or in the institutions responsible for the environment in which the behavior is learned. ... They do not deal with the antecedents or the predisposing factors that lead to the behavior, but only with the "outcome", or "symptom". [Dryfoos, 1990, pp. 3–4]

"Prevention interventions", she advises "should be directed toward the common *antecedents* of the categorical problem behaviors rather than at the separate manifest behaviors" (Dryfoos, 1990, p. 7). Identity needs, we have seen, are the common antecedents of our most serious social problems. These problems are symptoms of identity needs. The main reason the problems exist is because they provide various forms of identity support. Preventing these social symptoms thus requires interventions that affect identity in a positive way. There are five basic types of such interventions:

1. reducing traumatogenic social and cultural structures, institutions, practices, and conditions in order to prevent identity damage and impeded development;
2. promoting the development and enactment of multiple, diverse, prosocial identity contents;
3. reducing harmful social and cultural identity defences;
4. promoting integration of rejected elements of self, which reduces the need for defences and strengthens identity;
5. fostering the development of more complex and inclusive identity structures, which expands and strengthens identity, enables integration of diverse identity contents, and reduces the need for malignant defences.

The first of these strategies can be pursued by policies and practices that reduce the various traumatogenic factors discussed in the previous chapter. The rest of the strategies will be explored in this and the following three chapters.

Developing policies and practices that enact these various forms of identity support and development can help solve most social problems, including the meta-problem of our responding ineffectively or even counterproductively to our first-order problems. Using the identity-centred model of social symptoms can help us avoid ineffective and counterproductive interventions and formulate instead practices and policies that affect the identities involved in ways that help to reduce social problems while benefiting the individual perpetrators as well, rather than simply manipulating and exploiting the individuals for social ends, a practice that ultimately only exacerbates social problems.

As should already be evident from this model, various identity-affecting strategies, ranging from individual therapy to massive alterations in the nature and distribution of material resources, can be effective in altering identities in ways that make them stronger and more prosocial and thus render their destructive behaviours less necessary. The same is true of cultural interventions. Cultural resources are crucial for all of the identity elements we have discussed: the content of each identity register, as well as the structure, defences, and degree of integration of the various components, all depend in various ways on cultural resources for both their development and their maintenance. The provision of such identity resources, in fact, might be said to be the most fundamental and important function of culture in general. Indeed, a culture is nothing more, and nothing less, than the practices and artefacts of a society that have as their primary function the construction, development, integration, enactment, recognition, and defence of the identities of the members of that society. All of the institutions, practices, media, and artefacts of a culture work in one way or another to support one or more of these processes. There is, thus, a myriad of cultural resources potentially available for identity-based interventions. The following chapters identify some of the most promising interventions, which are meant to be illustrative rather than exclusive or comprehensive.

Allocation of recognition and enactment opportunities

One of the most powerful and direct forms of intervention into identity to reduce social problems is the allocation of recognition and enactment opportunities for specific identity contents. When people do not receive adequate recognition or enactment opportunities for benign identity contents, they will enact malignant contents or seek recognition through harmful actions. One of the most direct ways, then, to prevent people from engaging in destructive actions is to provide them with adequate recognition and enactment opportunities for identity contents that do not entail such actions.

That such identity support can prevent social problems has been demonstrated not only in empirical studies of the environmental factors that protect individuals against becoming violent, as we will see in the concluding chapter, but also by laboratory experiments. One experiment found that even a seemingly rather insignificant form of identity affirmation, such as prompting individuals to think about an identity-bearing value, resulted in a reduction in the expression of prejudice. Subjects who did not experience this moment of validation prior to evaluating a minority job candidate evaluated her more negatively than subjects who did experience such a moment (Fein & Spencer, 1997, p. 34). Other experiments have demonstrated that identity support also reduces biased perception and judgement, and resistance to new ideas:

Persistent biases in social judgment arise from identity-maintenance motivations. ... Such motivations pressure cognitive
processes to a desired end. ... Relieving these pressures fosters a
more rational and even-handed evaluation of the evidence. ... An
affirmation of an alternative source of identity both attenuated
resistance to persuasion and produced a more even-handed evaluation of evidence. Shoring up global self-worth, it seems, takes the
sting out of new ideas, making them less painful to accept as true.
... Participants felt less threatened by evidence that impugned
their attitudes, it seems, when they received an affirmation of an
alternative source of self-worth. As a result, they engaged in fewer
defensive manoeuvres aimed at protecting an identity. [Cohen,
Aronson, & Steele, 2000, pp. 1161, 1162, 1163]

In addition to demonstrating that identity security reduces
aggression and prejudice, studies have also shown that, in a given
situation, any one of a number of different modes of identity
support, or self-affirmation, can reduce or eliminate the problematic
behaviour (Steele, 1999, p. 374). That is, if a person is experiencing
the depletion of identity in a certain area, such as being a compe-
tent driver, that deficiency can be redressed by various means other
than becoming and/or being recognized as a good driver (Liu &
Steele, 1986, p. 539). "People can apparently adapt to self-threat",
Steele reports, "through actions that affirm the general integrity of
the self even when these adaptations do nothing to resolve the
provoking threat itself" (Steele, 1999, p. 375). Thus, as Steele further
explains, "any adaptation, cognitive or behavioral, that affirms self-
integrity can reduce the impact of specific threats to that integrity.
These adaptations can vary widely and are widely interchangeable,
allowing 'fluid compensation'" (ibid., p. 387).

What this means is that problematic behaviours such as prejudice, violence, and substance abuse, which we have seen to be
efforts to support identity, can be reduced or eliminated by providing people with recognition or enactment opportunities of benign
contents that provide identity support equal to or greater than that
provided by the problematic behaviour. The particular means of
identity support an individual chooses, Steele explains, will be
determined by its cost-effectiveness relative to other options and by
its relative availability, which means how accessible it is to a
person's perception, memory, and/or imagination (ibid., p. 389).

Providing benign alternative sources of identity support can thus range from providing material resources to facilitating social relations, engaging individuals in certain cultural activities, and promoting certain psychological associations, which in some cases can be as simple as making people aware of certain self-concepts (Steele, Spencer, & Lynch, 1993, p. 889).

One of the most powerful demonstrations of how identity support can prevent social problems is the Perry School project, implemented several decades ago in Ypsilanti, Michigan, which involved a battery of interventions to help parents provide nurturing, non-traumatic conditions—that is, optimum identity-development conditions—for their children. This programme was found to be not only effective in reducing various social problems, but also cost-effective, more than paying for itself by reducing the need that children from the programme had for expensive social services (such as remedial education, medical aid, welfare, or involvement with the criminal justice system) when they reached adolescence and adulthood. Reviewing the key findings of an evaluation done years after the interventions, when the subjects were twenty-seven, Elliot Currie concluded:

> The results were impressive: the Perry students were far more likely to be literate, off welfare, working and earning a decent living. They were only one-fifth as likely as the carefully matched control group to have become chronic criminal offenders (defined as having been arrested five or more times) and only about one-fourth as likely to have been arrested for drug-related crimes. [Currie, 1998, p. 92]

Another important means of preventing social problems would be to eliminate the grotesque disparities in wealth and income between the richest and the poorest of Americans, as well as between America and other parts of the world. Such an intervention, by dramatically increasing the recognition accorded the poor and reducing their identity-depleting shame, would significantly reduce violence, prejudice, substance abuse, and other social problems. As Gilligan observes,

> Cleaning up our social and economic system, by reducing the shame-provoking [i.e., identity-depleting] inequities in social and

economic status, will do far more to prevent physical violence than all the police, prisons and punishments in the world, all the prison psychiatrists we could possibly hire, and all the armies, armaments, and Armageddons we could mobilize. [Gilligan, 2001, pp. 99–100]

There is substantial empirical evidence to back up this claim, including significant correlations between inequality and violent crime (see Currie, 1998, pp. 120ff.).

One of the most basic things that can be done to provide people with adequate recognition is to eliminate conditions and practices that humiliate and shame them and thus deprive them of the quota of recognition normally available to anyone simply by virtue of being human. Gilligan points out that breaking the cycle of violence requires eliminating the shaming and humiliating (i.e., recognition-depriving, identity-damaging) treatment of criminals. Since violence is a result of damaged identity, experienced as shame, the best way to reduce violence, Gilligan argues, is to reduce the factors that cause shame. "The task before us now", Gilligan says, "is to integrate the psychodynamic understanding of shame and guilt with the broader social and economic factors that intensify those feelings to murderous and suicidal extremes on a mass scale" (Gilligan, 1996, p. 239) and work to "bring about fundamental changes in the social and cultural conditions that expose people to increased rates and intensities of shame and humiliation" (ibid., p. 225). Gilligan observes that "other cultures [who] have . . . altered their social conditions so as to protect their members from exposure to overwhelming degrees of shame and humiliation . . . have experienced the dramatic diminution in rates of violence . . ." (ibid., p. 226).

More generally, providing everyone, including foreign nations and other groups, with positive recognition in the form of respect would go a long way toward reducing both interpersonal and intergroup aggression and violence. Studies reveal that such respect is prominent in peaceful societies:

Respect permeates almost all levels of the peaceful societies—it is especially pervasive among peoples who want to avoid trouble with anyone. Respect for neighboring peoples is an important strategy that some of the peaceful societies realize will help to maintain external peace . . . an idea that appears to be largely ignored in the contemporary American approach to strategic international thinking. Within each peaceful society, respect permeates human relationships, no matter how closely people are related. . . . [A] strong respect for women prevails throughout the literature on peaceful societies . . . [and] family respect seems to be one of the most critical foundations for the all pervasive nonviolence in the peaceful societies. [Bonta & Fry, 2006, p. 184]

The same logic applies to other social problems. Public policies that reduce inequalities, signs of inequality, and other shame-producing phenomena, as well as policies that embody respect for everyone, especially currently disrespected groups, can significantly reduce social problems by reducing identity-damaging deficiencies in recognition.

The effectiveness of recognition in reducing social problems is also apparent in successful efforts to reduce conflicts between groups. Diplomatic negotiations often involve important forms of linguistic recognition of participants in the form of dramatic announcements, laudatory toasts, and use of prestigious titles. In addition, diplomatic meetings provide structural recognition for the participants' body–imagistic identity contents, in the form of the safe, comfortable, and sometimes luxurious physical settings that are provided for the meetings. And the provision of good food, drink, music, and other entertainment provides important tacit, structural recognition and opportunities for enactment of participants' identity-bearing affective–physiological states. In addition, structured dialogue between warring parties can support each party's large-group identity by providing recognition of several of its key contents by the opposing group and third-party facilitators. These identity contents include, in particular, the group's chosen trauma and its chosen glory, both of which attain recognition and validation by means of the discussions. By receiving such continuous and multifarious recognition, members are relieved of the pressure to extort recognition by aggressively performing their identity and asserting its worth—sometimes by violent means—in face of the other group.

One particularly significant form of recognition is recognition from the reality, in the form of hard evidence (as opposed to mere expressions from other people), that one's existence has made a difference in the world. Since such recognition comes as a result of enacting certain identity contents, there is, therefore, a need for opportunities to enact one's identity contents, and the provision of such opportunities can contribute significantly to the reduction of violence and other social symptoms. Thus, to reduce social problems, we need to make available the social, cultural, and material activities and resources necessary to enact signifiers like independence, courage, power, and perhaps even dominance in productive, non-violent ways, through academic, social, artistic, mechanical, or construction projects.

We also need to provide non-violent ways of attaining and performing bodily integrity, which can be done through dressing to change the appearance of one's body, by dieting and/or exercising in order to change the form or capacities of one's body, and by engaging in athletic activities that are themselves a performance of one's bodily powers, as well as through surrogate bodies—other human, animal, or inanimate bodies whose beauty, power, stamina, grace, or agility people can experience vicariously. People who have access to a wide range of spatial, architectural, technological, and artistic resources have important non-violence-entailing identity-sustaining possibilities that people who lack such access do not have, and any increase in such access for people who lack it will contribute to the reinforcement of body–imagistic identity contents and, thus, directly and indirectly to the reduction of violence and other social symptoms.

Increasing people's opportunities to engage in activities and acquire objects that produce their identity-bearing affective states will also aid in maintaining identity without the production of social symptoms. This can be done by providing people with greater opportunity to enact in a benign manner their identity-bearing affective–physiological states. Such opportunity can take multiple forms. One form is access to legal substances that directly intervene in the body's chemistry. Such substances include not only mood-regulating drugs such as tranquillizers and antidepressants, but also nutritious, physiology-stabilizing foods, in contrast to sugar-laced beverages and junk foods that are often the primary fare of the poor. Providing individuals with the material, social, and scheduling resources to engage regularly in endorphin-producing physical exercise or meditation or yoga is another means of helping them enact identity-bearing affective–physiological states. Opportunities to experience mood-regulating sights, sounds, smells, and tastes can also be provided—for example, in the form of individuals' own (often ethnic) music, food, and sights as well as through the reduction of noise pollution, air pollution, and the visual pollution caused by urban blight. Fostering positive social interactions, ranging from fleeting and anonymous contacts to ongoing relationships, will also help to enact identity-bearing affective states. Encountering acknowledgement and respect instead of indifference or utter disregard in even the most fleeting and anonymous contact with others—including clerks, waiters, fellow pedestrians, and other drivers—can make a significant difference, over time, in one's level of identity security, and altering cultural norms in this direction should be a priority. Furthermore, since sympathy from others can reduce the intensity and duration of identity-depleting affects while sharing one's joys or triumphs with another can intensify and extend the duration of positive affective–physiological states, providing formal (e.g., grief counselling) and informal opportunities for such interactions should also be a priority.

Promoting new identity contents

In addition to providing greater opportunity for recognition and enactment of benign identity contents people already possess, social problems can also be reduced by changes in identity contents. For example, individuals in peaceful societies have very different identity contents than individuals in the USA. In particular, identity contents such as brave, courageous, and aggressive are largely absent in peaceful societies (Bonta & Fry, 2006, pp. 183–186). Instead, individuals in these societies "define themselves as peaceful":

> For people in the most peaceful societies, avoiding violence—at least, thinking and feeling that they must avoid it—is not only real to many of them, it is defining for them. Individuals in some peaceful societies see themselves *as* peaceful, and they clearly take pride in that peacefulness, a striking contrast, in their minds, to other manifestly less peaceful societies with which they come in contact.

> For some of these societies, particularly the most highly peaceful
> ones, this very sense of definition of themselves as nonviolent is the
> most critical aspect of their worldviews. [*ibid.*, 2006, p. 180]

In addition to peaceful, other identity-bearing signifiers in peaceful
societies include nurturant, dependent, affiliative, and non-aggres-
sive, and one Malaysian tribe, the Chewong, "do not even have
words for fighting, war, aggression, or crime" (Bonta & Fry, 2006,
p. 180). Some non-violent societies also clearly embrace specific
non-violent affective–physiological and body-imagistic identity
contents as well, such as calmness, love, passivity, and compassion
(*ibid.*, pp. 180–181).

Another more benign type of identity content is one that enacts
a supraordinate self schema. The content of the androgynous or
"sensitive" man is an example. A man with such a supraordinate
identity content no longer has to be, or wants to be, "all man".
Rather, he can be, and desires to be, both "masculine" and "feminine". That is, he embraces, enacts, and in some cases even takes
pride in identity contents—such as sensitivity, tenderness, vulnerability, dependency, and passivity—that were previously identified
as "feminine" and excluded from his identity. A prime example of
the benefits provided by such a supraordinate identity content is
Gandhi, who "almost prided himself on being half man and half
woman" (Erikson, 1969, p. 402).

Twelve-step programmes promote another such supraordinate
content in their inculcation of "recovering alcoholic" (or "recovering addict") as a primary identity content. Such an identity-bearing
label helps to integrate the two warring sides of individuals who
have sought treatment for substance abuse: the part of themselves
that craves a drink or a fix and the part of themselves that hates and
fears the craving part and its behaviours and their consequences.
Identifying oneself as both recovering and alcoholic (or addict)
prevents dissociation or repression of the addictive elements of
one's self and affirms the positive sober side as well, with the
present participle ("recover*ing*" rather than "recovered" or "cured")
emphasizing the agentic and processual aspect of one's identity, as
well as its simultaneous self-efficacy (the self has the power to
recover) and vulnerability and finitude (one's agentic power is not
absolute or guaranteed).

The most effective means of shifting identity investments from malignant, antisocial to benign, prosocial contents is a fourfold approach involving:

1. reducing opportunities for enacting malignant, antisocial contents;
2. reducing recognition for malignant, antisocial contents;
3. creating opportunities for enacting benign, prosocial contents;
4. providing recognition for benign, prosocial contents,

Empirical evidence for the efficacy of steps one and two can be found in studies of negative reinforcement. The efficacy of steps three and four has been demonstrated by studies showing that engaging children in prosocial behaviours and then explicitly recognizing them as being altruistic individuals appears to promote prosocial identity contents that result in more prosocial behaviour (Eisenberg, 1995, p. 416). This strategy of feeding the benign identity contents with the material and cultural resources and opportunities necessary for enactment and recognition, while starving the malignant identity contents by withholding the psychological, social, and material resources and opportunities necessary for their enactment and recognition, simultaneously deprives malignant contents of support while reducing the need to enact them by compensating for their lost support with increased support for the benign identity contents. The strategy is based on Steele's principle of compensation, noted above, which holds that identity strength in one register or one content can make up for a lack or weakness in another register or content.

The operation of this process can be seen clearly in addictions. To begin with, both chronic and acute turning to drugs or alcohol in the first place is often a response to loss of support for another identity content. Virtually everyone has at one time or another sought and received identity support from drugs, alcohol, or food to compensate for a temporary loss of identity support experienced in a bad day at work or a dispute with a friend or loved one, and many people use such a tactic on a regular basis to compensate for a more general and diffuse deficiency of identity support that may manifest itself in anxiety or depression (Khantzian, 1999, pp. 575–576). This same principle of compensation can be seen operating in the opposite direction when people overcome their addictions by substituting other forms of identity support for those provided by the addiction. As Leon Wurmser observes, "potent meaning-giving factors can replace in highly motivated individuals the compelling role the drug exerts" (Wurmser, 1995, p. 78). There are instances, for example, in which religious conversion puts an end to drug abuse. In fact, twelve-step programmes tend to operate on much the same principle as religious conversion, providing new identity-supporting interpersonal relations, group membership and recognition, physical space, knowledge/belief systems, and identity-bearing signifiers, together with alternative affective–physiological states that may be produced by the group's dynamics and by the interpersonal relationships it establishes.

Real-world evidence of the efficacy of this method of changing identity contents on a broad, societal scale can be found in the effect of the feminist withdrawal of recognition and enactment opportunities for sexist identity contents and the creation of such opportunities for non-sexist contents: sensitivity and tenderness emerged as feasible identity contents for men, while contents such as brutishness, brutality, and dominance receded in prominence. Although the shift in investment has not been nearly as broad and deep as it needs to be, it has been significant and discernible, and this fact demonstrates the efficacy of the strategy. A renewal and extension of this effort is needed, both institutionally and interpersonally.

This same basic strategy is employed in other solutions to social symptoms as well, although it may be understood (in behaviourist terms) as providing positive reinforcement rather than alternative identity support. Big brother programmes, boys clubs, midnight basketball, and so on have beneficial personal and social effects not just because they provide positive role models, engage boys in benign activities that keep them out of trouble, or inculcate positive values, but also, and more importantly, because they provide opportunities to enact and be recognized for benign contents of identity while precluding such opportunities for malignant, violence-entailing contents. It is possible to formulate similar practices to address other social symptoms.

Similar practices might be used, for example, to promote new identity contents to prevent teenage pregnancy. In the linguistic register, this might involve providing recognition for, and opportunities to enact, identity-bearing signifiers other than woman and mother—signifiers like athlete, student, graduate, teacher, etc. It could also involve redefining, as a society, signifiers like woman and mother to involve more than just the biological functions that almost any teenage girl is capable of performing, redefining them to involve psychological, social, and economic functions as well. In the imagistic register, such an effort would mean providing opportunities for girls to develop a sense of their body beyond its function as a sex object and a reproductive organism. Sports, dance, and fashion programmes could play a significant role here.

Social symptoms such as poverty, inequality, crime, war, and terrorism can also be reduced by using one or more of the four strategies to promote an alteration of identity investments on a mass scale. For example, public recognition and valorization of actions promoting peace and equality would promote investment in the identity contents that produce these actions. One instance of such public expression would be the establishment of cabinet-level departments in government devoted to these ends. American Congressman and former presidential candidate Dennis Kucinich has advocated the establishment of a Department of Peace, and the logic of social symptoms strongly supports such a move—and the establishment of a Department of Social Justice as well. A Department of Peace would function as the inverse of the Department of Defense (formerly, and more aptly, named the Department of War), not only by forming a peace army (similar in certain ways, perhaps, to the current Peace Corps, but with much greater numbers, resources, visibility, and policy relevance) but also by providing millions of American youth with basic training in waging peace and justice. Such basic training, instead of constructing (as military training does) aggressive, violent identities around malignant affective, imagistic, and linguistic contents, would construct compassionate, beneficent identities around benign, empathic identity contents. In addition, instead of developing fighting and killing skills for enacting these violent identities, it would develop emotional and social intelligence skills such as perspective-taking and self-understanding for enacting compassionate identities. The extent to which such a programme seems Utopian, impractical, or unrealistic is directly proportionate to the degree to which we desperately need it.

Getting people to embrace alternative, benign identity contents requires the provision of enactment opportunities along with substantial recognition for embodying and enacting these contents. Two particularly powerful sources of recognition are idealized others and material recognition. Providing recognition from an idealized source is important, because if recognition comes from an individual or group that people do not look to as a primary source of recognition, there will be little incentive for them to invest in the alternative contents. This is a principle intuited by advertising and public relations experts, as well as by some educators, who have long understood that the statements and actions of athletes, recording artists, movie stars, other celebrities, and one's peers carry much more weight with many people, especially youth, than do the statements of teachers, preachers, law enforcement officers, and public officials. Hence the public service messages from athletes and other celebrities urging adolescents not to smoke, do drugs, or quit school.

Material forms of recognition are also very powerful, since they are a form of recognition from reality. Thus, any attempt to redirect social recognition would ideally include altering material compensation so that instead of providing the greatest rewards to possessors of the most malignant identity contents, as is too often the case in American society today, more benign identity contents would elicit greater material recognition.

Such a dramatic reversal of present formulas for allocating recognition is, of course, unlikely to occur any time soon, if at all. In the meantime, however, social and cultural critique can make a difference in the distribution of recognition by exposing the current regime of malignant contents and demonstrating their consequences, and at the same time illuminating socially more productive alternatives. Cultural productions, especially films and television programmes, can also contribute to such redirection through the types of identity content that get represented and hence recognized, and the context and manner in which they are presented. For example, divesting people's identities of violence-entailing contents and investing them in peaceful ones can be promoted by reducing the dissemination and celebration of gratuitous aggression in sports, films, and television programmes, as well as the more general celebration of traditional masculine identity contents (toughness, dominance, bravado, etc.). Feminists made significant inroads in this direction several decades ago, but the effort needs to be renewed.

Redefining toxic identity contents

Another basic tactic for altering identity contents is to redefine some of the malignant contents in terms of more benign qualities and behaviours. For example, altering (in light of psychoanalytic knowledge) a culture's model of a good, civilized, humane person to include, rather than exclude, negative thoughts, feelings, and impulses such as murderous hatred and "perverse" sexuality would significantly reduce the extent to which people need to repress such impulses and externalize them on to racial, ethnic, national, sexual, or economic subalterns in order to maintain their own identities. A prime candidate for such redefinition is masculinity. The prevailing definition of masculinity, as Gilligan points out, is a crucial factor in the production of violent behaviour:

> Men are honored for activity (ultimately, violent activity); and they are dishonored for passivity (or pacifism), which renders them vulnerable to the charge of being a non-man ("a wimp, a punk, and a pussy"). . . . The male gender role generates violence by exposing men to shame if they are not violent, and rewarding them with honor when they are. . . . Men . . . are taught that to want love or care from others is to be passive, dependent, unaggressive and unambitious or, in short, unmanly. . . . [Gilligan, 1996, pp. 231, 233, 237]

Given the role that this dominant definition of masculinity plays in producing violence, Gilligan concludes that "[w]e cannot think about preventing violence without a radical change in the gender roles to which men and women are subjected" (ibid., p. 233). Such change is eminently possible, Gilligan maintains: "Since culture is itself constructed, by all of us, if we want to take steps to diminish the amount of violence in our society, both physical and sexual, we can take those steps" (ibid.). Thus, to the extent that the secondary signifiers that define, and whose embodiment enacts, the master signifier man can be changed from signifiers like independent, tough, powerful, and aggressive to signifiers such as kind, caring, generous, protective, and nurturing, a person's linguistic–conceptual identity can still reside primarily in the master signifier man, but the exclusive capacity of aggressivity and violence to enact masculinity will be significantly reduced and the capacity to enact masculinity through benign, prosocial behaviours will be dramatically increased.

One of the best ways to promote such redefinitions is through messages from people (authorities, leaders, celebrities) to whom the people at issue look for recognition. Such a strategy would entail the production of messages from such individuals that said, in various ways, directly and indirectly: "Violence is not manly", "Killing someone is not a manly thing to do", "Real men don't need to kill other people, or hurt them", and conversely, "Real men care about other people", "Real men help, protect, and look after other people", "Sensitivity is masculine", "Calmness and cool [as opposed to aggressivity and violence] are masculine", and so on. In addition to direct messages of this sort, the redefinition of master signifiers in non-violent terms can also be promoted indirectly, through the actions of characters and personas in popular music, television programmes, films, and fiction.

Correlative alterations of ideal body images to redefine agency and power away from rivalry and dominance and toward resilience, flexibility, responsiveness, collaboration, and co-operation would probably reduce the need to enact collective national agency and power through economic competition and military aggression and enhance the feasibility of performing national power in the modes of co-operation and assistance. Such alteration can be promoted through increasing opportunities to enact such qualities (e.g., opportunities to sing and dance) and decreasing opportunities to enact competitive and violent qualities (e.g., opportunities to fight or struggle against other bodies), as well as the opportunity to construct and/or inhabit various surrogate bodies or bodily prosthetics involving co-operation and co-ordination with other bodies (as in painting, sculpting, cabinet making, construction, and landscaping) rather than competition and aggression towards them. Instead of enhancing their bodily integrity and agency through physical aggression and violence, people can do so through nurturing surrogate bodies, such as children and pets, and through hobbies involving construction or maintenance of houses, gardens, cars, computers, or other artefacts, machines, or appliances. Providing alternative, more benign means of enacting identity-bearing affective–physiological states, such as the rush, can also contribute to the reduction of social problems. Challenges involving struggle against inanimate objects rather than people, and requiring collaboration rather than competition, can produce such vitality affects without their negative consequences.

Such cultural interventions in identity contents can contribute significantly to the amelioration of social problems. Recognition and enactment opportunities for benign contents will reduce the need to enact malignant contents and gradually even replace malignant contents. And where such replacement may not be possible, redefinitions and redirections of malignant contents can render such contents more benign.

CHAPTER SEVEN

Decommissioning harmful defences

A second basic strategy for reducing social problems is to dissolve the defences that they rely on. Such dissolution can be promoted by developing, individually and collectively, the capacity for and habit of recognizing and exposing their operation in both individual and collective actions, attitudes, and emotions. To do so, we first need to educate people about the purpose and function of defences in general, explaining how they work to make identity more secure and how they are also often harmful and counterproductive. Second, it is important to disseminate knowledge about the sorts of elements that are typically defended against—namely, the negative qualities and passions that are embodied in every individual and group. Third, we need to help people understand how defences operate and how they can be detected—that is, how individuals' rejected impulses and qualities are unconsciously expressed and gratified in collective actions, policies, relationships, institutions, and cultural representations, including those that one does not directly cause or participate in. Finally, in addition to exposing collective defences and helping people achieve insight into their own defensive operations, defences can also be undermined by identifying and explaining the various types of social and cultural discourses, practices, institutions, and structures that facilitate and enact them.

Since it is always easier to recognize defences operating in others rather than in oneself, it is most effective to begin with examples of other individuals and groups with whom people have minimal identification (e.g., ethnically, ideologically, and/or historically distant examples), and then work through examples that are increasingly closer (historically, ideologically, ethnically, etc.) to the individuals themselves, until finally they are able to recognize the defence operating in the actions, discourses, and attitudes of their own group(s) and even perhaps of themselves individually. This final, most difficult, level of insight can be facilitated by helping people to reflect, in response to examples of the defence in others, "Have I (or has my group) ever acted in a similar way, or in such a way that someone might conclude that I was under the sway of this defence?"

Decommissioning defences should be pursued by educators, through explicit instruction about defences in high school and university humanities and social science courses. It should be prominent in media criticism, demonstrating how, for example, the content, focus, format, and structure of television, film, and other media mobilize and reinforce various defences that seriously distort users' understanding of themselves and others in ways that lead to harmful and counterproductive social attitudes and policies. Deactivating defences should also be prosecuted through public discourse wherever possible, including critical analyses of political discourse, the positions and actions of government officials, and the operations of political and social policies, practices, institutions, and structures.

Avoidant defences

Repression

An effective starting point for lifting collective repression is with commonly recognized examples of repression and the return of the repressed elements in disguised form, such as the oft repeated insight that people who are sexually repressed often express their unconscious sexual desires in disguised ways, like crusades against pornography or sexual promiscuity, which allow the crusader voyeuristic and other sexual gratifications. As this example reveals, eagerness, excitement, or zeal in activities that would not seem inherently to entail such feelings for the individual or group engaging in them can be a signal that the activities are providing gratification of repressed impulses.

Having understood the principle of repression and the nature and signs of its operation in this instance, people can then be helped to discover more socially destructive instances of it, such as the repressed aggression that pervades the USA's policies, both domestic and foreign. Our collective passion for ignorance (as Jacques Lacan phrased it) concerning the violence and brutality of our own collective actions and their consequences is one of the key instances of repression that needs to be exposed. Just as repressed sexuality is signalled by the excitement with which people respond to occasions of its disguised expression, so the disguised expression of repressed aggression is often signalled by the enthusiasm, excitement, or zeal with which people respond to the harm or misfortune of others or pursue violence against supposedly evil targets. Such responses include not only the celebrations that sometimes take place at executions, but also the more widespread and often fervent support of capital punishment, the cheering at violent action in films, the criminalization and punishment of the use of certain drugs, and punitive economic policies, including regressive taxation, declining support for education and welfare, and the refusal of universal healthcare. Helping people to recognize the aggression embodied in these social policies can help to lift our collective repression.

Other means of facilitating the lifting of repression are to give voice to common thoughts and feelings that are not openly discussed and to call out political leaders, religious leaders, educators, leading intellectuals, and other public voices who remain silent on some of the nation's most important collective thoughts, feelings, and motives. Public silence is a major facilitator of collective repression, and attending to and pointing to topics that do not get talked about at all, and to what remains unsaid when the topics are discussed, will help to undermine such collective repression. Various feminist consciousness-raising activities of the 1960s and 1970s, which spoke explicitly about impulses and feelings that most women had but that many women were largely unconscious of, are exemplary in this regard.

Denial

It is also important to expose and explain the operation of the social and cultural apparatuses that enable and enact collective denial, which works hand in hand with repression. These include, first and foremost, the numerous ways in which the media manage the news in order to enable denial by keeping unpleasant truths from public attention and awareness. A scandalous instance is the total absence from the television screen of screaming, wailing, moaning, shrieking, vomiting, bleeding, burning, and dismembered military and civilian victims of war. This grotesque omission enables the entire populace of the USA and its leaders to deny the horrendous consequences of their own action of promoting, supporting, and/or acquiescing in unnecessary and unjustifiable torture and slaughter of human beings. Pointing out this omission whenever it occurs, and countering it with graphic accounts and pictures and sounds of the unbearable human suffering that is occurring at this very moment and at every moment can help to dissolve this denial and thus reduce the facility with which the USA perpetrates horrors on its own people and the rest of the world. Here, too, calling out public figures on their silence on these issues, and pointing out the motives driving these silences, can render denial less effective, on balance, in maintaining identity.

Reaction formation

People can be introduced to reaction formation through the familiar situation from romantic films in which actors such as Cary Grant and Katherine Hepburn think they loathe each other and fight like cats and dogs until they realize they love each other. Important signals of reaction formation should also be identified, such as going out of the way to assert or demonstrate one's supposed feeling when such a manifestation is not called for, or insisting on one's feeling with more intensity than is warranted (i.e., protesting too much). When this basic understanding of reaction formation is operative, one can then move to confront social realities influenced by it—for example, recognizing that the public's violent treatment of criminals and various other minority groups may be due in part to a repressed attraction to them (a conclusion supported by the fascination many people feel for brutal athletes and film action heroes who are not very different from criminals). Similarly, asking whether professed love and concern for some groups might hide a deeper hostility toward them can help people to seek and find indications of animosity and disgust behind expressions of concern and pity for the poor and acts of charity and philanthropy toward them. Informed by such examples, people may then be helped to recognize the same defence in positions that members of their own society, including they themselves, take toward various outgroups, such as the profession of concern for the disadvantaged by people who support the very policies that create the disadvantaged.

Undoing

Undoing can be introduced and explained through the familiar example of apologizing and being especially nice or helpful to people after one has harmed them in some way, as well as through the well known metaphor of closing the barn door after the livestock have escaped. Undoing can often be pointed out as well in the same situations in which reaction formation is involved. For example, when reaction formation manifests itself as expression of concern for individuals towards whom one is really indifferent or even hostile, it is often followed with undoing, an action designed to reverse the negative consequences of one's neglect or hostility. Historical examples of such undoing include the philanthropic activities of robber barons who established libraries, universities, and foundations with money gained through ruthless, rapacious, and brutal treatment of workers, competitors, and the general public. Currently, much disaster relief functions as an undoing for public figures as well as for ordinary citizens, and this function can be made evident to people fairly easily. Examples include George W. Bush's failures of leadership in preventing the 9/11 attacks and the suffering resulting from Hurricane Katrina. Bush's attempt to undo these failures can be seen by his waging war against Osama bin Laden and Saddam Hussein after his inattention to, and neglect of, the warning signals of an imminent terrorist attack, and in his flying to New Orleans to make a show of providing assistance to the victims of Hurricane Katrina after critical days of inattention and neglect by him and his administration.

Social and cultural practices and institutions supporting undoing should also be exposed and critiqued. These include policies that lower taxes for the rich and services for the poor while touting the virtues of philanthropy, volunteerism, and "faith-based initiatives". Such policies provide a windfall for the rich while allowing them to undo their greed and rapacity through giving away a tiny portion of the wealth they have selfishly and unscrupulously accumulated. Public rituals with flags and ceremonies honouring dead and wounded military personnel also frequently serve as a means of undoing the reckless and self-indulgent decisions of those who sent them to their deaths and injuries.

Displacement

Recognition of displacement, too, can be promoted by asking people first to consider its operation in common experiences of relative insignificance. Everyone is familiar with the "kick the dog" phenomenon: hitting or kicking a non-human object when one is angry at a person—such as when a baseball player who is angry at an umpire kicks the trash can in the dugout or throws his bat against the wall. Also familiar are cases in which people who are angry at their supervisor direct their aggression at members of their family. The phenomenon of post traumatic stress disorder (PTSD) can also be usefully invoked, for it demonstrates how traumatized individuals will often displace their fear and/or anger on to an innocent third party.

From such examples it is but a small step to instances of the collective displacement of aggression that are almost as familiar. Here, one might consider the well-known fact that oppressed groups often direct their aggression not at those in power, who are responsible for the oppression, but at individuals, institutions, and properties of their own group or a subaltern group, who are both more accessible and safer targets than the real culprits. An example is rioters looting stores owned by members of their own community instead of directing their anger toward its true targets. From spontaneous displacements of this sort by informal groups one can recognize how more systematic and sustained scapegoating embodies the same process, only here operating in conjunction with projection. Historical instances of xenophobia can provide instructive examples: the German oppression of Jews, the persecution of foreign workers and immigrants in post-war Europe, and so on.

Having become familiar with displacement through such examples, people will be more capable of recognizing similar processes operating in their own country and perhaps even in their own minds—in, for example, the way many individuals in the USA blame their lack of economic prosperity on the recipients of affirmative action or, more recently, the presence of undocumented workers, rather than on corporate executives who make tens of millions of dollars per year or move jobs to other countries, or on an increasingly regressive system of taxation and the individuals who promote it. Obvious examples of displacement at the international level include George W. Bush's redirecting his aggression and that of his followers from Osama Bin Laden to Saddam Hussein, and, to a lesser extent, towards North Korea and Iran as well.

Recognizing the operation of displacement in such instances can enable people to detect its operation in other instances, such as the concern with the USA's torture policy. While such concern is certainly legitimate, it also functions to distract attention from the much greater physical and psychological torture being inflicted on the citizens of Iraq by the USA's invasion and occupation: while victims of American torture may number in the hundreds or even thousands, victims of the torture produced by the USA's military operations in Iraq number in the hundreds of thousands (Burnham, Lafta, Doocy, & Roberts, 2006, p. 1421).

Digesting such examples can prepare people, finally, to apprehend how various policies, institutions, and cultural phenomena involving suffering or aggression—including violent films, violent songs, and violent sports, as well as poverty, incarceration, war, and terrorist attacks—are displaced enactments of repressed aggression that virtually everyone harbours but does not own. Achieving such recognition requires seeking out the secret gratifications one gets from these phenomena and then discerning how the victims of these instances of violence are substitutes for the true targets of one's aggression, those who are really doing one harm or have done so in the past.

It is also useful to help people realize explicitly and fully that, since virtually everyone, as we have seen, has sustained traumatic experiences of one sort or another, we all have a reservoir of fear, anger, and aggression (Strean & Freeman, 1991) that we are seeking to enact. Since we usually do not (and often cannot) enact this rage against its true objects, we now must either sublimate it—for example, by directing it toward suffering and injustice—or displace it onto substitute objects, such as other nations, races, or groups of people to whom our nation, race, or group does harm.

Providing prosocial opportunities, channels, and expressions of sublimated anger and rage can reduce the need for displacement and other defences while giving impetus to worthy social causes. Proponents of social justice often ask, "Where's the outrage?" in response to blatant instances of injustice. The answer is that it is being directed at substitute targets, and often with unjust, destructive results. Expressing outrage, and organizing events (protests, marches, demonstrations, sit-ins) for the expression of outrage, can help redirect people's displaced anger and rage toward prosocial rather than destructive ends.

Minimizing defences

When avoidant defences are deactivated or absent, minimizing defences are often used to keep from recognizing the full significance of a threatening internal or external reality. It is, thus, important to help people develop the ability and habit of recognizing and rejecting minimization when it manifests itself in themselves and others. Intellectualization, one of the most prominent forms of minimization, can be confronted first through historical instances, such as the cold rationality with which Nazi scientists experimented on and exterminated Jews and other subalterns. People can also be led to examine more generally the lack of emotion with which government and military leaders plot the extermination of their enemies, or with which the well-to-do discuss the plight of the desolate. But, finally, people will need to recognize how they are induced into intellectualization by public discourse and the media—by every euphemistic government announcement or media report of human suffering or misfortune that presents just certain abstract facts or statistics concerning human misery without including the physical and emotional details—in the form of photos, videos, audio recordings, and vivid descriptions—of the experiences of suffering human beings. This final and crucial realization can be elicited by asking people to contemplate the lack of feeling and empathy with which they normally listen to news reports of child abuse, rape, murder, illness, hunger, poverty, and military and civilian mutilations and deaths in war. Such minimization can be diminished by continually countering the euphemisms with graphic, imagistically rich and affectively laden accounts of the human suffering that euphemism and intellectualization minimize.

Rationalization, which often operates synergistically with intellectualization to minimize the negative consequences of one's individual or collective action, must also be continually exposed and countered with the hard facts of human suffering that result from one's actions. Rationalization must also be addressed through exposing the full consequences of the actions and their hidden motives. For example, the official reasons given for the invasion of Iraq (to prevent the use of weapons of mass destruction), domestic spying (to catch terrorists), tax cuts for the wealthy (to help the economy, or "fairness"—i.e., letting people keep "their" money), and to prevent stem cell research (to preserve life) must be countered with the hidden motives and the full range of consequences involved in these policies. This is a task not only for educators at all levels, but also for the news and entertainment media, politicians, and the relevant government agencies.

Dissociative defences

Dyselaboration

Dyselaboration is a key defence in social symptoms because it prevents people from connecting social problems to their root causes and their optimal solutions. To promote recognition and understanding of dyselaboration, attention can be directed to historical failures to acknowledge the causal relations between social conditions such as poverty and inequality, on the one hand,

and the problems of violence, crime, and substance abuse on the other, or the failure during the Cold War of both the USA and the USSR to recognize how their own behaviours were important causes of the other's belligerence. Examining such a case retrospectively, in light of recently declassified documents, can throw into relief the blindness of each side concerning the causes of the other's behaviours. On the basis of such understanding, people can then be helped to recognize how their own responsibility for current social problems is similarly defended against by dissociating these problems from the deeper causes constituted by behaviours of one's own group. Examples include the failure of most Americans, including (and especially) George W. Bush, Dick Cheney, and Condoleeza Rice, to acknowledge our own contributions (spelled out in Honderich, 2002) to the conditions that led to the terrorist attacks on September 11, 2001, as well as the general failure to recognize how the USA's prosecution of the war against Iraq is an important causal factor in the continued operations of Iraqi insurgents and al-Qaeda against American personnel. Ultimately, people must be helped to recognize how their own personal failure to enquire into the causes of the actions of other groups and into the deep motives and more distant effects (including "blowback") of the actions of their own group is both a product of and a contributor to the general social and cultural defence of dissociation, which protects their identities but in doing so causes great harm.

In addition to being exposed, dyselaboration can be further undermined by education and other discourses that promote the pursuit and connecting of facts concerning all causes of a problem or phenomenon and all the effects of a practice, action, or institution, and by confronting public discourse with the facts, concrete details, and affective realities that these defences are excluding from the discourse. Such counter-discourse develops internalized cognitive scripts that seek multiple chains and levels of cause and effect for every event, action, and condition that one encounters (Bracher, 2006). The decommissioning of dissociation is, thus, simultaneously a reinforcement of rigorous, inductive, and logical thinking, and as such it contributes not only to identity development and (thereby) to social change, but also to the development of reasoning capacities and fuller understanding of complex issues.

Affectualization

While intellectualization can enable conditions and practices of profound social injustice, the same is true of the opposite defence, affectualization, which involves immersion in an affective reaction as a way to avoid recognizing both the causes of social problems, including one's own complicity in them, and potential solutions to them, including actions that one might oneself take to ameliorate them. The operation of affectualization can be made evident to people not only in the frenzy of Hitler's rallies or current demonstrations against the USA around the world, but also in the emotional responses at many political rallies in the USA today. After seeing how affectualization and its consequences operate when Islamic fundamentalist crowds chant "Death to America", Americans should be encouraged to recognize the same destructive defensive process in their own emotional responses to the attacks of 9/11: an outpouring of hatred at the expense of any reflection on the causes of such attacks or on what the most effective ways of preventing future attacks might be. One might foster a similar recognition of how affective responses to political speeches or to American military actions, victories, and losses preclude thought, reflection, and analysis.

Compartmentalization

Institutional and structural aids to dissociation should also be exposed, counteracted, and ultimately eliminated. Most notable is the bureaucratic compartmentalization of knowledge that prevents policy-makers and the general public from recognizing the full battery of causes of problems, acknowledging all the motives driving policy decisions, or encountering the full range of consequences of these decisions. Such impediments include the classification of knowledge that might prove embarrassing to policy-makers as well as inter-agency isolation and lack of communication.

Also significant are American media formats that concentrate on today's events and leave their causes and consequences out of account, separate "news" from "context" and "background", focus on political events and relegate social and cultural realities to the margins, and attend almost exclusively to events in which the USA is directly involved while largely ignoring the misery and hopelessness in which so many of the planet's inhabitants find themselves. Most serious of all is the media focus on spectacle in isolation from the rich and complex underlying reality and its sequestration of events from their multiple causes and consequences. Deactivating such dissociations can be accomplished by helping people to recognize again and again—and thus develop the capacity and habit of realizing spontaneously on their own—how the entire significance of an event or action can be transformed by learning of a single new cause or consequence: for example, learning that an act of aggression by one party was preceded by an attack from another party, or realizing that a policy touted as prudent non-intervention was followed by a Holocaust that might have been prevented.

Externalizing defences

Projection

As we have seen, projection is one of the most immediately destructive defences, functioning as an integral component of group hatred and the violence that often accompanies it. Making projection less feasible can be accomplished in several ways. First, increasing the general awareness of the mechanism of projection and helping the public at large recognize it in various situations will increase the effort necessary for people to remain unconscious of their own reliance on this defence. As with the other defences, when people are ignorant of the mechanism of projection or of what it looks like in operation, it is much easier for them to use it themselves, individually and collectively, than when they are aware of its existence and function and are familiar with its appearance. People who can see projection operating in other people will not automatically recognize it in themselves, but they will be more capable of doing so and more likely to do so. Thus, educating people about the need for enemies and other subalterns, and about the ways in which subalterns are systematically constructed to meet that need, as described in Chapter Four, can help to disable projection. A histor-

ical demonstration might show how European settlers and coloniz-
ers in Asia, Africa, and the Americas who viewed indigenous
peoples as savages were often themselves guilty of much greater
savagery than the natives. After recognizing the operation of projection in such examples, people can be enlisted in examining their
own group's current characterizations of various outgroups for
signs of projection.

Since culture facilitates projection by providing negative representations of outgroups, which establishes these groups as suitable
receptacles for the in-group's rejected elements of self, deactivating
group projections can be promoted by demonstrating that the
outgroup does not actually possess the negative qualities being
attributed to it. Sometimes, the most effective way of doing this is
to put the prejudiced people in direct contact with members of the
outgroup, as in the school integration that has been pursued in the
USA for the past half century. One of the main reasons this intervention works, when it does work, is that it succeeds in correcting
the false images that people have of the outgroup and thus reducing the opportunity for projection.

In addition, demonstrating that some of the positive attributes
(e.g., honesty, courage, intelligence, empathy, nurturance) previously thought to be possessed only by members of the in-group are
also possessed by members of the outgroup also renders the image
of the outgroup less accommodating of the projection of negative
qualities. This result can be produced through various forms of
public discourse that provide information about the history, the
achievements, the living conditions, and the subjective experiences
of targets of projection.

A third strategy for dissolving projections is to help people
recognize that certain negative qualities are just as characteristic of
members of their own group as they are of the opposing group.
Such characteristics include vengefulness, rigidity, extremism,
viciousness, hatefulness, laziness, greed, and so on. By recognizing
through historical evidence as well as current events that these and
other negative qualities previously attributed exclusively to
members of the outgroup are also possessed by some members of
the in-group, people reconstitute their own group identity in a form
that is more capacious and thus able to include the previously
rejected, projected elements and become less reliant on projection

and on the violence that is directed on to the objects receiving the projections.

These three types of awareness can also be promoted by fostering identifications in each register with members of an outgroup. Such identification can be facilitated by intergroup contact. By meeting face-to-face with members of an opposing group and sharing for a period of time all the multifarious and continuous experiences of a particular place (weather, setting, architecture, sounds, smells), members of each group achieve a certain familiarity, and even identification, with members of the other group at the level of the visual and spatial orientation constituting their body–imagistic identities. Similarly, by sharing food, drink, music, dance, and other forms of entertainment and recreation, they form provisional identifications with members of the opposing group at the level of their affective–physiological identity contents, of the same type that constitute the most fundamental and powerful components of their own group identities. In addition, through their discussions, they discover various identity-bearing signifiers (ideals, values), beliefs, and narratives that they share with members of the opposing group. The result of such recognitions is a reduction in projection and hatred directed at the other group.

Projective identification

It is not always possible to expose projection by revealing a discrepancy between one's perception of others and their reality, however. For sometimes projection operates not just on one's perception, but on the reality itself. Such an operation, known as projective identification, occurs when one unconsciously and surreptitiously manipulates other individuals or groups in ways that induce them to actually enact the negative behaviours or qualities that one has projected on to them. A historical example can be provided in the interactions between European invaders and the indigenous peoples of Asia, Africa, and the Americas: after being cheated, lied to, brutalized, and butchered, some indigenous peoples began to reciprocate the savagery to which they had been subjected, thus providing a factual basis for the European claims that these peoples were violent and dangerous. On the basis of such examples, contemporary white middle-class people might begin to see how various behaviours of their own—including the social, political, and economic structures, institutions, and policies they support—produce crime, squalor, poverty, drug addiction, and other states of being and behaviours, including terrorism, that they then excoriate and attempt to eliminate with a viciousness that can only be called savage. They can recognize, that is, the projective identification through which the dominant class or nation manipulates and coaxes its subalterns to constitute and position themselves as fitting objects of externalization for the rejected impulses and qualities of the dominant group, how their society as a whole creates the class of criminals and an underclass of unemployed, homeless, substance abusers, drug dealers, prostitutes, pimps, and "trailer trash" as receptacles and targets for the negative qualities of the majority. And also how their country, through its policies and public discourse, elicits belligerence and terrorism on the part of other countries and groups—how, for example, by accusing another nation of being a nuclear threat and thus establishing it as a potential target of American military action, the USA provokes this potential target to actually acquire nuclear weapons in order to protect itself from us.

Externalization

Externalization is more difficult to expose and decommission than projection and projective identification, because it involves the attribution of one's own negative qualities to others who actually, objectively possess these qualities prior to and apart from one's own intervention. Externalization, therefore, cannot be reduced by evidence that the negative assessment of the other is not true (as in projection), or that the negative qualities have been provoked by one's own group (as in projective identification). What must be done instead is to demonstrate how one's own group itself possesses the very qualities that it is attempting to attribute exclusively to the other group. This involves repeatedly discerning and proclaiming the ways in which, for example, George W. Bush's own statements and policy decisions manifest many of the negative qualities he attributes to "terrorists". Thus, his various domestic spying operations and the suspension of habeas corpus can be shown to demonstrate a fear, and even hatred, of freedom, his "faith-based" rejection of life-saving stem-cell research and his declaration of a "Crusade" against al-Qaeda manifest a religious fanaticism, and his prosecution of a war that has to date killed hundreds of thousands of civilians in Iraq as well as over 4,000 American soldiers (as compared with the 3,000 civilians killed by the 9/11 attacks) can be exposed as the product of his own "axis of evil": Cheney–Rumsfeld–Bush.

But while working to eliminate suitable targets of externalization and reducing the relative feasibility of externalizing defences can be very important interventions, neither of them will be able to overcome projection to a satisfactory degree unless people also come to own their rejected impulses and integrate them into their identities. For if one is unable to own the externalized impulses, it will be difficult, and in some cases impossible, to dissolve the projections or to eliminate suitable targets for them, no matter how many facts might be marshalled against the projection-distorted images of an outgroup. When the need is present, a suitable target for externalizing the rejected impulses will be either found, constructed, or imagined. This is one reason why contact with the subaltern and multi-cultural education often do not eliminate racism: the need for externalization often overrides the reality principle. It is, thus, crucial to help people recognize and own the rejected parts of themselves that they have externalized on to the subaltern. Indeed, deactivating any of the defences will be significantly enhanced by the acknowledgement and integration of the qualities that are being defended against. It is this task that the next chapter addresses.

CHAPTER EIGHT

Promoting identity integration

P romoting identity integration reduces social problems in several ways. First, the increase in the number and diversity of contents results in a more secure identity, which has less need of socially problematic behaviours to maintain itself. Integration of previously disconnected or excluded elements of the self strengthens identity not only by eliminating opposing forces through incorporation, but also by expanding, as a result of this incorporation, the repertoire of actions through which identity can be enacted and recognized.

Second, integration of rejected impulses eliminates the return of the repressed, the process by which excluded elements of the self are acted out unconsciously and often in harmful ways. Being integrated into identity deprives these forces of much of their invisibility and autonomy and puts them more under the control of conscious decision-making.

Third, integrating the self's negative qualities into identity reduces the need for externalizing and other defences that contribute to social symptoms. For example, owning one's tenderness, passive impulses, weaknesses, and vulnerabilities, eliminates the need for reaction formation, in which one attempts to demonstrate one's toughness and dominance through individual or collective violence of the physical, institutional, structural, or cultural variety. Finally, the resultant awareness and acceptance of one's own negative qualities enables one to understand, and thus respond with sympathy and assistance rather than antipathy and opposition to, the immediate perpetrators of social problems, resulting in less punitive, more productive responses to such problems. For example, owning one's desire for and enjoyment of violence renders externalization of these impulses not only less necessary but also less feasible, since it is hard to condemn someone else for qualities that one knows oneself to possess as well.

The social benefits of relieving identity of its need to defend itself against excluded elements of self can be seen in the treatment of substance abusers. Research on substance abusers reveals that such individuals often exclude affects from their identities. As Krystal and Raskin note, "Often 'having feelings' is experienced as a threat to one's adult, especially masculine identity" (Krystal & Raskin, 1970, p. 89). One of the reasons Alcoholics Anonymous is effective for many people is that it provides an environment of recognition in which individuals are encouraged to identify, acknowledge, and accept affects, impulses, and other personal qualities that they had previously rejected and/or regulated with the aid of chemical substances (Khantzian, 1999, pp. 581–597). The inclusion and integration of previously excluded elements strengthens identity not only by relieving it of the burden of defending itself against these elements but also by providing it with more contents. As one recovering alcoholic put it, "I really have started to get an identity that I never had before. I don't have to put on as many airs. I don't have to lie to people, I don't have to do anything like I used to try to create a person" (quoted in Khantzian, 1999, p. 584).

The social benefits of a reduced need for projection following integration can be seen in a study that found that individuals in a high school psychology class who increased their acceptance of previously rejected elements of their selves (through group discussions that fostered self-understanding) manifested a decrease in racist attitudes, even though racism itself was not discussed at all in the course. The study's principal investigator concluded that the reduction in prejudiced attitudes was due to a diminished need to project negative attributes that had previously been disowned (Jones, 1961, pp. 108–109). One unexpected but significant finding was that while in the experimental group both prejudiced beliefs and prejudiced attitudes ("the action-prone aspects of prejudice" [*ibid.*, p. 104]) decreased, in the control group the prejudiced beliefs declined over the course of the semester but the action-prone tendencies did not, suggesting that the reduction of prejudiced beliefs in the control group "may have been caused by uncontrolled socio-cultural pressures toward 'anti-intolerance'" (*ibid.*, p. 109). This result indicates that, in addition to applying pressures of anti-intolerance through politically correct speech codes or other cultural diversity requirements, an effective strategy for undermining racism and other forms of hate and intolerance must also help prejudiced people integrate into their own identities those disturbing qualities of their own selves that they are currently externalizing on to the objects of their intolerance and hatred. Without such integration, behaviour toward subalterns is often even more hostile after anti-prejudice admonitions than it was before, a phenomenon known as the rebound effect (Jones, 1997, pp. 194–195).

A number of psychologists have argued that such integration is also crucial for preventing terrorism. John Mack observes that it is crucial that we recognize

> that violence and hatred are not a monopoly of terrorists, but a property of mind and heart that we all share—perpetrators, retaliators, and bystanders. . . . Once we begin to look at the private aggressor or terrorist in ourselves, and at our contribution as a nation to creating the hostility of which we find ourselves to be the object, other kinds of knowing become possible. . . . Only then can we see the aggression and ignorance that underlies our dominance and neglect and perceive our own role in the creation of victims far from our own shores. [Mack, 2002, p. 181; see also Abdullah, 2002, p. 135; McCarthy, 2002, pp. 137–139; Olweean, 2002, pp. 121–122]

Acceptance and integration of rejected elements into identity can be promoted on a collective level by several types of intervention, including:

1. educating the general populace regarding the existence of rejected qualities of self, the harm resulting from their

exclusion from one's sense of self (identity), and the benefits resulting from their acceptance and integration;

2. confronting the general populace with evidence of their collective embodiment of rejected elements and of the harm done by their failure to recognize, accept, and integrate these elements;

3. modelling and testimony, by leaders and public figures, of their possession of these rejected elements, of the harm produced by their exclusion, and of the benefits of their acceptance and integration.

Education to promote awareness and understanding

Sexual impulses and fantasies

Although virtually all adults today are familiar with the idea of the unconscious, many have only a vague notion of the nature and significance of unconscious elements. When most laypersons think of unconscious contents, they think of more or less conventional sexual impulses and desires, unaware of the fact that the most significant unconscious elements for most people today are aggressive and passive impulses and desires, along with homosexual contents.

Rejection of homosexual and other "queer" sexual impulses, wishes, fantasies, and thoughts remains rampant, due largely to the cultural stigma that is still attached to non-heterosexual acts and the anxiety that follows from this stigma. This cultural stigma is fed by, and in turn feeds, a general ignorance concerning the ubiquity and naturalness of non-heterosexual thoughts and feelings. Our society needs a universal sex education that enlightens people concerning what Freud called the polymorphous perversity—which has now become known as the queerness—of all sexuality, in order to relieve individuals of the burden and consequences of rejecting their own sexual feelings, fantasies, impulses, and desires that run counter to their dominant sense of themselves as sexual beings. Once individuals understand that it is "natural" and "normal" for everyone to have thoughts, fantasies, and impulses to do things with parts of their own and/or others' bodies that they experience as being outside their comfort zones and perhaps even downright disgusting, "abnormal", "sick", or "unnatural", and that acknowledging them does not mean that one is defined by them or that one has to enact them, they will feel much less threatened by such mental contents and will be able to accept them and thus free themselves (and others) of the burdens and consequences of defending against them.

People also need to be educated that intense emotional opposition to non-heterosexuality is generally an indicator of strong non-heterosexual thoughts or feelings, a principle supported by research, cited earlier, showing that the most aggressive responses to homosexuality are produced by those heterosexual males who are most easily aroused by viewing films of male homosexual activities (Adams, Wright, & Lohr, 1996). Broad cultural acknowledgement of these facts concerning sexuality would significantly reduce not only direct verbal and physical attacks on non-heterosexual individuals, but also the various forms of cultural, institutional, and structural violence that our society currently perpetrates against them. Such knowledge should be part of a comprehensive sex-education course taken by every student. So should an understanding of the negative consequences for self and other that follow from the repression of non-heterosexual impulses and ideas. Such understanding can be fostered by the testimony of non-heterosexual individuals who have struggled with accepting their own "non-normativity", and by the presentation of cases of gay-bashing in which the perpetrators were clearly responding to a perceived threat to their own constricted, uncompromisingly heterosexual identities.

Aggressive and violent impulses

Perhaps the most crucial unconscious contents for people to become aware of and accept responsibility for are their own aggressive impulses and murderous wishes. Freud was, no doubt, correct in his assessment that human aggression "constitutes the greatest impediment to civilization" (Freud, 1930a, p. 69)—and, he might well add today, the survival of life on this planet. Thus, we have at least as much need for aggression education or violence education as we have for sex education, and it is encouraging that such education is no longer as rare in public schools as it once was. However, much more education concerning aggression and violence is needed. People need to understand that, like "perverse" sexual impulses, violent and even murderous impulses are normal, natural, and universal and that there should thus be no shame in having such impulses. It is crucial to help people realize that

> being human means that to some degree we are all murderers in the inner core of our being. . . . Whenever we feel unloved, rejected, threatened by the possible loss of someone we need desperately, we will feel intense rage. The more desperate our need for love and the more vulnerable we feel, the more we will hate. Since none of us can feel loved all the time, all of us [have such feelings and thus] are potential murderers. [Strean & Freeman, 1991, pp. 262, 12]

When we realize that

> we are all potential murderers—[that] the difference between a Hinckley who really tries to kill the President of the United States and a depressed, jealous lover who sits in his room and just fantasies killing his rival, is a matter of degree . . . we will be much more understanding of and empathic toward the one who actually murders his parents, [realizing that] he is not all that different from everyone else except that his early life has been more tormenting and more traumatic. [ibid., pp. 37, 156]

Such a realization that everyone harbours murderous feelings and impulses, Strean and Freeman point out, enables people to become more accepting of both themselves and others (ibid., p. 267), and such acceptance, if widespread, will lead to a reduction in cultural, institutional, and structural violence, as well as interpersonal physical violence.

People also need to be educated that acknowledging and integrating such impulses into their sense of self does not mean they have a duty, or even a licence, to enact them. On the contrary, they should be helped to understand that such acceptance makes it less likely that they will act out their violent impulses either directly, in the form of physical violence, or indirectly, in the form of cultural, institutional, or structural violence directed toward various societal subalterns. For when one recognizes that one harbours in oneself the same urges to and capacity for aggression and violence that one condemns in others, one comes to realize, as Hannah Arendt put it, "that in one form or another men must assume responsibility for all crimes committed by men and that all nations share the onus of evil committed by all others" (Arendt, 1945, p. 2111). Such recognition that being human entails harbouring evil, murderous impulses

> is the only guarantee that one "superior race" after another may not feel obligated to follow the "natural law" of the right of the powerful, and exterminate "inferior races unworthy of survival"; so that at the end of an "imperialistic age" we should find ourselves in a stage which would make the Nazis look like crude precursors of future political methods. [*ibid.*]

Only individuals who have integrated their own capacity for evil into their sense of themselves are capable of resisting the externalizing operations underwriting crimes against humanity.

> Upon them and only upon them, who are filled with a genuine fear of the inescapable guilt of the human race, can there be any reliance when it comes to fighting fearlessly, uncompromisingly, everywhere against the incalculable evil that men are capable of bringing about. [*ibid.*, p. 2112]

Feelings and wishes of tenderness, passivity, and dependency

A third major category of rejected elements contributing to social problems includes feelings of tenderness and impulses of passivity and dependency, which for many men conflict with important identity contents such as toughness, independence, strength, and dominance. As with other excluded elements of self, the general populace needs to be educated concerning the fact that everyone has such feelings and wishes and that there is no shame in this fact. Feminist and other critiques of gender have made significant contributions to educating the public in this regard. New forms of manhood such as the sensitive man, the vulnerable man, the metrosexual man, and the androgynous man have reduced the stigma attached to dependency, passivity, tenderness, and gentleness in men. However, the prominence of counterphobic behaviour in public as well as in private makes it clear that much remains to be done in the area of public education and cultural transformation. Such changes can be furthered by informing people of examples such as the murderer, described by Gilligan, who engaged in violence because of the shame he felt regarding his wish to be taken care of by his mother. People's attention can also be directed to less catastrophic examples of the bravado and belligerence that are often clearly efforts to compensate for underlying feelings of weakness, passivity, or dependency that the belligerents are afraid to own and integrate into their identities. Children provide ready examples of such shaky bluster, as do characters in many film and television comedies. From such examples one can move to somewhat less obvious instances of the excessive bravado sometimes exhibited by military personnel, politicians, and government officials, and to the recognition that much risk-taking and belligerent behaviour is a counterphobic response to feelings of fear and/or rejected desires to flee or seek protection in the arms of a stronger party.

Contemporary and historical examples can also be provided of how unconscious wishes for passivity and dependency lead people to submit to various totalitarian regimes, such as fascist governments, violent gangs, and fundamentalist religious sects and cults, which then often collectively act out their counterphobic defences on scapegoated individuals and groups. Such examples can be used to help people understand that dependency on others, and hence the need and wish to submit to the norms of some group, are universal and must be met, and that the rejection of these needs often results in their being pursued surreptitiously, and defended against in ways that are harmful to oneself as well as to others.

Confrontation to promote acceptance

Education concerning the existence, the nature, and the "normalness" of these types of rejected elements of self will significantly reduce resistance to them by removing the stigma attached to them, and education about the negative consequences of leaving them unintegrated into identity will motivate people to acknowledge them as part of themselves. To fully own and accept such a rejected quality of self, however, most people must encounter compelling evidence that they themselves actually possess this quality and that its rejection is more harmful to their identity than its integration would be. The most effective confrontations are often those produced in individual psychotherapeutic treatment, in which individuals encounter convincing evidence, in the form of either their transferential interactions with their therapist or their self-defeating behaviours outside of treatment, of the presence of such rejected qualities in themselves and the harm that results from the rejection. Collective confrontation can also be effective, however. Such confrontation can take several forms, including historical analysis and analysis and critique of contemporary social and cultural phenomena. And such analyses can occur in several venues, including education, the media, religious institutions, and political discourse and policy making.

Historical analysis can be very effective in helping individuals admit negative qualities into the collective aspects of their identities, whence they can gradually come to greater personal acceptance of these qualities as part of their individual identities as well. De-idealizing, critical histories of a nation or ethnic group, by exposing the negative elements of people's collective past self, can pave the way for people to recognize and accept similar negative qualities in their contemporary collective self and, in some cases, in their individual self as well. American history, both distant and recent, is rife with manifestations of the most inhuman and evil of qualities, beginning with Columbus's barbaric and sadistic treatment of indigenous peoples of the New World—such as cutting off the hands of Indians who failed to provide him with gold and letting them bleed to death (Zinn, 1995, p. 4)—and including the subsequent genocide of North American peoples, the enslavement and brutalization (including starvation, whipping, rape, and murder) of millions of Africans, and more recent wartime atrocities, such as the use of atomic bombs in Japan and the firebombing of German population centres during the Second World War, the My Lai massacre during the Vietnam War, and the torturing of prisoners at Abu Ghraib, Guantanamo, and various secret sites around the world during the War on Terrorism.

Analysis of contemporary social phenomena can also contribute significantly to helping people recognize and accept negative qualities in themselves. Social analyses such as those presented in Parts II and III of this book can help people to recognize the ways in which their own political attitudes, positions, and actions involve various forms of aggression and violence towards other groups, as well as the identity needs that motivate these actions and the negative consequences that follow from them. The exultation of the public at large upon news of the death or suffering of a Public Enemy, such as Saddam Hussein, Fidel Castro, or the criminal celebrity *du jour*, should be offered as evidence that we have the same hateful feelings and violent and sadistic impulses that we tend to recognize only in our enemies. Educators, public intellectuals, and other culture workers need to confront the general public with the fact that when we condemn another individual or group, we are often ourselves harbouring the very quality we are condemning (Strean & Freeman, 1991, p. 93). People should also be helped to recall instances in which they have hoped for, or rejoiced in, the suffering of another human being. When people realize that "when [they] hear about a murderer, rarely do [they] want to understand what drove him to murder; more often [they] wish to kill him" (Strean & Freeman, 1991, p. 244), they are face to face with their own murderous impulses.

Concerning the presence of wishes for passivity and dependency, various mass movements and behaviours, both historical and contemporary, can be brought forward. The attraction and submission to strong leaders is one powerful piece of evidence for the presence of such wishes in the selves of many Americans. Confronting people with this phenomenon, in the form of blind submission to religious figures, real and mythic, who tell people what to think and what to do, political leaders who tell them whom to hate and invade, and cultural leaders who tell them what to buy, can help people discern these same wishes in themselves, in so far as they can recognize their own participation in such phenomena. Crowd behaviour provides another, related type of evidence for the presence of passive and submissive wishes: anyone who has ever felt ecstatic, gratified, or even merely comfortable being caught up in the collective emotions, thoughts, and behaviour of sports events, concerts, rallies, religious ceremonies, demonstrations, marches, or riots has experienced, and should be able to acknowledge and own, the existence in him- or herself of the wish to be passive or submissive to a stronger force.

The most powerful evidence that people have unconscious non-normative sexual wishes, fantasies, and impulses, which then produce aggressive behaviours towards non-heterosexual individuals and groups, is constituted by the aggression itself. The fact that this aggression is caused by the presence of such unconscious impulses is not widely recognized; most people who express such aggression believe that they do so not because they themselves have "perverse" or non-heterosexual impulses or fantasies that they find extremely threatening, but, rather, because they have beliefs or values that condemn such impulses in others. It is, thus, necessary to confront people with evidence that something besides their beliefs and values is motivating their aggression. Such evidence can be found in the fact that other violations of their beliefs and values—including more serious ones—do not elicit from them the same visceral intensity, hatred, and violence. Examples include crimes of theft, robbery, and even assault—not to mention cutthroat business and labour practices—that cause great human harm and suffering yet elicit less intense aversion, less strident denunciation, and less frequent and intense violence than do non-normative sexual identities and behaviours.

One of the most direct routes to recognizing rejected qualities of the collective self is through popular culture. Helping people examine their attraction and responses to films, television programmes, music, and sports can enable them to recognize much about their unconscious impulses, wishes, and fears. Popular culture, like all culture, is a mechanism for enacting, being recognized for, defending, and/or rejecting various elements of self. One major function of popular culture is to enable disguised enactment of unconscious impulses and wishes. Thus, directing people's attention to their emotional reactions to specific types and elements of music, films, or sports events can help them become aware of their rejected elements of self. The presence of emotion indicates that identity is in some way at stake in the situation, and the particular emotion indicates how the situation is experienced as bearing upon identity. Thus, being attracted to a particular cultural experience, such as a certain type of film or a particular sport, and having positive emotions in relation to it, indicate that the experience functions to enact, elicit recognition for, and/or defend some aspect of one's identity. Such defence can include sublimation: unconsciously enacting or rehearsing, in a disguised, socially acceptable form, rejected elements of self that would otherwise threaten identity.

Many cultural experiences provide such disguised gratification of unconscious wishes (Holland, 1975). War films and sports events, for example, engage viewers' aggressive and violent impulses as well as their fantasies of dependency and subordination to a more powerful force (in this case, the group). Confronting the general public, through media commentaries as well as public education, with their enjoyment of such spectacles, can help them to recognize and accept their own aggressive and violent impulses as well as their passive and dependency wishes. Helping people to enquire, "Why is there so much violence in sports, a violence obviously appealing to millions who look forward eagerly to watching their team destroy another team as if it were a fight to the death?" and "What does a baseball game mean to me personally that I sink into a depression because the Mets don't win?" (Strean & Freeman, 1991, p. 253) can help them come to recognize that, in competing in sports either directly (as players) or vicariously (as fans), they "both avenge themselves for past hurts and discharge the hatred and murderous fantasies they have endured many times in life when they felt like losers" (ibid., p. 252). Similarly, teachers, media critics, and other culture workers and public intellectuals can help people reflect on their attraction to, and enjoyment of, violent films and televisions programmes and to come to recognize that a "very strong part of [themselves] exults in the act of murder as [they] identify with the killer . . . [as the killer] acts out the revenge within [their own] hearts" (ibid., p. 38).

Feelings of aversion to certain kinds of cultural experiences also provide evidence of unconscious, rejected elements of self with which to confront people. Many men are averse to sad, sentimental movies, as well as to "chick flicks" that elicit tender, romantic feelings, because such feelings threaten their sense of self. Helping men to focus on the feelings such movies elicit can help them to reclaim these rejected parts of their selves. The same is true of homoerotic movies. Men can be confronted with the evidence mentioned earlier that the men who are most stridently anti-gay exhibit the greatest sexual arousal when exposed to gay male pornographic images. Men can be reassured that having such feelings is "normal" and that the harm of such impulses comes not from having them but from repressing them and externalizing them. Then they can be asked to recall instances when they have experienced anxiety or aversion when encountering representations of non-heterosexual eroticism and to reflect on the possible causes of such aversion. Claims that their aversion is due to the "immoral" or "unnatural" nature of homosexual acts can be countered by pointing out that they fail to experience the same aversion to other acts that are equally or more "immoral" or "unnatural."

Modelling integration

In addition to education and confrontation concerning rejected elements of self, modelling the process and struggles of integration can also be effective in promoting it among the general public. Well known examples of such modelling include the testimonies of recovering addicts in the meetings of twelve-step programmes, the testimonies and biographies of saints, religious leaders, celebrities, convicted felons, and other individuals detailing their struggles to acknowledge troubling parts of themselves, and novelistic accounts of integration achieved by certain literary characters. Women have been aided immensely in recent decades by "strong women" role models, both real and fictional, who have embraced their culturally proscribed sexual and aggressive impulses and integrated them productively into their identities as women. Men today can receive similar assistance from masculine celebrities and stereotypes (athletes, soldiers, policemen, firemen, etc.) who embrace feelings of tenderness, weakness, dependency, vulnerability, and so on. Indeed, for a time in the second half of the twentieth century, the figure of the male antihero in literature and film served such a purpose for a small minority of individuals. Individuals of both sexes can benefit from models of recognizing and accepting murderous impulses and feelings of rage and hate, as well as testimonies of the respective consequences of failed and successful integration.

*   *   *

Integrative activities such as those described here can have several effects of considerable social value beyond their benefits to people at risk for criminal behaviour, substance abuse, or teenage pregnancy. By helping the perpetrators of all types of violence—which means virtually everyone in our society—integrate previously excluded elements of self, such activities reduce the need for them to maintain their identities through various types of violence, including punitive and unfair social institutions and structures and the production or promotion of harmful cultural forces. In addition, such integration can help the majority of people who are not the immediate perpetrators of first-order social problems to understand how the immediate perpetrators are at the mercy of unconscious identity needs that led them to ruin. Such understanding on the part of the empowered is fostered, first, by their newly acquired experience of having similarly been the pawns of their own uninte-grated elements of self, and second, by their newly acquired under-standing of the types of identity needs that are likely to be motivating the disempowered in their various destructive and self-destructive behaviours. People with such understanding, in turn, are more likely to support the types of social and political actions that are necessary to solve these problems. As Abdullah notes,

> To defuse the terrorist, we must understand the mind of the terror-ist. To understand the mind of the "other," we must understand our own mind. The seeds of terrorism lie within each of us. . . . To stare terrorism in the face is to look in the mirror. [Abdullah, 2002, p. 135]

The same is true for all other social symptoms as well. We can take a major step toward the solution of our major social problems by helping everyone to realize this fact.

CHAPTER NINE

Promoting more inclusive identity structures

I dentity integration both produces and is facilitated by more complex and inclusive identity structures. Developing such structures requires three types of experience, Kegan notes. The key experience is that of a frustration or crisis that can be resolved only through the development of a more inclusive structure. At the same time, however, ongoing support must be available to identity as it abandons its old structure and develops the new one. And third, opportunities to engage in modes of cognition and affect that bridge or combine the old and the new, more complex and inclusive structures are often necessary as well. Each of these functions can be performed by social realities, cultural artefacts, and various types of intervention. We can promote structural development by making sure that cultural support for each of these three functions is available for each of the four stages of transition to a more inclusive structure.

Support for identity structures

In order for people to develop more inclusive structures, the frustration they experience in their current structure must not threaten their sense of self to the point that they revert to even simpler structures in order to maintain their identities. To prevent such regression, they must experience adequate support for their currently structured identity even as they are moving (usually unwittingly) into a more complex, inclusive, and adequate structure. A basic task for anyone who wants to promote structural development of identities is thus to make certain that the individuals involved have this support in adequate measure.

One quite fundamental and ubiquitous form of support is language. In addition to supporting impulsive identity through its expressive function, language supports the imperial, ongoing self through the permanence of its substantives (nouns) and through verb tenses denoting ongoing states of being as well as past and future states. It supports the interpersonal form of identity by establishing the permanence of other beings and of our relationships with them, in so far as it allows us to name them and hence make them present to ourselves and thus sustain our relationship to them even in their absence. Furthermore, it helps to sustain institutional, systemic identity by positioning individuals in relation to networks of relationships, or systems. Even interindividual identity structures are supported by language, in so far as language provides the medium for conceptualizing this position (e.g., "universal love", "global village", "world community", "love for humanity", "generativity", and so on). Literacy, and subsequently printing, further enhance each of these functions by rendering specific utterances of language permanent and accessible to anyone at any time.

Painting, sculpture, and architecture also serve to support each of the various identity structures. The permanence of visual and spatial artefacts such as cave paintings and of Greek statues may have helped to construct and support an imperial identity structure (i.e., an ongoing sense of self) out of the pulsations of the impulsive self, which are themselves supported through the expressive functions of art. Monuments like the Roman emperors' tombs and the Egyptian pyramids not only serve as permanent visual reminders of the continuous identities of their occupants, but also summon the subjects of these empires to enact an ongoing relationship to these rulers and, by extension, their empires, thus enacting not only imperial but also interpersonal and institutional/systemic forms of identity.

Music, too, provides major support for all structures, sustaining the impulsive through its expressive dimension, enacting the imperial through its melodic lines, the interpersonal through its harmonic dimensions, and the systemic through symphonic complexities, both synchronic and diachronic. The affective resonance it provides and enacts is both a model and sometimes a facilitator of interindividual empathy that transcends systemic identity differences.

Sports also provide support of each identity structure for both participants and spectators. Impulsive identities are sustained through opportunities in sports for spontaneous physical action expressing the feelings and impulses of the moment. But sports also offer multiple opportunities for enacting an imperial self, in the form of perseverance in training ranging from a few seconds (e.g., doing one more repetition in weight training) to many years (e.g., training for a high school, college, or professional athletic career), as well as in the form of executing a game plan or a career strategy instead of just acting impulsively. The interpersonal bonds formed between athletes, between athletes and coaches, and between fans and athletes sustain the corresponding identity structure, while the institutional structure is supported through identification with a team and putting the interests of the team (e.g., winning) ahead of one's own individual concerns (e.g., personal statistics). Sports even provide support for the interindividual identity structure, in those moments when players and fans recognize the humanity of members of the opposing team, a recognition that occurs outside the framework of the game, such as when an opposing player is seriously injured.

One of the richest cultural resources for enacting the various identity structures is literature, including films and television programmes. Support for the impulsive structure is found in genres in which impulsive and expressive actions and discrete events overshadow plot, character, relationships, and thematic concerns. Such genres include certain types of animated cartoons, video games, action films, situation comedies, stand-up comedy, and pornography. These genres offer audiences the opportunity to identify with highly impulsive, expressive, and self-indulgent characters, such as Shakespeare's Falstaff, *Sesame Street*'s Cookie Monster, and *Seinfeld*'s Kramer, and they sometimes offer thematic reinforcement of the impulsive structure as well, through themes such as *carpe diem*.

The imperial structure is supported by literary genres that focus on the pursuit of goals, including the goal of attaining or enacting a certain identity. These include *Bildungsromanen* such as *David Copperfield* or rags-to-riches Horatio Alger novels, tales of the sustained efforts and repeated accomplishments of military and sports heroes, detective novels and police dramas in which the investigators' perseverance and endurance solve the crime, and other narratives with themes of commitment, steadfastness, integrity, duty, anticipation, and planning, ranging from *The Odyssey* to the story of Jesus' death and resurrection, to revenge novels such as *The Count of Monte Cristo*.

Genres supporting the interpersonal identity structure include those that focus on and valorize interpersonal relationships, including romantic films, buddy films, romance novels, and Shakespeare's romantic comedies. The protagonists of these identity-defining relationships can range from devoted lovers or fast friends, on the one hand, to friendly competitors, intense rivals, and even bitter foes or sworn enemies, on the other hand. Themes and values of love and fidelity dominate in such stories, which sometimes express quite explicitly the notion that nothing else matters besides the other's devotion and presence, as suggested by the title of John Dryden's play about Anthony and Cleopatra: *All for Love, or The World Well Lost*.

The institutional, or systemic, identity structure is supported by stories with a broad social panorama and/or long historical view, in which the fate of a group or society is equally or more important than that of an individual or a couple. Such stories often present multiple interacting characters and plots that emphasize the extent to which each action, event, and character are inextricably interwoven with other, sometimes quite distant (chronologically and/or geographically) actions, events, and characters. Clear examples include stories such as Virgil's *Aeneid*, in which national leaders, military commanders, prophets, religious leaders, or other champions of the collective see the big picture—the entire system—and act to maximize the good of the collective. Themes include patriotism, nationalism, and self-sacrifice.

Support for the interindividual identity structure can be found in narratives with empathic, compassionate protagonists operating with an inter-systemic social, historical, environmental, or cosmological perspective and emphasizing the fundamental sameness of all individuals and groups, sympathy for all people, and transcultural understanding and co-operation. Characters such as Atticus in *To Kill a Mockingbird*, Jim Casy and (later) Tom Joad in *The Grapes of Wrath*, the socialist orator in *The Jungle*, and the transformed Bigger Thomas at the end of *Native Son* provide cultural models for readers to emulate as they try to enact this most inclusive of identity structures.

People who are immersed in a rich array of cultural resources such as these that provide multiple and readily available support for each identity structure will be more likely to have the structural security necessity to develop the more inclusive and complex structures, including, ultimately, the interindividual structure.

Frustration of simpler structures

For such development to occur, however, the simpler, narrower structures must encounter frustrations and impasses. Such impediments are present in certain domains of the social order itself, but achieving optimal frustration in certain crucial domains requires specific cultural interventions as well.

Social realities challenging simpler structures

Even the simplest form of social life frustrates impulsively and imperially structured identities. Traditional societies, as Kegan points out, demand identities that have developed beyond the atomistic structure of the impulsive stage through the temporally continuous structure of the imperial stage to the trans-categorical structure of the interpersonal stage. To function in a traditional society, that is, a person's identity must reside not in a multiplicity of discrete impulses, or even in an ongoing awareness of oneself and others as enduring entities, but rather in a sense of oneself as a function of one's role in relation to other people—roles immortalized in surnames (e.g., baker, tailor, farmer, carpenter, smith, carter, wheelwright, etc.).

In traditional social orders, one can function perfectly well without going beyond this level of complexity. Modernity, however, confronts the interpersonal identity structure of traditional orders with a crisis: it demands that individuals occupy multiple social roles and integrate the often quite diverse values and dispositions associated with those roles. To meet this demand, identity must take the form not of a role or relationship, but, rather, of a system that organizes the variegated roles, values, and dispositions a person must enact, adjudicates among their competing claims, and integrates them into a reasonably coherent and continuous mode of being.

The postmodern, global world, in turn, confronts modernity with a crisis of its own: the need to adjudicate among competing systems—in order, for example, to work co-operatively with individuals and groups whose group identities and systematic beliefs are significantly different from one's own. Postmodern life thus demands that people move the foundation of their identities up yet another level, from a particular system to a position supraordinate to all systems that constitutes a vantage point for comprehending, comparing, and judging multiple systems of cultural meaning, social organization, or governance.

Cultural challenges to narrower structures

Specific cultural phenomena and artefacts can also challenge or frustrate simpler identity structures in a number of ways. First, they can involve people in situations in which the simpler structure proves inadequate. Sports, for example, can confront people with the inadequacy of the impulsive structure by providing experiences in which following one's impulses and breaking training make it more difficult in subsequent performances to gratify these impulses. The same is true of impulsive behaviours during competition, which can result in penalties and other negative consequences. In addition, while an imperial identity structure is more effective than an impulsive one, athletes who operate with an imperial structure and focus more on their own personal performance than on the team's success often suffer personally in the form of team failure and loss of respect from team-mates.

Similarly, cautionary tales such as those found in fables, myths, proverbs, parables, and novels depict the destructive consequences of impulsive actions or imperial pride and self-aggrandizement, as well as interpersonally defined identities. Examples of the latter include Dante's treatment of Paolo and Francesca, the film *Elvira Madigan*'s depiction of the social expulsion and eventual starvation and suicide of the romantic couple who spurn the rest of the world and live only in each other, and *Madame Bovary*'s portrayal of the consequences of living impulsively, imperially, and interpersonally, in complete disregard of the long-term personal and interpersonal consequences of such an orientation or its harm to other individuals outside the romantic couple.

History, too, demonstrates the harm that can be produced by impulsive, imperial, interpersonal, and systemic identity structures, whether it be the impulsive actions or self-aggrandizing obsessions of generals or heads of state, or their interpersonal loyalties and animosities, or even their systemically structured identities of patriotism or nationalism.

The operation of simply structured identities can also be impeded by authoritative cultural forces declaring them unacceptable. Notable instances include religious and legal proscriptions of impulses such as lust, violence, and covetousness; of imperial identity qualities such as pride, selfishness, and ruthless self-aggrandizement; and of interpersonal allegiances that override loyalty to the group, such as nepotism and aiding and abetting a felon. In addition, cultural artefacts can block the enactment of more simply structured identities by being constructed in such a way that they cannot be comprehended or enjoyed by such identities, thus motivating the development of more adequate, complex structures. For example, characters motivated by interpersonal, institutional, or interindividual identity needs frustrate readers whose identities are primarily impulsive or imperial. The absence of attractive characters with impulsive or imperial identities can also encourage readers and viewers to assume a more complex identity structure.

Such impediments do not succeed in moving most people to the most inclusive identity structure, however. The reason is not only because it is difficult to do so, but also because impulses, personal agendas, interpersonal relationships, and participation in groups and systems remain essential components even of interindividually structured identities and are thus always capable of becoming the totality of one's sense of self when one's internal or external circumstances fail either to demand or to provide adequate resources for enacting a more complex and inclusive identity structure. Indeed, each of the structures in various ways depends upon or presupposes each of the others, so that it is never a question of leaving a particular orientation behind but, rather, as Kegan (1982, 1994) puts it, coming to *have* the simpler structures rather than *being* them. Thus the identity structure one operates with can vary dramatically according to social context and psychological circumstances, and most adults operate as each of the five structures at different times.

While various social and cultural factors can provide sufficient frustration and challenge of simpler structures in some domains, in other domains such forces are largely absent, and hence many adults can quite easily operate in these domains out of a simpler, more restrictive identity when in fact a more complex and inclusive structure is necessary. This is particularly the case regarding most of the social problems we have been discussing in this book. Many people, for example, when they take political positions on drug addiction, poverty, or violent crime, operate out of an impulsive identity (a visceral aversion to the individuals involved in these problems), an imperial identity (rigid adherence to certain moral principles), or an interpersonal identity structure (regarding these others as personal enemies), rather than through either a systemic identity, which would enable them to see the full array of causes of these problematic behaviours and the complete picture of the consequences of specific policies regarding such behaviours, or an interindividual structure, which would reveal the perpetrating others as fully human individuals whose behaviours make perfect sense given their formative backgrounds and present circumstances. The same is true of international relations such as war. George W. Bush's War on Terrorism, for example, is largely a product of an impulsive structure (aggression deriving from fear, humiliation, anger, and hatred), an imperial structure (blind and arrogant American unilateralism), and an interpersonal structure (Bush's desire both to avenge and vindicate, and also to surpass, his father by invading Baghdad and toppling Saddam Hussein).

Interventions

What is needed, then, are specific interventions precisely in the domains of these social problems that will

1. stymie the operation of the simpler, narrower identity structures in these domains, by confronting people with information or implications concerning the harm produced by the actions or conclusions derived from these structures;
2. script the cognitive activities that stymie enactment of the simpler, narrower identities in these contexts by modelling and reflexively describing, explaining, and advocating these cognitive activities, which include searching for the negative effects and cognitive distortions produced by the narrower identity structures;
3. demonstrate to people the general inadequacy of their simpler, more restrictive identity structures for dealing with social problems;
4. criticize the more restrictive structures on the basis of specific identity contents, such as fairness, generosity, intelligence, and so on.

Such interventions can be variously performed by the media, education, cultural commentary and analysis, and political and cultural leaders.

Anger management, for example, helps individuals develop the capacity to refrain from impulsively lashing out at a noxious stimulus by first taking a slow, deep breath or slowly counting to ten and then consciously identifying several different potential responses and asking, "What will be the consequences if I do this, and how will I feel then?" Such a process extends one's sense of self, or identity, beyond the immediate present and into the (proximal or distal) future; or, rather, it makes one's future sense of self part of one's present sense of self and thus prevents or at least moderates the harmful behaviour that the immediately present, impulsive sense of self is inclined to as a means to maintain itself.

A similar temporal extension of identity is promoted by twelve-step programmes, in which alcoholics and addicts are taught to resist the impulses of the moment by focusing on the relatively short-term (and hence more easily attainable) future state of pride in the accomplishment of making it through the day without giving in to the impulse of the moment (the "one day at a time" approach), and their keeping count of how many days (or weeks, months, or years) they have remained sober develops greater extension of their identity or sense of self into the past. Thus whenever they experience the impulse to drink, instead of being composed entirely of this impulse, their sense of self will comprise their (actual) past and (anticipated and wished for) future state of sobriety and the pride—heightened sense of self—that is its result.

Collective operations of the impulsive structure can be similarly stymied by providing information about the negative consequences of impulsive actions, such as the human and financial costs of the War on Terrorism (hundreds of thousands of deaths and injuries, trillions of dollars) or by asking questions that cause people to contemplate the future consequences of impulsive actions. Simply asking the question, "Where will this action lead?" can introduce anticipation and thus substitute an imperial identity structure for an impulsive one for the issue at hand. Posing more specific questions such as "What obstacles might this action encounter?" or "What undesirable, negative consequences might result from indulging in such behaviour?" can be even more effective in getting people to extend their sense of self beyond the present moment. Such questions need to posed consistently and vigorously by the media, by educators, by public officials, and by other leaders.

Frustrating the imperial identity can be achieved by confronting people with the impossibility of absolute independence, the unavoidability of other people, and the inevitability of dealing with them, as well as with the harm done to others—and often to oneself as well—when one operates in single-minded pursuit of one's own aims. People can be confronted with the inevitability of engaging with other people simply by asking them who is likely to be affected by a particular imperial project—such as policies aiming to reduce crime, substance abuse, welfare spending, or terrorist threats—and what the experience of these various others is likely to be. The issue can be pressed by providing accounts of innocent victims of such policies and practices, such as the parents, siblings, spouses, and children of incarcerated substance abusers or of targets of federal terrorist investigations (not to mention the abusers and targets themselves), or presenting stories and videos of dead and mutilated veterans or civilians and their families who have suffered their fates as the result of the imperial identity of a president and populace determined to "stay the course" in an imperialist war. News reports of the Vietnam War, complete with photos and film of wounded and dead soldiers and civilians, performed this function effectively; similar reports have been conspicuously absent—and systematically repressed by the Bush administration, with the collusion of the media—during the present wars in Iraq and Afghanistan.

Confronting people with information concerning the harm done to themselves by such actions and policies can be an even more effective means of frustrating the operation of their imperial identity. Examples include the tremendous financial cost as well as the severe reduction of the USA's prestige and influence around the world resulting from its imperial unilateralism in the War in Iraq and elsewhere, the increase in violence resulting from the criminalization of drug use and the severe punishment of criminals, and the climate change and other looming environmental disasters resulting from the imperial expansion of industry in the single-minded pursuit of immediate wealth. An effective intervention of this sort in the latter issue is Al Gore's film *An Inconvenient Truth*, which graphically demonstrates the self-destructive consequences of this instance of collective imperial identity operation.

The interpersonal identity structure can be impeded by evidence of the harm caused by promoting the welfare of one's personal friends and family at the expense of society as a whole, as well as the impasse that arises when one is caught between competing loyalties. An example is the cronyism and personal loyalty that characterized the Bush administration, where personal relationships trumped the greater social welfare, as exemplified in Bush's praise of FEMA director Brown ("Heckuva job, Brownie!") in the midst of Brown's disastrous mismanagement of the federal response to Hurricane Katrina, Bush's awarding the Presidential Medal of Freedom to outgoing CIA Director George Tenant in the wake of Tenant's providing a false intelligence cover for the administration's case for invading Iraq, and Bush's stubborn support of his egregiously incompetent and dishonest Attorney General, Alberto Gonzales. Being confronted with the cost of such interpersonal loyalties to their own country and the rest of the world, as well as to Bush himself, can prompt American citizens (if not Bush himself) to seek and demand a firmer and broader foundation for public policy than the interpersonal identity structure. In addition, continually introducing, through education, the media, and other public discourse, a broad social perspective incorporating the needs and concerns of multiple others to whom one can relate interpersonally can produce an impasse of conflicting loyalties that can be resolved only by shifting one's identity to a systemic/institutional structure.

Harmful operations of the institutional/systemic identity structure can be stymied by confrontation with another, alternative system that challenges people's identification with their current system. One form of such a confrontation is to challenge people to explain the superiority of their nation, religion, political system, ethnicity, or culture *vis-à-vis* specific alternatives. Efforts to produce such an explanation can then be scrutinized to reveal the absence within these systems themselves of grounds for such a defence, as well as the spontaneous evocation, in producing such a defence, of grounds transcending the specific system (nation, religion, etc.) itself—grounds relating to human suffering and flourishing and thus involving an interindividual identity structure.

Another form of challenge to a systemic identity is the encounter with people having different religious beliefs, political convictions, food preferences or eating habits, and so on. Sustained engagement with such others will separate many people from their own systemic identities by demonstrating both the inability of such identities to provide a basis for interacting with such others and the existence within oneself of a more fundamental and inclusive form of identity, the interindividual structure, which is the basis upon which one is able to relate to others who are operating out of a different systemic identity.

Confronting people with the human suffering and injustice produced by systems with which they have identified can also be effective in moving them beyond their systemic identities. Historically, this function has been performed powerfully by novels. By confronting her white readers with what she called "the real presence of distress" (Stowe, 1852, p. 76) in her slave characters, Harriet Beecher Stowe helped these readers move beyond their identification with the American system of slavery. Upton Sinclair and John

Steinbeck used accounts of the suffering of immigrant labourers in *The Jungle* and displaced Oklahoma farmers in *The Grapes of Wrath*, respectively, to a similar effect with regard to the American economic and political system, as well as its underlying social Darwinist ideology of *laissez-faire* capitalism. Such narratives are particularly effective when they elicit identification with individuals from an opposing group or system, for in such identifications readers enact and demonstrate the existence of an identity structure more fundamental and inclusive than their systemic/institutional identity—namely, the interindividual identity. What is lacking in America today, and desperately needed, are similar widely read novels that expose the enormous human costs of the identity-bearing economic, political, ideological, and religious systems of "the American way of life".

Bridges to more inclusive structures

Cultural models

In addition to stymieing the operations of the narrower structures while maintaining support for identity, another means of promoting more inclusive and complex structures is to provide "bridges" from a narrower to a more inclusive structure. One of the simplest bridges is a cultural representation of the movement from one structure to the next. Cultures sometimes model these transitions in the struggles of heroes that people are encouraged to emulate. Such representations provide a significant motivation to attain the more complex structure, in the form of the implicit but powerful recognition they embody of the struggle and the attainment. The heroes of Homer's epics, for example, model the struggle to overcome the impulsive self and establish an imperial and then an interpersonal identity. According to Bruno Snell (1953) and Julian Jaynes (1976), the identities of the ancient Greeks tended to be less integrated than our own, with the Greeks experiencing their impulses as autonomous, divine forces in relation to which they were largely powerless. The movement from this disjointed sense of self (impulsive identity) to a more or less continuous and unified sense of self (imperial identity) was long and arduous, and is both modelled and chronicled in Homer's epics. *The Iliad*'s account of the Trojan war models the subordination of the impulsive self's violent impulses to the imperial identity's long-term purpose of defeating Troy. And in the representation of Achilles' relationship to Patroclus (and more specifically in Achilles' forsaking battle to mourn Patroclus's death), *The Iliad* also models the supersession of imperial identity by the more complex interpersonal structure of identity.

The Odyssey presents the same struggle of imperial identity to overcome the impulsive self in the form of the various temptations (Circe, the Sirens, the Lotus Eaters) that Odysseus must resist in order to stay the course back to Ithaca. And the epic's audiences vicariously experience the subordination of this imperial dimension of identity to an interpersonally defined identity embodied in Odysseus's devotion to his ultimate goal of being reunited with Penelope. This same structure of identity is also modelled by Penelope, in her steadfast resistance of the suitors for a period of twenty years.

In Virgil's *Aeneid*, the hero transcends not only the impulsive and imperial dimensions of identity but the interpersonal dimension as well. The Roman Empire required subjects who derived their sense of self from their identification with the entire social system rather than simply with their interpersonal relationships or their personal tasks or goals. Aeneas models this institutional or systemic identity by renouncing his love for Queen Dido and leading his people onward in pursuit of their collective destiny, the founding of Rome.

Religion offers models of more complex identities as well. It does so, on the one hand, in the form of the actions it commands: "Love thy neighbour as thyself" admonishes the hearer to leave behind the simpler impulsive and individualist/imperial forms of identity and assume an interpersonal form, and "Love thine enemy" urges the listener to transcend the interpersonal and even the institutional identity structure (in so far as it refers to group enemies as well as personal ones) and take on an interindividual form of identity in which one identifies with the whole of humanity. Religion also offers numerous examples of figures—gods, saints, prophets, disciples—who have assumed the more complex identity structures. The story of Jesus, for example, inspires believers to transcend, as Jesus did, not only their impulses and personal ambitions but also their interpersonal relations (Jesus urged his listeners to leave their families and follow him) and even their insti-tutional/systemic identities (Jesus' refusal to become King of the Jews) and embrace an identity that includes within itself the entirety of humanity ("the kingdom of God").

Philosophy, too, models these identity structures. Hegelian philosophy, for example, describes an inevitable progress from the simplest, most limited forms of being to the most complex and inclusive. Moral philosophers such as Lawrence Kohlberg (1980), Peter Singer (1985, 2004), and Richard Rorty (1999) describe moral progress as a widening of one's circle of care, and epistemologists and psychologists such as William Perry (1999) and Robert Kegan (1982) articulate the models upon which our present discussion is based.

In the social realm, more complex structures of identity are modelled by famous people of all sorts. Any leaders (political, reli-gious, intellectual, military), entertainers, celebrities, athletes, or wealthy individuals who (a) embody the American Dream, (b) engage in philanthropy, (c) work for social justice, and (d) work to humanize rather than demonize, aid rather than harm, opposing groups function as models, respectively, of (a) imperial, (b) inter-personal, (c) institutional/systemic) and (d) interindividual forms of identity.

More complex structures as means to enact simpler ones

Another type of bridge between two structures is the presentation of the more complex structure as a means of maintaining or enhanc-ing the more simply structured identity. Thus, the imperial struc-ture can be presented as a means of gratifying one's impulses. For example, athletes who may pursue football or hockey because they enjoy gratifying their aggressive impulses learn that the imperial structure that enables them to put in the long hours of training that result in such gratification is a superior means of maintaining their impulsive self. Through being enacted more and more, and receiv-ing recognition from others, the imperial structure may gradually eclipse the impulsive structure, even though impulse gratification may remain an important part of one's identity.

The interpersonal structure, similarly, can be presented as a means for realizing one's imperial aims or enacting one's roles.

Athletes often come to realize that their individual performances can be enhanced by close interpersonal relationships with teammates both on and off the court or field. Through such sustained co-operation with others, the relationship can gradually become an end in itself—and the framework of one's sense of self—rather than merely an instrument for the realization of one's projects. This same transition can be seen working in many other domains besides athletics, including academics and interracial and international relations.

A systemic or institutional identity structure can, in turn, manifest itself as a means for maintaining interpersonal identity, such as when marriage or community involvement is entered into as a way to secure one's interpersonal relationships with one's romantic partner and one's children.

Additionally, today, the trans-systemic, interindividual structure is increasingly revealing itself as the only means of maintaining certain systems, and even life itself. Thus, surviving and prospering as a nation, as an ethnic group, as a religious group, and even as the species homo sapiens is increasingly recognized as being dependent upon our entering into co-operative relationships with other nations, ethnic groups, religious groups, and species. Emphasizing this interdependency, and pointing out at every turn its many manifestations—environmental, economic, political, social, and cultural—is one powerful way to promote the development of the interindividual structure.

Content bridges

Finally, some identity contents require certain structures for their enactment, and therefore foregrounding, advocating, and providing recognition for these contents can contribute significantly to the development of their corresponding structures. This is most obvious in the case of identity-bearing signifiers, all of which entail at least an imperial structure, in so far as they designate an ongoing quality and not just a momentary impulse. But some specific signifiers entail more complex structures as well. Thus, "loyal" and "partner" entail at least an interpersonal structure, "patriot" and "team player" entail an institutional structure, and "kind" and "compassionate" point to an interindividual structure.

Promoting such signifiers thus also promotes the development of the corresponding identity structure.

Identity-bearing knowledge and belief systems as such entail at least the rudiments of an institutional, systemic structure, but the particular content of knowledge or belief can entail other structures, including even the impulsive (as in hedonistic beliefs) and imperialist (as in social Darwinism). Knowledge of the basic sameness of all humans despite their differences, as well as the (religious or ethical) belief in universal values or in the right of every human being to be treated with respect and love, and as an end and not a means, promote development of the interindividual structure.

All scripts and narratives entail at least an imperial structure, since they both represent and establish the continuing being of objects, characters, and actions through time. But narratives can also potentiate, and summon their readers or bearers to enact, interpersonal, institutional, and interindividual identities. They can do so in several ways. First, by presenting a particular identity structure as the endpoint, goal, or culmination of a series of actions or chain of events, a narrative can present a more inclusive and complex identity structure as the logical entailment or natural development of a simpler, more restrictive structure. Such narratives constitute the heart of novels such as *The Jungle* (Sinclair, 1906), *The Grapes of Wrath* (Steinbeck, 1939), *Native Son* (Wright, 1940), and *Invisible Man* (Ellison, 1952), whose protagonists begin with primarily impulsive and imperial identities and then evolve, out of necessity, to various degrees of interindividual structure.

Second, narratives and smaller scripts can promote structural development by engaging their readers or bearers in enacting the behaviours that constitute the higher structures. In the treatment of Attention Deficit/Hyperactivity Disorder (ADHD), children learn simple scripts to follow that enable them, for example, to remember their homework and to complete it on time, thus enacting the imperial structure in the academic domain. Proverbs provide similar scripts for adults, articulating prescriptions and proscriptions for specific behaviours that, when followed, enact a surmounting of impulses and a consolidation of imperial identity in particular domains of life. Thus, "Haste makes waste", and "A stitch in time saves nine", cue individuals to transcend their impulses (the impulses to act and to remain inactive, respectively). Other examples of

such prescriptions and proscriptions include the ten command-
ments, which variously direct their adherents to transcend the
impulsive and the imperial structures by either enacting or avoiding particular behaviours (e.g., to honour one's parents and the
Hebrew god, and to refrain from killing, stealing, and fornicating).
All the various forms of the golden rule operate in the same
manner: they provide a general prescription for behaviour that,
when followed, enacts the interindividual identity structure.
Promoting the embodiment and internalization of such signifiers,
knowledge systems, and scripts, by providing opportunities for
their repeated rehearsal and enactment, can contribute significantly
to the development of the more complex and inclusive identity
structures in all domains of life.

Even affective–physiological identity contents can entail certain
identity structures. Most notably, the empathic impulse—which, as
we will see in the next chapter, is arguably the most primal of all
impulses—enacts at a prereflective level the interindividual identity
structure. Here, in the reflexive empathy that we are born with, we
find the chief instance of what Erikson called the "resources for
peace even in our 'animal nature'" (Erikson, 1964, p. 230): the
inborn, affective–physiological basis for the most inclusive of identity structures. And recognizing, modelling, and providing opportunities for the enactment of empathy, along with the other identity
contents entailing interindividuality, can contribute significantly to
the development of this identity structure as well as key prosocial
identity contents, and hence to the amelioration of our most serious
social problems.

The identity development imperative

T he exposition to this point has shown how social problems are symptoms of the identity issues of their immediate perpetrators, how these identity issues are themselves the consequences of various social and cultural forces, and how these forces are, in turn, the product of the identity issues of "normal, law-abiding citizens", whose identities have themselves been rendered vulnerable or deficient by many of these same social and cultural forces. The previous four chapters have sketched out strategies of social and cultural identity interventions that could significantly reduce the social symptoms by removing or reducing the identity issues that give rise to them. I will conclude by explaining why societies should pursue a vigorous and systematic project of identity support and development such as the one I have outlined here. There are four fundamental reasons.

1. Providing identity support and development is the best, and ultimately the only, way to solve our most serious social problems.
2. Social justice requires optimal identity support and development opportunities for everyone.

3.   Morality—our own and that of other people—requires that we protect ourselves and each other from identity damage and insecurity and promote identity development, because consistently moral behaviour is possible only on the foundation of a secure and adequately developed identity.
4.   Our own individual, personal fulfilment requires helping others achieve optimal identity security and development.

The practical imperative

That supporting and developing identity is the most effective way of solving the social problems we have discussed is a basic conclusion to be drawn from the evidence presented in Part II of this book, where we saw how the behaviours constituting these problems were motivated primarily by the need to defend, maintain, or enhance a threatened, damaged, or deficient identity. Another body of evidence pointing to this same conclusion comes from interventions that have been successful in preventing or reducing these problems. Analysis of successful interventions reveals that they all involve one or more operations on identity, including:

1.   undermining malignant identity contents (by withholding recognition and enactment opportunities);
2.   supporting benign identity contents (with recognition and enactment opportunities);
3.   undermining harmful defences;
4.   promoting integration of identity components;
5.   promoting structure development.

That socially destructive behaviours can be prevented by providing adequate identity support, and that this identity support can take numerous different forms, is evident from the findings of research into the multiple factors that have been found to prevent violent and other delinquent behaviour among children and adolescents who have been exposed to significant doses of the traumatizing, identity-damaging experiences discussed in Chapter Five. These preventive factors (summarized in Dryfoos, 1990, pp. 228ff.; Garbarino, 1999, pp. 150–176; Lerner, 1994, pp. 68–72) include:

1. a sense of deeper meaning or purpose for life;
2. authentic self-esteem;
3. positive values;
4. androgyny;
5. constructive coping strategies;
6. an ability to seek out social support from outside the family;
7. the capacity to respond actively rather than passively;
8. intelligence;
9. positive relationships;
10. social stability;
11. economic equality.

These factors are of two basic types: personal qualities and capacities, and social and cultural conditions. Consider first the personal factors.

1. A sense of deeper meaning or purpose for life, which Garbarino identifies as one of the most significant protective factors, is a kind of definition of identity itself: it is precisely the sense of oneself as a force that matters in the world. It is often based on an implicit institutional or systemic recognition of central identity components by an Other (society, nature, god, reality). Religious people, for example, get profound identity support from the belief that the ultimate force in the universe made them, and perhaps watches them, responds to them, and even loves them. If the ultimate force in the universe takes one's own ongoing being-in-the-world into account, then that being must matter a lot. A similar implicit recognition is experienced by those who define a purpose (usually less cosmic) for themselves, such as social change, community building, teaching, or child rearing, which is one reason why some troubled adolescents are able to turn their lives around when they have children. Any activities or situations that provide, or offer, opportunities to develop meaning or purpose will provide identity support and thus help to prevent violence and other social symptoms.

2. Authentic self-esteem is correlated with a reduced tendency to violence because *authentic* self-esteem is an indication that identity is already strong. As discussed in Appendix II, self-esteem is not coterminous with identity. A severe superego, for example, can result in low self-esteem even when one's identity as a whole—that is, one's ongoing sense of oneself as a force in the world—is fairly strong and secure. And deficient reality testing can, conversely, produce an illusory sense of one's own significance. Authentic self-esteem, however, is positively correlated with secure identity, a sense that one's existence matters, which results in a reduced propensity to violence and other antisocial behaviours. Such self-esteem results from agency and accomplishment, which accrue recognition from reality.

3. *Positive values* reduce one's propensity to perpetrate social problems because they are identity-bearing signifiers the performance of which requires behaviour that is prosocial rather than antisocial. Moreover, the very fact that society has deemed certain qualities to be positive and valuable means that whoever embodies or enacts these qualities automatically experiences the tacit recognition of her society, together with the approval of her superego, the internalized representative of society. In so far as a society successfully inculcates values such as honesty, responsibility, and compassion, it contributes to this mode of recognition and identity support.

4. *Androgyny* is associated with a reduced propensity to violence and other antisocial behaviours because it involves a larger and more diverse set of identity contents than either masculinity or femininity by itself. Moreover, for boys, androgyny includes a group of ("feminine") identity contents that entail non-violence. To the extent that a boy is androgynous, he is freed from the tyranny of the violence-entailing masculine identity components that are prominent in each register of a more narrowly masculine identity. For a boy who is androgynous, the master signifier "man" either does not have the same prominence as it does for boys who are not androgynous, or, if it is prominent, it is not defined for him as tough, dominant, and unfeeling. Androgyny usually also means that the boy's body–imagistic identity accords less prominence to a sense of bodily agency involving brute force, size, or domination and greater prominence to grace, co-ordination, and aesthetic sensibility. And, in the affective–physiological register, an androgynous boy will in all likelihood accord less centrality to vitality affects such as anger and rage. What these differences mean is that such boys can receive recognition for identity contents that do not entail aggression to the same degree that the contents of traditionally masculine boys do.

5. *Constructive coping strategies* are, by definition, capacities to maintain one's identity—one's sense of oneself as an ongoing force that matters in the world. Since identity vulnerability is a major cause of antisocial behaviour, the capacity to protect and maintain one's identity would inevitably lessen one's inclination to such behaviour. In addition, the successful coping that results from these strategies enhances one's sense of agency, one's ability to make things happen, which involves a tacit recognition by reality itself.

6. *An ability to seek out social support from outside the family* is a specific coping strategy. This ability, when acted upon, not only supports identity by enacting agency, it also results in the attainment of various forms of identity-supporting recognition, as well as resources and opportunities to develop and enact positive identity contents. Just being involved or connected with other people constitutes a tacit recognition of one's existence, and to the extent that these others manifest interest in one's activities, skills, or attributes, concern for one's problems or general welfare, or reliance upon one's activities, they are providing significant identity-supporting recognition. Since such social support helps to maintain one's identity, the ability to find such support leads to a reduction in identity vulnerability and hence also in socially harmful behaviours.

7. *The capacity to respond actively rather than passively* is correlated with reduced propensity to harmful behaviours because it, too, is an essential component of a relatively strong identity: it is the capacity for agency, which produces recognition from reality. It is based on the conviction that one's intentions can be acted upon and that these actions will make a difference in reality, including the reality of one's own situation and of others' responses.

8. *Intelligence* overlaps with a number of the previous factors. In the first place, it is related to coping strategies, in so far as it allows one to cope more effectively (or, alternatively, one could say that effective coping strategies are themselves a type of intelligence). Similarly, intelligence increases one's capacity to elicit social support (or alternatively, we could say that such an ability is itself "social intelligence"). Intelligence is also related to one's capacity to integrate the various components of one's identity and to the complexity of one's identity structure. And intelligence often elicits identity-supporting recognition in and of itself, as well as

providing the means for performing all sorts of identity contents, particularly in the linguistic register—for example, constructing a purpose for one's life and conceiving a strategy for realizing that purpose.

Just as these protective personal qualities all entail some form of identity support, so, too, the major environmental factors that have been identified as protective against antisocial behaviour can be seen to have this effect, because they provide significant identity support in one or more forms: they provide recognition (direct or indirect, express or tacit) and/or opportunities and resources for developing or enacting benign identity contents.

9. *Positive relationships* constitute one of the most powerful protections against antisocial behaviour. As Garbarino observes, "Being the center of someone's universe is hard to beat as a resilience factor" (Garbarino, 1999, p. 164). Being at the centre of someone's universe supports identity by providing the richest and most direct and powerful form of identity-establishing and identity-supporting recognition: cherishment (Young-Bruehl & Bethelard, 2002).

10. *Social stability* is protective for similar reasons. It supports identity first of all by providing an enduring context replete with all forms of recognition: direct, express interpersonal recognition; tacit interpersonal recognition; and various forms of structural, institutional, and cultural recognition in relation to which each register of identity can engage in an ongoing enactment of a repertoire of contents. A stable social situation provides multiple stable linguistic contents to enact, opportunities to enact them, and multiple sources of recognition for their enactment. It also provides ongoing resources and opportunities for the productive performance of positive body–imagistic identity components (recreational facilities, fashion, grooming materials and techniques, familiar buildings, public places, and personal spaces) and affective–physiological components (restaurants, concerts, movies, recreation).

11. *Economic equality* supports identity by providing a powerful structural and institutional recognition of the worth of anyone who has such equality—an effect diametrically opposed to that of poverty, which, as we saw in Chapter Five, sends an equally powerful message that one is ultimately unworthy or deficient. Economic equality also supports one's identity by eliciting interpersonal

recognition: people who are economically established receive much more positive attention than people who are not. In addition, money enables one to procure and enact linguistic identity contents (signifiers), by purchasing material goods attached to particular labels (brand name, social class, etc.), and to procure and perform most other identity contents as well, including certain modes of enjoyment or other affects, via specific types of food, drink, entertainment, and sexual activity (affective–physiological identity contents), as well as a particular body regime involving one's appearance and sense of bodily integrity and agency, via clothes, exercise, nutrition, health care, body prosthetics, and even surrogate bodies (body–imagistic identity contents).

The fact that each preventive factor for socially harmful behaviours contributes in one way or another to identity security constitutes strong evidence that the best way—indeed, the only way—to solve our most serious social problems is to more effectively promote identity security and development. And this means providing the material, social, and cultural conditions that (a) promote the development of benign identity contents and structures and (b) provide optimum opportunities to enact and be recognized for these identity contents.

The social justice imperative

A second reason that promoting identity security and development is imperative is that it is a prerequisite for social justice. As political philosophers Axel Honneth and Emmanuel Renault have recently argued, the essence of social justice is the provision of all individuals with adequate resources and opportunities for optimal identity development. Personal identity-formation, in Honneth's view, is the ultimate good, the ultimate goal: "the purpose of social equality is to enable the personal identity-formation of all members of society; . . . enabling individual self-realization constitutes the real aim of the equal treatment of all subjects in our societies" (Fraser & Honneth, 2003, p. 177). Since identity maintenance is a fundamental human need, it follows that being deprived of adequate means for developing and maintaining one's identity is a profound injustice. "The justice or well-being of a society", Honneth contends, "is

proportionate to its ability to secure conditions of mutual recognition under which personal identity-formation . . . can proceed
adequately" (*ibid.*, p. 174).

Renault makes the same basic argument. It is our personal identity, he observes, that gives our life its value. "Our identity", he
says, "is the ensemble of characteristics that, for us, constitute our
essence . . . [and,] we believe, . . . the value of our life" (Renault,
2004b, p. 78). The most fundamental right is the right to demand an
identity, and this right is the foundation of justice (Renault, 2004a,
pp. 276–277). Renault maintains that "the concept of a positive relation to one's self", which entails personal identity, "constitutes the
centre of the normative conception of justice and the good life"
(*ibid.* p. 359).

Since optimal identity-formation requires adequate recognition,
both Honneth and Renault focus on recognition as the key to social
justice. Honneth argues,

> Subjects as it were deserve the amount of social recognition
> required for successful identity-formation. [I]ndividual identity-
> formation generally takes place through stages of internalizing
> socially standardized recognition responses . . . and the disappear-
> ance of such relations of recognition results in experiences of disre-
> spect or humiliation that cannot fail to have damaging
> consequences for the individual's identity-formation. [Fraser &
> Honneth, 2003, p. 173]

Given this understanding of social justice and a just society as
providing everyone with recognition that is equal, valorizing, satisfying, and non-alienating, it follows that social justice requires "the
transformation of the entirety of the institutional conditions (material and symbolic) that structure the denial of recognition" (Renault,
2004a, p. 210). But while Honneth and Renault emphasize the
central role of recognition in social justice, it is clear from their arguments that recognition is important only because it is crucial to the
formation and maintenance of identity. Recognition is simply a
means to the end of identity maintenance, which is the primary
value. Moreover, as Renault points out, lack of recognition is not, in
and of itself, unjust; it is unjust only in so far as it affects one's
psycho–physical integrity, the heart of one's personal identity
(Renault, 2004a, p. 360). Social justice is, therefore, a function not of

recognition *per se* but, rather, of all the social factors—of which recognition is but one, albeit probably the most obvious and important one—that affect an individual's ability to develop and maintain a secure identity. It follows that a society is just to the extent that it provides its members with equal resources and opportunities for the optimal development and maintenance of their identities, and it is unjust to the extent that it impedes optimal identity development, damages identities, threatens identities, or withholds resources and opportunities for enactment or recognition of benign identity contents. What this means is that anyone who is committed to social justice is also necessarily committed to the establishment of social conditions that foster optimal identity development and maintenance for everyone.

The moral imperative

Providing everyone with adequate means and opportunity to develop a secure, well-integrated and structured identity is also a moral imperative. In addition to being an end in itself, moral behaviour is a prerequisite for solving social problems and producing social justice. Solving social problems requires moral behaviour on the part of those who are now committing crimes and engaging in other antisocial behaviours. And producing social justice requires moral behaviour on the part of those in power, who are primarily responsible for the social, economic, political, and cultural realities in which everyone else attempts to survive and flourish. More specifically, those who demand moral behaviour from others (e.g., from criminals) have the moral obligation of providing these others with the means and opportunity to develop and maintain a secure identity. As Renault points out, it is unrealistic, hypocritical, and immoral to demand moral behaviour from individuals who lack the capacity for such behaviour (Renault, 2004b, p. 25). Moreover, the moral behaviour required in each instance itself requires a relatively secure and integrated identity.

Recent work from various disciplines points to identity, or one's sense of self, as the key to moral action. From the perspective of the understanding of identity developed in the preceding chapters, of course, these findings are to be expected, since identity maintenance is the fundamental motivation of every behaviour. But the dominant view of morality has been that it involves not an expression, but a repression of identity and a submission to an external moral injunction, such as the golden rule. As Zygmunt Bauman explains, much of modernity, from Kant onward, has operated with the assumption that morality requires the overriding of irrational impulses. But it is not the case that morality is a product of socialization that overrides all the impulses of the self. Rather, it is only because of the existence of the moral impulse as a primal given and a universal feature of human subjectivity that any sociality (and hence, subsequently, socialization) is even possible (Bauman, 1993, pp. 1–15, 34–36). As Bauman explains,

> Moral impulses . . . supply the raw material of sociality and of commitment to others in which all social orders are molded. . . . [M]oral responsibility—being *for* the Other before one can be *with* the Other—is the first reality of the self, a starting point rather than a product of society. . . . [T]here is no self before the moral self, morality being the ultimate, non-determined presence. [Bauman, 1993, p. 13]

It is only on the basis of the moral self that moral behaviour and social justice exist. Social justice is nothing more and nothing less than the extension of the primal impulse of the moral self to include others beyond the interpersonal dyad. Following Lévinas, Bauman maintains that social justice arises

> not from the demands of the Other, but from the moral impulse and concern of the moral self which assumes the responsibility for justice being done. . . . [I]t is that moral impulse which makes justice necessary: it resorts to justice in the name of self-preservation. [Bauman, 1997, pp. 224, 235]

Thus, Bauman argues,

> the key to a problem as large as social justice lies in a problem as (ostensibly) small scale as the primal moral act of taking up responsibility for the Other nearby, within reach. . . . It is here that moral sensitivity is born and gains strength, until it grows strong enough to carry the burden of responsibility for any instance of human suffering and misery [in the entire world]. [*ibid.*, pp. 243–244]

The fact that "we are not moral thanks to society . . . [but rather] *are* society, thanks to being moral" (Bauman, 1993, p. 61), means that our fate depends on the moral capacities of persons and not on the various ethical codes and legal prescriptions and proscriptions on human behaviour. This fact, in turn, means that the modern effort to supplant the irrational, emotional individual moral self with universal codes of behaviour is extremely dangerous (*ibid.*, p. 12). The moral self is the only force that can prevent the murderous treatment of the other when such treatment is legitimized by laws and ethical codes, as has been the case for many human atrocities throughout history, including the Inquisition, slavery, and the Holocaust (*ibid.*, pp. 35, 239, 249–250).

That the moral self, rather than systems of ethics, is the primary cause of moral action is demonstrated by research into the motives of altruistic and help-giving individuals, including, most notably, individuals who risked their lives and fortunes helping Jews escape the Holocaust. Kristen Monroe's extensive interviews with rescuers revealed that these individuals rarely acted on the basis of moral values, ethical principles, or religious beliefs. Indeed, many of them never even considered such questions before acting. They simply acted because the situation they were faced with seemed to offer no alternative, and they felt compelled to act as they did in rescuing potential victims from the Holocaust (Monroe, 1996, 2004). Moral exemplars studied by Colby and Damon exhibited this same quality:

> Time and again we found our moral exemplars acting spontaneously, out of great certainty, with little fear, doubt, or agonized reflection. They performed their moral actions spontaneously, as if they had no choice in the matter. In fact, the sense that they lacked a choice is precisely what many of the exemplars reported. [Colby & Damon, 1992, p. 303]

Findings such as these led Monroe to conclude that moral action is primarily a function of an individual's identity, or sense of self:

> Ethical political action emanates primarily from one's sense of self in relation to others. . . . The prime force behind ethical acts is not conscious choice but rather deep-seated intuitions, predispositions, and habitual patterns of behaviour related to our central identity.

> ... Our actions in situations that tap into ethical concerns are moti-
> vated more by our sense of self than by any conscious calculus.
> [Monroe, 1996, pp. 218–220]

Monroe explains that acting morally is felt to be the only possible
course of action because it is the only way of maintaining one's
identity:

> Certain situations present choices that affirm or deny one's basic
> perception of self in relation to others. As a general rule, ethical
> political behaviour flows naturally from this core perspective. To
> pursue an action that deviates in any significant regard from this
> necessitates a personal shift in identity that can occur only at great
> psychological cost and upheaval for the actor. [*ibid.*, p. 217]

Other research on moral action has reached the same basic conclusion. Augusto Blasi concludes that moral action is motivated by
the need for self-consistency, and that acting otherwise would constitute "a fracture with the very core of the self" (Blasi, 1983, p. 201).

Moral responsibility, upon which rest the possibilities for social
justice and the amelioration of our most serious social problems,
thus itself derives from the nature and particular features of individuals' identities. These features include the presence of particular
prosocial identity contents, the absence of certain defences, and the
achievement of a certain degree of self-integration and inclusiveness
of others within one's sense of self. Significant identity contents
include not only one's values and ideals, but also one's world view,
self-concept, and identity-bearing affects. Monroe emphasizes the
concept of a shared humanity and a world view in which all people
are one as key identity contents of Holocaust rescuers (Monroe,
1996, pp. 197–198, 202, 204, 216–217). Certain affects are also key to
the moral impulse, including those involved in moral indignation
and anger, as well as those present in sympathy and compassion.

People's defensive organizations, too, are crucial determinants
of the type and degree of moral behaviour they are capable of.
People with significant dissociative or externalizing defences will
never recognize the harmful effects of their actions, particularly
when those effects are not immediate and tangible. Yet, it is
precisely such recognition that has become increasingly necessary
as a basis for moral action. Modern technology has enormously

increased the reach of human action, both temporally and spatially, and as a result, we need to be able to anticipate the distant and long-term consequences that our motives and actions might produce (Bauman, 1993, pp. 217ff.).

In addition to dissociation among motives, actions, and consequences, there is another major type of dissociation that undermines moral action. This is the sequestration of morality as such from social, political, commercial, and economic motives, actions, and their consequences. This dissociation, so prominent in ideologies such as *Realpolitik* and social Darwinism, has allowed actions, practices, and policies causing terrible human suffering and monstrous injustices to proceed unchecked by the moral self (Bauman, 1993, p. 219, 1997, pp. 226–229). The moral impulse is allowed expression only in "the well-spaced and short-lived public rituals of collective empathy with other people's collective calamities" (Bauman, 1993, p. 243), such as providing relief for victims of natural disasters, and is inactive in all personal and collective decisions and actions that fail to prevent or ameliorate structural and institutional oppression.

A final identity factor that is crucial for moral behaviour is an inclusive structure—ideally, the interindividual structure. An ethics adequate to the postmodern condition, according to Bauman, is "one that readmits the Other as neighbor . . . into the hard core of the moral self" (*ibid.*, p. 84), and this is truly the case only with the interindividual identity structure. Erikson, too, argues that ethics requires "a more inclusive human identity", and he declares that "a truly universal ethics, such as has been prepared in the world religions, in humanism, and by some philosophers," requires "a species-wide identity" (Erikson, 1964, p. 242), which recognizes "the responsibility of each individual for the potentialities of all generations and of all generations for each individual" (*ibid.*, p. 157) and which "makes every child conceived a subject of universal responsibility" (*ibid.*, p. 238). "Ethics . . . cannot be fabricated", Erikson warns. "They can only emerge from an informed and inspired search for a more inclusive identity" (*ibid.*, p. 242). The kind of ethics demanded by the postmodern condition thus requires the most inclusive of identities, the interindividual identity, which, in the words of the Upanishads, "sees all beings in [one's] own self and [one's] own self in all beings" (*ibid.*, p. 221).

The self-fulfilment imperative: care and generativity

Finally, in addition to being necessary for promoting moral action, providing social justice, and solving social problems, promoting the identity development of others is also necessary for one's own ultimate fulfilment. Jacques Lacan touches on this point when he suggests that the moral impulse is a primal quality of subjectivity similar to "that search for an archaic . . . quality of indefinable pleasure which animates unconscious instinct" (Lacan, 1986, p. 42). But this point is developed most fully in Erikson's notion of generativity, which refers to "the instinctual power behind various forms of caring" (Erikson, 1964, p. 131) and derives from the infant's earliest responses to being recognized and affirmed by a caregiver (*ibid.*, p. 231). Generativity manifests itself as the need to be needed (*ibid.*, p. 130), the need to be of use to others, and its paradigmatic instance is found in the parent–child dyad, where the parent's gratification and fulfilment are a function of the help he or she is able to give the child:

> a parent dealing with a child will be strengthened in *his* vitality, in *his* sense of identity, and in *his* readiness for ethical action by the very ministrations by means of which he secures to the child vitality, future identity, and eventual readiness for ethical action. [*ibid.*, p. 232]

But generativity extends far beyond the care for one's own children; it "potentially extends to whatever a [person] generates and leaves behind, creates and produces" and ultimately involves "a universal sense of generative responsibility toward all human beings" (*ibid.*, p. 131).

Such generativity, as Don Browning notes, dramatically alters "the relationship between self and society, between the public and the private," such that one's "innermost private satisfaction and the outermost public relevance are found in one and the same reality—the individual confirmation that rebounds to [one] from the recognition and affirmation of that which [one] has generated" (Browning, 1973, p. 146). When one is operating out of an interindividual identity structure, one's greatest fulfilment is to be found in those actions that contribute most to the well being of others. And since, as we have seen, people's well-being ultimately depends, in multiple ways, on the degree of identity security they and everyone else have achieved, the most fulfilling actions are those that contribute most to the identity development and security of others.

Thus, even a purely self-interested approach to life will, if pursued in an enlightened and rigorous manner, lead one to engage in actions that support and develop the identities of others and thereby promote moral action, enhance social justice, and reduce social problems. Maintaining one's sense of self, or identity, requires taking care of others, and maintaining one's fullest sense of self, one's interindividual identity, requires promoting the security and development of all other identities, present and future. For an interindividual identity, the vicious circle of social problems described in the introduction becomes a beneficent, self-reinforcing circle of generativity, social justice, and social problem resolution, as shown in Figure 5.

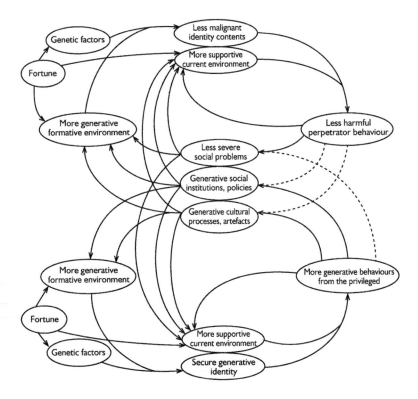

Figure 5. The circle of generativity.

Psychological symptoms as expressions of identity needs

Concerning the nature of psychological symptoms, Freud states:

> In obsessional neurosis and paranoia the forms which the symptoms assume become very valuable to the ego because they obtain for it, not certain advantages, but a narcissistic satisfaction which it would otherwise be without. The systems which the obsessional neurotic constructs flatter his self-love by making him feel that he is better than other people because he is specially cleanly or specially conscientious. [Freud, 1926d, p. 99]

This sort of identity support ("narcissistic satisfaction") provided by symptoms is seen by Freud as a secondary gain (*ibid.*, pp. 99–100), and the claim that symptoms are not only secondarily but also *primarily* means of identity support might seem hard to square with Freud's statements that "a symptom is a sign of, and a substitute for, an instinctual satisfaction which has remained in abeyance" (*ibid.*, p. 91), that "unconscious day-dreams are . . . the source . . . of neurotic symptoms" (Freud, 1916–1917, p. 373), and that fear of castration is a major determinant of symptoms, at least in phobias (Freud, 1926d, pp. 108, 122, 124, 143). But when we place these comments in the context of other, more definitive statements Freud makes about symptom formation, and when we examine more closely what "instinctual satisfaction" and "castration" mean, not only in general, but for Freud himself, these very comments of Freud's point to identity needs as being the root cause of psychical symptoms in individuals. In the first place, Freud's own gloss of "instinctual needs" as "honour, power, wealth, fame, and the love of women" (Freud, 1916–1917, p. 376) and of daydreams as "imagined satisfactions of ambitious, megalomaniac, and erotic wishes" (*ibid.*, p. 372) foregrounds narcissistic gratifications, which function precisely as supports of one's identity. Similarly, when Freud declares that "the generating of anxiety sets symptom formation going and is, indeed, a necessary prerequisite of it" and that "symptoms are created in order to remove the ego from a situation of danger," including the danger of "a constantly increasing instinctual demand" (Freud, 1926d, p. 144), we can see that psychical symptoms are primarily attempts to defend identity from forces that would disrupt or destroy it. Each of the three types of threat—loss of love, castration, and superego criticism—which Freud sees as triggering, respectively, the symptoms of hysteria, phobia, and obsessional neurosis, is a particular form of threat to identity. Loss of love deprives us of the recognition and validation that are crucial for maintaining identity; superego criticism deprives us of the sense of unity between our ideal and actual identities; and castration, which might seem to involve loss of just pleasure or power, is actually, as Freud himself notes, a threat to one's masculinity (*ibid.*, p. 115)—that is, one's identity as a man. Indeed, the reason that castration anxiety is such a prominent determinant of symptoms is because it constitutes a threat to identity in each of the three Lacanian registers: it deprives a man of his most intense, identity-defining jouissance (identity in the Real), of an essential component of his body image (identity in the Imaginary), and of the key signifier of masculinity (identity in the Symbolic).

The claim that psychological symptoms function primarily (and secondarily) to support an individual's identity, or sense of self, is also supported by a more recent analysis of four different categories of symptoms by Mary Connors. The four types of symptoms are addictive disorders, anxiety disorders, dissociative/somatoform disorders, and depressive states/work inhibitions (Connors, 1994,

p. 509). In addictive disorders, according to Connors, impending fragmentation is warded off through involvement with a substance or activity:

> addictive behaviours may be seen as efforts to stave off fragmentation in a vulnerable self by establishing a selfobject relationship with a substance or activity which then becomes habitual and destructive. . . . The symptomatic behaviour is both a manifestation of fragmentation and an effort at restitution through non-relational means. [*ibid.*, pp. 512–13]

Anxiety disorders prevent fragmentation through avoiding a feared stimulus, which "may be a cognition, as in obsessive–compulsive disorder; a sensation, as in panic disorder; or an external object or situation, as in simple phobia and social phobia" (*ibid.*, pp. 514). In dissociative disorders,

> the integrative functions of consciousness have been split to protect the self from unbearable pain. Patients with multiple personality disorder, fugue states, psychogenic amnesia, and other dissociative disorders have found ways to survive often horrific experiences, but at the expense of a sense of full continuity of identity in time. [*ibid.*, pp. 516–17]

And depression and work inhibitions involve "two dissociated motivational systems that exist side by side: one organized around the requirements of needed others and one that contains the hidden true self, with its disavowed affects and developmental strivings" (*ibid.*, pp. 518). Connors concludes that "common to all [four ways of symptom formation] is the notion of a vulnerable self in a relational matrix that is or was somehow inadequate" (*ibid.*, p. 510). My argument is that social symptoms, too, are the result of vulnerability of self or identity in a relational (or social) matrix that is, or was, somehow inadequate.

Multiple self-motives
and self-esteem

In addition to the findings of self-affirmation theory and other research discussed in Chapter One, the motivational primacy of identity maintenance has also been supported by quantitative research demonstrating the existence of additional self-motives, including processes of self-enhancement, self-verification, self-assessment, and self-improvement. The self-enhancement motive, which involves "the need to achieve and maintain a positive sense of self" (Taylor, Neter, & Wayment, 1995, p. 1278), is demonstrated by studies showing that people process, interpret, and remember information pertaining to themselves in ways that enhance their sense of self, that they go out of their way to impress others, and that they select social situations that place them in a good light (Sedikides & Strube, 1995, p. 1330). The self-verification motive, which involves people's desire for confirmation of their sense of self, including its negative aspects, manifests itself in findings that people with a negative sense of self prefer conversation partners and even life partners who confirm this negative sense of self rather than partners who provide more positive feedback, and by the fact that, when life hands them a state of good fortune that contradicts their negative sense of self, they often become depressed and even physically ill (Swann, 1999). The self-assessment motive, which involves the quest for certainty regarding one's traits and abilities, whether the feedback is positive or negative (Sedikides & Strube, 1995, p. 1330), can be inferred from the fact that people seek out and often prefer to engage in tasks that will allow them to discern the degree to which they possess a given trait or ability, as opposed to tasks that do not provide such information (Sedikides & Strube, 1997, pp. 220–221). The self-improvement motive, which aims to change personal qualities for the better, rather than just feeling better (the self-enhancement motive) (Taylor, Neter, & Wayment, 1995, pp. 1278–1279), is most evident when people feel threatened or inadequate. Such feelings "are more likely to instigate the self-improvement motive ... than any other motive" (Sedikides & Strube, 1997, p. 222).

Then there is the phenomenon of self-esteem. Social scientists who research the causes of social problems usually ignore psychological causes and focus instead on social conditions. In those relatively rare instances when they do focus on the question of psychological causes, they often settle on self-esteem rather than identity maintenance as the key psychological force behind social problems (Crocker & Park, 2003, p. 291; Vignoles, Golledge, Regalia, Manzi, & Scabini, 2006, p. 308) and conclude that raising individuals' self-esteem will contribute to the prevention of social problems (Hewitt, 1998; Smelser, 1989; Swann, 1999, pp. 5–6). A prominent example is the research of sociologist Howard Kaplan, who has concluded that "the self-esteem motive" is the main motivational cause of all human behaviour (Kaplan, 1975, pp. 10, 52) and that people turn to deviant behaviours when their conventional behaviours have failed to produce adequate self-esteem, leaving deviant behaviours as "the only remaining promise for satisfying the self-esteem motive" (Kaplan, 1975, p. 54). Deviant behaviour enhances self-esteem by allowing the individual (1) to avoid the self-esteem-damaging normative environment, (2) to attack and reduce the status of the esteem-damaging normative standards, and (3) to substitute "new group memberships and normative standards" that are more easily attainable and that "offer greater promise of positive attitudinal responses from other group members" (*ibid.*, p. 55).

Kaplan is right to find the motivation for deviant behaviour in certain vulnerabilities concerning the self. In this respect, his explanation of deviant behaviour is quite congruent with the research discussed in the previous section as well as with the general thrust of my argument. However, his locating this motivation in low self-esteem rather than identity maintenance is both incorrect and practically disadvantageous. That it is incorrect is indicated by both logic and empirical evidence. Logically, it does not make sense that individuals with a low sense of self-worth would reject the system that they have been socialized to value and believe in. Rather than rejecting the system, they should be inclined to reject themselves, or those parts of themselves that they experience as unworthy, and replace these parts with new, worthier elements of self. Such behaviours, in fact, are readily observable in individuals with low self-esteem, who are often depressed, self-critical, or self-abnegating. Rather than engaging in socially deviant behaviour, people with low self-esteem tend to suffer in silence and humility, because they do not believe that they deserve better than they have got. Deviant behaviour is the logical course of action for individuals with *high* self-esteem who feel that the dominant social order has not given them the wealth, status, respect, recognition, or opportunities to enact and display their virtues that they believe is their due. They believe they are worth more than society is acknowledging, and they therefore reject the social system through various forms of deviant behaviour, including violence.

This is precisely what Roy Baumeister discovered in his survey of research on aggression and violence. He found individuals with low self-esteem to be "shy, modest, emotionally labile (and having tendencies toward depression and anxiety), submitting readily to other people's influence, and lacking confidence in themselves"— all characteristics, Baumeister, Bushman, and Campbell observe (2000, p. 26), that are more likely to prevent aggression than to produce it. In contrast, the research revealed aggressive and violent individuals to have high self-esteem plus an "inflated sense of being superior to others and being entitled to special privileges" (*ibid.*, p. 28). They conclude that

> Aggression is most likely when people with a narcissistically inflated view of their own personal superiority encounter someone who explicitly disputes that opinion. Aggression is thus a means of

defending a highly favourable view of self against someone who
seeks (even unwittingly) to deflate it. Threatened egotism, rather
than low self-esteem, is the most explosive recipe for violence. [*ibid.*,
pp. 28–29]

In addition to being incorrect, the assumption that low self-
esteem is a significant cause of social problems is also disadvantageous from a practical standpoint, because it encourages people
to see the causes of social problems as residing "inside people's
heads" (Hewitt, 1998; Swann, 1999) and therefore to seek solutions
to social problems in programmes that bolster self-esteem through
such techniques as providing indiscriminate praise for children in
school and having them repeat esteem-bolstering statements such
as "I am worthy", "I am capable", and "I am likeable" (Baumeister
& Boden, 1998, p. 132; Hewitt, 1998, pp. 8ff., 56ff.; Swann, 1999,
pp. 4–5). Unfortunately, there is little evidence that such an
approach works (Hewitt, 1998; Smelser, 1989). Baumeister and
Boden conclude that such an approach is "quite fundamentally
misguided", and that "boosting self-esteem by itself might even
increase violence" (Baumeister & Boden, 1998, p. 132).

While Baumeister and colleagues' analysis refutes the idea that
low self-esteem is the key cause of, and therefore the most effective
target for intervention in, aggression, violence, and other social
problems, their focus on threatened egotism—which they define as
"favourable views of self that are disputed or that in some other
way encounter an external appraisal that is far less favourable"
[*ibid.*, p. 114]—is itself too narrow. Not only research on the causes
and cures of violence, but also recent research on human motivation in general, indicate that the key factor is identity vulnerability
rather than threatened egotism. Baumeister and Boden's threatened
egotism, or "favourable views of self that are disputed" is, like
Kaplan's "low-self esteem" and "negative self-attitudes", a manifestation of identity vulnerability or insecurity, but the two are not
coextensive, because identity, as one's sense of self, includes but
also exceeds one's sense of self-worth, or self-esteem.

Other recent research on self-esteem also strongly suggests that
it is identity maintenance rather than self-esteem maintenance that
is the fundamental need and motivating force behind human
behaviour. William Swann, for example, has found that, when

confronted with a choice between (a) partners, activities, or situations that provide them with positive feedback about themselves and (b) partners, activities, or situations that provide them with negative feedback, people with negative self-views tend to choose the latter. "In study after study", Swann reports, "people made it clear that although they do indeed enjoy praise and adoration, they also want *self-verification* in the form of evaluations that confirm and validate their own views of themselves" (Swann, 1999, p. 23). While the desire for self-verification and the desire for positive feedback often work together, Swann found that when the two motives conflict, as they often do for people with low self-esteem, the self-verification motive generally prevails. As Swann explains, "The key seems to be that firmly held self-views provide people with a sense of personal coherence that they value even more than they value positive changes" (*ibid.*, p. 52). Michael Kernis's investigation of various types of self-esteem also points to identity maintenance as the fundamental need, which, when met, often contributes to self-esteem and, when not met, often leads to attempts to bolster self-esteem. True self-esteem, that is, arises from the enactment of one's core identity contents, "the unobstructed operation of one's true, or core, self in one's daily enterprise" (Kernis, 2003, p. 13), and it is the maintenance of this identity, rather than self-esteem, that is the fundamental human motivation.

Kernis distinguishes between fragile and secure forms of high self-esteem, with the former being defensive, unstable, contingent on continual validation from others, and coexistent with unconscious low self-esteem, and the latter being genuine, independent of external validations, stable, and co-existent with unconscious high self-esteem. Individuals with fragile high self-esteem "are especially caught up in how they feel about themselves and will take a variety of measures to bolster, maintain, and enhance these self-feelings", including "the adoption of an aggressively self-enhancing presentational style that includes self-aggrandizing and self-promotion", as well as denial of responsibility for their failures, derogation of people who threaten their sense of worth, self-handicapping, and excessive risk-taking (*ibid.*, p. 3). Secure high self-esteem, in contrast, is neither dependent on continuous validation by others nor contrary to one's unconscious sense of worth:

True high self-esteem is not "earned," nor can it be "taken away." It is not "overinflated," nor is it "undeserved." Doing well is valued because it signifies effective expression of one's core values and interests, and it is this effective expression that is valued, not high self-esteem per se. [*ibid.*, p. 9]

REFERENCES

Abdullah, S. (2002). The soul of a terrorist: reflections on our war with the "Other". In: C. E. Stout (Ed.), *The Psychology of Terrorism, Vol. 1: A Public Understanding* (pp. 129–141). Westport, CT: Praeger.

Adams, H. E., Wright, L. W., & Lohr, B. A. (1996). Is homophobia associated with homosexual arousal? *Journal of Abnormal Psychology, 105*: 440–445.

Aizenman, N. C. (2008). New high in U.S. prison numbers. *Washington Post*, 29 February: A1.

Anderson, K. (2000). Erich Fromm and the Frankfurt School critique of criminal justice. In: K. Anderson & R. Quinney (Ed.), *Erich Fromm and Critical Criminology: Beyond the Punitive Society* (pp. 83–119). Urbana, IL: University of Illinois Press.

Ardila, R. (2002). The psychology of the terrorist: Behavioral perspectives. In: C. E. Stout (Ed.), *The Psychology of Terrorism, Vol. 1: A Public Understanding* (pp. 9–15). Westport, CT: Praeger.

Arendt, H. (1945). Organized guilt and universal responsibility. Reprinted in: S. Lawall (Ed.), *The Norton Anthology of Western Literature, Vol. 2* (8th edn) (pp. 2108–2112). New York: Norton, 2006.

Atwood, J. (Ed.). (1996). *Family Scripts*. Washington, DC: Taylor and Francis.

Bandura, A. (1998). Mechanisms of moral disengagement. In: W. Reich (Ed.), *Origins of Terrorism: Psychologies, Ideologies, Theologies, States of Mind* (pp. 161–191). Washington, DC: Woodrow Wilson Center Press.

Baum, D. (1996). *Smoke and Mirrors: The War on Drugs and the Politics of Failure*. New York: Little, Brown.

Bauman, Z. (1993). *Postmodern Ethics*. New York: Blackwell.

Bauman, Z. (1997). Morality begins at home: or, can there be a Levinasian macro-ethics? In: H. Jodalen & A. J. Vetlesen (Eds.), *Closeness: An Ethics* (pp. 218–244). Boston: Scandinavian University Press.

Baumeister, R. F., & Boden, J. M. (1998). Aggression and the self: high self-esteem, low self-control, and ego threat. In: R. G. Geen & E. Donnerstein (Eds.), *Human Aggression: Theories, Research, and Implications for Social Policy* (pp. 111–137). New York: Academic Press.

Baumeister, R. F., & Vohs, K. D. (2001). Narcissism as addiction to esteem. *Psychological Inquiry, 12*: 206–210.

Baumeister, R. F., Bushman, B. J., & Campbell, W. K. (2000). Self-esteem, narcissism, and aggression: does violence result from low self-esteem or from threatened egotism? *Current Directions in Psychological Science, 9*: 26–29.

Blasi, A. (1983). Moral cognition and moral action: a theoretical perspective. *Developmental Review, 3*: 178–210.

Bloom, S. L., & Reichert, M. (1998). *Bearing Witness: Violence and Collective Responsibility*. New York: Haworth.

Bonta, B. D., & Fry, D. P. (2006). Lessons for the rest of us: learning from peaceful societies. In: M. Fitzduff & C. E. Stout (Eds.), *The Psychology of Resolving Global Conflcits: From War to Peace, Vol. 1: Nature vs. Nurture* (pp. 175–210). Westport, CT: Praeger.

Bracher, M. (2006). Teaching for social justice: reeducating the emotions through literary study. *JAC: a Quarterly Journal for the Interdisciplinary Study of Rhetoric, Writing, Multiple Literacies, and Politics, 26*: 463–512.

Breakwell, G. M. (1986). *Coping with Threatened Identities*. New York: Methuen.

Browning, D. (1973). *Generative Man*. Philadelphia, PA: Westminster.

Burke, P. J. (1991). Identity processes and social stress. *American Sociological Review, 56*: 836–849.

Burnham, G., Lafta, R., Doocy, S., & Roberts, L. (2006). Mortality after the 2003 invasion of Iraq. *The Lancet, 368*: 1421–1428.

Burton, J. (1997). *Violence Explained*. New York: Manchester University Press.

Bushman, B. J., Baumeister, R. F., & Phillips, C. M. (2001). Do people aggress to improve their mood? Catharsis beliefs, affect regulation opportunity, and aggressive responding. *Journal of Personality and Social Psychology, 81*: 17–32.

Carpenter, L. M. (1998). From girls into women: scripts for sexuality and romance in *Seventeen* magazine, 1974–1994. *The Journal of Sex Research, 35*: 158–168.

Carveth, D. L. (1984). Psychoanalysis and social theory: the Hobbesian problem revisited. *Psychoanalysis and Contemporary Thought, 7*: 43–98.

Chancer, L. S. (2000). Fromm, sadomasochism, and contemporary American crime. In: K. Anderson & R. Quinney (Eds.), *Erich Fromm and Critical Criminology: Beyond the Punitive Society* (pp. 31–42). Urbana, IL: University of Illinois Press.

Cohen, G. L., Aronson, J., & Steele, C. M. (2000). When beliefs yield to evidence: reducing biased evaluation by affirming the self. *Personality and Social Psychology Bulletin, 26*: 1151–1164.

Colby, A., & Damon, W. (1992). *Some Do Care: Contemporary Lives of Moral Commitment*. New York: Free Press.

Connors, M. E. (1994). Symptom formation: an integrative self psychological perspective. *Psychoanalytic Psychology, 11*: 509–523.

Costanzo, M. (1997). *Just Revenge: Costs and Consequences of the Death Penalty*. New York: St Martin's Press.

Cottle, T. J. (2001). *Hardest Times: The Trauma of Long-Term Unemployment*. Amherst, MA: University of Massachusetts Press.

Crenshaw, M. (2003). The causes of terrorism, past and present. In: C. W. Kegley, Jr (Ed.), *The New Global Terrorism: Characteristics, Causes, Controls* (pp. 92–105). Upper Saddle River, NJ: Prentice Hall.

Crocker, J., & Park, L. E. (2003). Seeking self-esteem: construction, maintenance, and protection of self-worth. In: M. R. Leary & J. P. Tangney (Eds.), *Handbook of Self and Identity* (pp. 291–313). New York: Guilford.

Currie, E. (1998). *Crime and Punishment in America*. New York: Henry Holt.

Currie, E., & Skolnick, J. H. (1997). *America's Problems: Social Issues and Public Policy* (3rd edn). New York: Longman.

Damasio, A. (2000). *The Feeling of What Happens*. New York: Harcourt.

Dash, L. (1989). *When Children Want Children*. New York: William Morrow.

Delgado, R. (1995). Words that wound: a tort action for racial insults, epithets, and name-calling. In: R. Delgado (Ed.), *Critical Race Theory* (pp. 159–168). Philadelphia, PA: Temple University Press.

Dryfoos, J. G. (1990). *Adolescents at Risk: Prevalence and Prevention*. New York: Oxford University Press.

Duncan, M. G. (1999). *Romantic Outlaws, Beloved Prisons: The Unconscious Meanings of Crime and Punishment*. New York: New York University Press.

Eagleton, T. (2000). *The Idea of Culture*. Malden, MA: Blackwell.

Edelson, M. (1992). Telling and enacting stories in psychoanalysis. In: J. W. Barron, M. Eagle, & D. Wolitzky (Eds.), *Interfaces of Psychoanalysis and Psychology*, (pp. 99–124). Washington, DC: American Psychological Association.

Eisenberg, N. (1995). Prosocial development: a multifaceted model. In: W. M. Kurtines & J. L. Gewirtz (Eds.), *Moral Development: An Introduction*. Boston: Allyn and Bacon.

Ellens, J. H. (2002). Psychological legitimization of violence by religious archetypes. In: C. E. Stout (Ed.), *The Psychology of Terrorism, Vol. 3: Theoretical Understandings and Perspectives* (pp. 149–162). Westport, CT: Praeger.

Ellison, R. (1952). *Invisible Man*. New York: Vintage, 1995.

Erikson, E. H. (1964). *Insight and Responsibility*. New York: Norton.

Erikson, E. H. (1968). *Identity: Youth and Crisis*. New York: Norton.

Erikson, E. H. (1969). *Ghandi's Truth: On the Origins of Militant Nonviolence*. New York: Norton.

Erikson, E. H. (1974). *Dimensions of a New Identity*. New York, Norton.

Fabick, S. D. (2002). Us & them: reducing the risk of terrorism. In: C. E. Stout (Ed.), *The Psychology of Terrorism, Vol. 2: Clinical Aspects and Responses* (pp. 225–241). Westport, CT: Praeger.

Faludi, S. (1999). *Stiffed: The Betrayal of the American Man*. New York: Morrow.

Fein, S., & Spencer, S. J. (1997). Prejudice as self-image maintenance: affirming the self through derogating others. *Journal of Personality and Social Psychology, 73*: 31–44.

Fetterley, J. (1978). *The Resisting Reader: A Feminist Approach to American Fiction*. Bloomington, IN: Indiana University Press.

Fisher, S. (1974). *Body Consciousness*. New York: Jason Aronson.

Fonagy, P., Moran, S. J., & Target, M. (1993). Aggression and the psychological self. *International Journal of Psychoanalysis, 74*: 471–485.

Forster, E. M. (1971). *Maurice*. New York: Norton.

Fraser, N., & Honneth, A. (2003). *Redistribution or Recognition?*, J. Golb, J. Ingram, & C. Wilke (Trans.). New York: Verso.

Freud, S. (1916–1917). *Introductory Lectures on Psycho-analysis. S.E., 16.* London: Hogarth.

Freud, S. (1926d). *Inhibitions, Symptoms and Anxiety. S.E., 20.* London: Hogarth.

Freud, S. (1930a). *Civilization and Its Discontents. S.E., 21.* London: Hogarth.

Fromm, E. (1931). On the psychology of the criminal and the punitive society, H. D. Osterle & K. Anderson (Trans.). In: K. Anderson and R. Quinney (Eds.), *Erich Fromm and Critical Criminology: Beyond the Punitive Society* (pp. 129–156). Urbana, IL: University of Illinois Press, 2000.

Fromm, E. (1955). *The Sane Society.* New York: Henry Holt.

Gaertner, L., Sedikides, C., Vevea, J. L., & Iuzzini, J. (2002). The "I", the "we", and the "when": a meta-analysis of motivational primacy in self-definition. *Journal of Personality and Social Psychology, 83*: 574–591.

Gallimore, T. (2002). Unresolved trauma: fuel for the cycle of violence and terrorism. In: C. E. Stout (Ed.), *The Psychology of Terrorism, Vol. 2: Clinical Aspects and Responses* (pp. 143–164). Westport, CT: Praeger.

Garbarino, J. (1999). *Lost Boys: Why our Sons Turn Violent and How We Can Save Them.* New York: Free Press.

Gilbert, H. (1994). Selfobjects throughout the life span: research with nonclinical subjects. In: A. Goldberg (Ed.), *Progress in Self Psychology, Vol. 10: A Decade of Progress* (pp. 31–51). Hillsdale, NJ: Analytic Press.

Gilligan, J. (1996). *Violence: Reflections on a National Epidemic.* New York: Random House.

Gilligan, J. (2001). *Preventing Violence.* New York: Thames & Hudson.

Glasser, M. (1998). On violence: a preliminary communication. *International Journal of Psychoanalysis, 79*: 887–902.

Glassner, B. (1999). *The Culture of Fear: Why Americans Are Afraid of the Wrong Things.* New York: Basic Books.

Grand, S. (2000). *The Reproduction of Evil: A Clinical and Cultural Perspective.* Hillsdale, NJ: Analytic Press.

Grossman, D. (1996). *On Killing: The Psychological Cost of Learning to Kill in War and Society.* New York: Little, Brown.

Hawkins, J. D., Farrington, D. P., & Catalano, R. F. (1998). Reducing violence through the schools. In: D. S. Elliot, B. A. Hamburg, and K. R. Williams (Eds.), *Violence in American Schools* (pp. 188–216). New York: Cambridge University Press.

Hedges, C. (2002). *War is a Force that Gives us Meaning*. New York: Public Affairs.

Herman, J. (1997). *Trauma and Recovery*. New York: Basic Books.

Hewitt, J. P. (1998). *The Myth of Self-Esteem*. New York: St. Martin's Press.

Hillman, J. (2004). *A Terrible Love of War*. New York: Penguin.

Holland, N. N. (1975). *The Dynamics of Literary Response*. New York: Norton.

Honderich, T. (2002). *After the Terror*. Edinburgh: Edinburgh University Press.

Honneth, A. (1995). *The Struggle for Recognition: The Moral Grammar of Social Conflicts*. Cambridge, MA: MIT Press.

Hoover, K. (2004a). Introduction: The future of identity. In: K. Hoover (Ed.), *The Future of Identity: Centennial Reflections on the Legacy of Erik Erikson* (pp. 1–14). New York: Lexington.

Hoover, K. (2004b). What should democracies do about identity? In: K. Hoover (Ed.), *The Future of Identity: Centennial Reflections on the Legacy of Erik Erikson* (pp. 97–109). New York: Lexington.

Horowitz, M. (1998). *Cognitive Psychodynamics*. New York: Wiley.

Horowitz, M., Milbrath, C., Reidboc, S., & Stinson, C. (1993). Elaboration and dyselaboration: Measures of expression and defense in discourse. *Psychotherapy Research, 3*: 278–293.

Jaynes, J. (1976). *The Origin of Consciousness in the Breakdown of the Bicameral Mind*. New York: Houghton Mifflin.

Jones, J. M. (1997). *Prejudice and Racism*. New York: McGraw-Hill.

Jones, R. M. (1961). *An Experiment in Psychoanalytic Education*. Chicago, IL: Charles C Thomas.

Jost, J. T., & Banaji, M. R. (1994). The role of stereotyping in system-justification and the production of false consciousness. *British Journal of Social Psychology, 33*: 1–27.

Judges, D. P. (2000). Scared to death: capital punishment as authoritarian terror management. *Dissertation Abstracts International, 60*: 4228.

Juergensmeyer, M. (2001). The logic of religious violence. In: D. C. Rapoport (Ed.), *Inside Terrorist Organizations* (pp. 172–193). Portland, OR: Frank Cass.

Kaplan, H. B. (1975). *Self-Attitudes and Deviant Behavior*. Pacific Palisades, CA: Goodyear.

Kaplan, H. B., & Liu, X. (2000). Social movements as collective coping with spoiled personal identities: Intimations from a panel study of changes in the life course between adolescence and adulthood. In: S. Stryker, T. J. Owens, R. W. White (Eds.), *Self, Identity, and Social Movements* (pp. 215–238). Minneapolis, MN: University of Minnesota Press.

Katz, J. (1988). *Seductions of Crime: Moral and Sensual Attractions in Doing Evil*. New York: Basic Books.

Kegan, R. (1982). *The Evolving Self: Problem and Process in Human Development*. Cambridge, MA: Harvard University Press.

Kegan, R. (1986). The child behind the mask: sociopathy as developmental delay. In: W. H. Reid, D. Dorr, J. I. Walker, & J. W. Bonner, III (Eds.), *Unmasking the Sociopath* (pp. 45–78). New York: Norton.

Kegan, R. (1994). *In Over Our Heads: The Mental Demands of Modern Life*. Cambridge, MA: Harvard University Press.

Kernis, M. H. (2003). Toward a conceptualization of optimal self-esteem. *Psychological Inquiry, 14*: 1–26.

Kfir, N. (2002). Understanding suicidal terror through humanistic and existential psychology. In C. E. Stout (Ed.), *The Psychology of Terrorism, Vol. 1: A Public Understanding* (pp. 143–157). Westport, CT: Praeger.

Khantzian, E. J. (1999). *Treating Addiction as a Human Process*. Northvale, NJ: Jason Aronson.

Kohlberg, L. (1981). *The Philosophy of Moral Development*. New York: Harper & Row.

Krueger, D. W. (1989). *Body Self & Psychological Self*. New York: Brunner/Mazel.

Krystal, H. (1994). Self- and object-representation in alcoholism and other drug-dependence: implications for therapy. In: J. D. Levin & R. H. Weiss (Eds.), *The Dynamics and Treatment of Alcoholism: Essential Papers* (pp. 300–309). Northvale, NJ: Jason Aronson.

Krystal, H. (1997). Self representation and the capacity for self care. In: D. L. Yalisove (Ed.), *Essential Papers on Addiction* (pp. 109–148). New York: New York University Press, 1997.

Krystal, H., & Raskin, H. A. (1970). *Drug Dependence: Aspects of Ego Function*. Detroit, MI: Wayne State University Press.

Lacan, J. (1966). *Ecrits: The First Complete Edition in English*. Bruce Fink (Trans.). New York: Norton, 2007.

Lacan, J. (1986). *The Ethics of Psychoanalysis*. J.-A. Miller (Ed.), D. Porter (Trans.). New York: Norton, 1997.

Leary, M. R. (1996). *Self-Presentation: Impression Management and Interpersonal Behavior*. Boulder, CO: Westview.

Lerner, R. M. (1994). *America's Youth in Crisis*. Thousand Oaks, CA: Sage.

Levin, J. D. (1999). *Primer for Treating Substance Abusers*. Northvale, NJ: Jason Aronson.

Levitt, S. D., & Dubner, S. J. (2006). *Freakanomics: A Rogue Economist Explores the Hidden Side of Everything*. New York: William Morrow.

Lewis, B. (2003). The roots of Muslim rage. In: C. W. Kegley, Jr (Ed.), *The New Global Terrorism: Characteristics, Causes, Controls* (pp. 194–201). Upper Saddle River, NJ: Prentice Hall.

Lewis, M. (1993). *The Culture of Inequality* (2nd edn). Amherst, MA: University of Massachusetts Press.

Lichtenberg, J. D., & Schonbar, R. A. (1992). Motivation in psychology and psychoanalysis. In: J. W. Barron, M. N. Eagle, & D. L. Wolitzky (Eds.), *Interface of Psychoanalysis and Psychology* (pp. 11–36). Washington, DC: American Psychological Association.

Lichtenstein, H. (1977). *The Dilemma of Human Identity*. New York: Aronson.

Linville, P. (1985). Self-complexity and affective extremity: don't put all of your eggs in one cognitive basket. *Social Cognition, 3*: 94–120.

Liu, T. J., & Steele, C. M. (1986). Attributional analysis as self-affirmation. *Journal of Personality and Social Psychology, 51*: 531–540.

Lockley, P. (1995). *Counseling Heroin and Other Drug Users*. London: Free Association.

Long, D. E. (1990). *The Anatomy of Terrorism*. New York: Free Press.

Mack, J. E. (2002). Looking beyond terrorism: transcending the mind of enmity. In: C. E. Stout (Ed.), *The Psychology of Terrorism, Vol. 1: A Public Understanding* (pp. 173–184). Westport, CT: Praeger.

Mahalik, J. R., Englar-Carlson, M., & Good, G. E. (2003). Masculinity scripts, presenting concerns, and help seeking: implications for practice and training. *Professional Psychology: Research and Practice, 34*: 123–131.

Mauer, M. (1999). *Race to Incarcerate*. New York: New Press.

Massing, M. (1999). Beyond legalization: new ideas for ending the war on drugs. *The Nation*, 20 September, pp. 11–15.

McCarthy, S. (2002). Preventing future terrorist activities among adolescents through global psychology: a cooperative learning community. In C. E. Stout (Ed.), *The Psychology of Terrorism, Vol. 4: Programs and Practices in Response and Prevention* (pp. 131–156). Westport, CT: Praeger.

McCauley, C. (2002). Psychological issues in understanding terrorism and the response to terrorism. In: C. E. Stout (Ed.), *The Psychology of Terrorism, Vol. 3: Theoretical Understandings and Perspectives* (pp. 3–29). Westport, CT: Praeger.

Milburn, M., & Conrad, S. D. (1996). *The Politics of Denial.* Cambridge, MA: MIT Press.

Mills, N. (1997). *The Triumph of Meanness.* New York: Houghton Mifflin.

Mirow, D. (1989). Teen mother wanted babies, reporter finds. *The Plain Dealer,* 13 February, pp. 1C–3C.

Mitchell, S. A. (1993). Aggression and the endangered self. *Psychoanalytic Quarterly, 62:* 351–382.

Monroe, K. R. (1996). *The Heart of Altruism: Perceptions of a Common Humanity.* Princeton, NJ: Princeton University Press.

Monroe, K. R. (2004). Identity and choice. In: K. Hoover (Ed.), *The Future of Identity: Centennial Reflections on the Legacy of Erik Erikson* (pp. 77–94). New York: Lexington.

Musick, J. S. (1993). *Young, Poor, and Pregnant: The Psychology of Teenage Motherhood.* New Haven, CT: Yale University Press.

Olweean, S. S. (2002). Psychological concepts of the "Other": embracing the compass of the self. In: C. E. Stout (Ed.), *The Psychology of Terrorism, Vol. 1: A Public Understanding* (pp. 113–128). Westport, CT: Praeger.

Perlman, D. (2002). Intersubjective dimensions of terrorism and its transcendence. In: C. E. Stout (Ed.), *The Psychology of Terrorism, Vol. 1: A Public Understanding* (pp. 17–47). Westport, CT: Praeger.

Perry, W. G., Jr. (1999). *Forms of Ethical and Intellectual Development in the College Years: A Scheme.* San Francisco, CA: Jossey-Bass.

Pine, F. (1970). *Drive, Ego, Object, and Self: A Synthesis for Clinical Work.* New York: Basic Books.

Piven, J. S. (2002). On the psychosis (religion) of terrorists. In: C. E. Stout (Ed.), *The Psychology of Terrorism, Vol. 3: Theoretical Understandings and Perspectives* (pp. 119–148). Westport, CT: Praeger.

Pollan, M. (1999). The way we live now: a very fine line. *New York Times Magazine,* 12 September, pp. 27–28.

Post, J. M. (1998). Terrorist psycho-logic: terrorist behavior as a product of psychological forces. In: W. Reich (Ed.), *Origins of Terrorism: Psychologies, Ideologies, Theologies, States of Mind* (pp. 25–40). Washington, DC: Woodrow Wilson Center.

Pyszczynski, T., Greenberg, J., & Solomon, S. (1997). Why do we need what we need? A terror management perspective on the roots of human social motivation. *Psychological Inquiry, 8:* 1–20.

Pyszczynski, T., Greenberg, J., & Solomon, S. (1999). A dual-process model of defense against conscious and unconscious death-related thoughts: An extensioin of terror management theory. *Psychological Review*, 106: 835–845.

Radosh, P. (2000). Gender, social character, cultural forces, and the importance of love: Erich Fromm's theories applied to patterns of crime. In: K. Anderson & R. Quinney (Eds.), *Erich Fromm and Critical Criminology: Beyond the Punitive Society* (pp. 59–82). Urbana, IL: University of Illinois Press.

Rangell, L. (1994). Identity and the human core: the view from psychoanalytic theory. In: H. A. Bosma, T. L. G. Graafsma, H. D. Grotevant, & D. J. de Levita (Eds.), *Identity and Development: An Interdisciplinary Approach* (pp. 25–40). Thousand Oaks, CA: Sage.

Real, T. (1997). *I Don't Want to Talk About It: Overcoming the Secret Legacy of Male Depression*. New York: Simon & Schuster.

Renault, E. (2004a). *L'experience de l'injustice: reconnaissance et clinique de l'injustice*. Paris: Editions La Découverte.

Renault, E. (2004b). *Mépris social: ethique et politique de la reconnaissance* (2nd edn). Paris: Editions du Passant.

Retzinger, S., & Scheff, T. (2006). Emotion, alienation, and narratives in protracted conflict. In: M. Fitzduff & C. E. Stout (Eds.), *The Psychology of Resolving Global Conflicts: From War to Peace. Vol. 1: Nature vs. Nurture* (pp. 239–255). Westport, CT: Praeger.

Rorty, R. (1999). Human rights, rationality, and sentimentality. In: O. Savic (Ed.), *The Politics of Human Rights* (pp. 67–83). New York: Verso.

Rubenstein, R. E. (2003). The psycho-political sources of terrorism. In: C. W. Kegley, Jr (Ed.), *The New Global Terrorism: Characteristics, Causes, Controls* (pp. 139–150). Upper Saddle River, NJ: Prentice Hall.

Ryan, W. (1971). *Blaming the Victim*. New York: Pantheon.

Sachs, J. (2005). The end of poverty. *Time*, 14 March, pp. 42–54.

Schimel, J., Simon, L., Greenberg, J., Solomon, S., Pyszczynski, T., Waxmonsky, J., & Arndt, J. (1999). Stereotypes and terror management: evidence that mortality salience enhances stereotypic thinking and preferences. *Journal of Personality and Social Psychology*, 77: 905–926.

Schorr, L. B. (1988). *Within Our Reach*. New York: Anchor.

Schorr, L. B. (1998). *Common Purpose: Strengthening Families and Neighborhoods to Strengthen America*. New York: Anchor.

Schweickart, P. P. (1986). Reading ourselves: toward a feminist theory of reading. In: E. A. Flynn & P. P. Schweihart (Eds.), *Gender and Reading: Essays on Readers, Texts, and Contexts* (pp. 31–62). Baltimore, MD: Johns Hopkins University Press.

Sedikides, C., & Strube, M. J. (1995). The multiply motivated self. *Personality and Social Psychology Bulletin, 21*: 1330–1335.

Sedikides, C.. & Strube, M. J. (1997). Self-evaluation: to thine own self be good, to thine own self be sure, to thine own self be true, and to thine own self be better. *Advances in Experimental Social Psychology, 29*: 209–269.

Sennett, R. (1998). *The Corrosion of Character*. New York: Norton.

Sinclair, U. (1906). *The Jungle*. New York: Norton, 2003.

Singer, P. (1995). *How Are We to Live: Ethics in an Age of Self-Interest*. Amherst, NY: Prometheus.

Singer, P. (2004). *One World: The Ethics of Globalization* (2nd edn). New Haven: Yale University Press.

Smelser, N. J. (1989). Self-esteem and social problems: an introduction. In: A. M. Mecca, N. J. Smelser, & J. Vasconcellos (Eds.), *The Social Importance of Self-Esteem* (pp. 1–23). Berkeley, CA: University of California Press.

Snell, B. (1953). *The Discovery of the Mind*, T. G. Rosenmeyer (Trans.). Cambridge, MA: Harvard University Press.

Staub, E. (1989). *The Roots of Evil*. New York: Cambridge University Press.

Steele, C. M. (1999). The psychology of self-affirmation: sustaining the integrity of the self. In: R. F. Baumeister (Ed.), *The Self in Social Psychology* (pp. 372–390). Philadelphia, PA: Psychology Press.

Steele, C. M., Spencer, S. J., & Lynch, M. (1993). Self-image resilience and dissonance: the role of affirmational resources. *Journal of Personality and Social Psychology, 64*: 885–896.

Steinbeck, J. (1939). *The Grapes of Wrath*. New York: Penguin, 1997.

Stern, D. N. (1985). *The Interpersonal World of the Infant: A View from Psychoanalysis and Developmental Psychology*. New York: Basic Books.

Stowe, H. B. (1852). *Uncle Tom's Cabin*. New York: Norton, 1994.

Strean, H., & Freeman, L. (1991). *Our Wish to Kill: The Murder in All Our Hearts*. New York: St Martin's.

Swann, W., Jr. (1999). *Resilient Identities*. New York: Basic Books.

Taylor, C. (1991). *The Ethics of Authenticity*. Cambridge, MA: Harvard University Press.

Taylor, D. M., & Louis, W. (2004). Terrorism and the quest for identity. In: F. Moghaddam & A. J. Marsella (Eds.), *Understanding Terrorism: Psychosocial Roots, Consequences, and Interventions* (pp. 169–185). Washington, DC: American Psychological Association.

Taylor, S. E., Neter, E., & Wayment, H. A. (1995). Self-evaluation processes. *Personality and Social Psychology Bulletin, 21*: 1278–1287.

Thombs, D. L. (1999). *Introduction to Addictive Behaviors* (2nd edn). New York: Guilford.

Toch, H. H. (1969). *Violent Men: An Inquiry into the Psychology of Violence.* Chicago, IL: Aldine.

Todorov, T. (2001). *Life in Common*, K. Golsan & L. Golsan (Trans.). Lincoln, NE: University of Nebraska Press.

Tololyan, K. (2001). Cultural narrative and the motivation of the terrorist. In: D. C. Rapoport (Ed.), *Inside Terrorist Organizations* (pp. 217–233). Portland, OR: Frank Cass.

Trzebinski, J. (1995). Narrative self, understanding, and action. In: A. Oosterwegel & R. A. Wicklund (Eds.), *The Self in European and North American Culture: Development and Processes* (pp. 73–88). Boston: Kluwer.

Turner, J. H. (1987). Toward a sociological theory of motivation. *American Sociological Review, 52*: 15–27.

Vandello, J. A., & Cohen, D. (2003). Male honor and female fidelity: implicit cultural scripts that perpetuate domestic violence. *Journal of Personality and Social Psychology, 84*: 997–1010.

Vignoles, V. L., Golledge, J., Regalia, C., Manzi, C., & Scabini, E. (2006). Beyond self-esteem: influence of multiple motives on identity construction. *Journal of Personality and Social Psychology, 90*: 308–333.

Volkan, V. (1988). *The Need to Have Enemies and Allies: From Clinical Practice to International Relationships.* Northvale, NJ: Jason Aronson.

Volkan, V. (1997). *Bloodlines: From Ethnic Pride to Ethnic Terrorism.* New York: Farrar, Straus and Giroux.

Volkan, V. (1998). A psychoanalytic perspective on intergroup hatred. *Journal for the Psychoanalysis of Culture & Society, 3*: 78–80.

Wessells, M. (2002). Terrorism, social injustice, and peace building. In: C. E. Stout (Ed.), *The Psychology of Terrorism, Vol. 4: Programs and Practices in Response and Prevention* (pp. 57–73). Westport, CT: Praeger.

Westen, D., & Heim, A. K. (2003). Disturbances of self and identity in personality disorders. In: M. R. Leary & J. P. Tangney (Eds.), *Handbook of Self and Identity* (pp. 643–664). New York: Guilford.

Wicklund, R. A., & Gollwitzer, P. M. (1981). Symbolic self-completion, attempted influence, and self-deprecation. *Basic and Applied Social Psychology*, 2: 89–114.

Winterson, J. (1985). *Oranges Are Not the Only Fruit*. New York: Grove.

Woodward, B. (2003). *Bush at War*. New York: Simon & Schuster.

Woodward, B. (2006). *State of Denial*. New York: Simon & Schuster.

Wright, R. (1940). *Native Son*. HarperCollins, 1998.

Wurmser, L. (1995). *The Hidden Dimension: Psychodynamics of Drug Use*. Northvale, NJ: Jason Aronson.

Young-Bruehl, E., & Bethelard, F. (2002). *Cherishment: A Psychology of the Heart*. New York: Free.

Zinberg, N. E. (1997). Addiction and ego function. In: D. L. Yalisove (Ed.), *Essential Papers on Addiction* (pp. 147–165). New York: New York University Press.

Zinn, H. (1995). *A People's History of the United States: 1492–Present* (revised and updated edn). New York: HarperPerennial.

INDEX